TROUBLED WATER

TROUBLED WATER

The poisoning of America's drinking water—how government and industry allowed it to happen, and what you can do to ensure a safe supply in the home

Jonathan King
Research assistance by
Matt Rothman

 Rodale Press, Emmaus, Pennsylvania

Printed in the United States of America on recycled paper, containing a high percentage of de-inked fiber.

Book design by Acey Lee

Library of Congress Cataloging in Publication Data

King, Jonathan.
    Troubled water.

    Bibliography: p.
    Includes index.
    1. Drinking water—United States—Contamination.
2. Environmental health—United States.   3. Consumer education—United States.   4. United States.   Environmental Protection Agency.   I. Rothman, Matt.
II. Title.
RA592.A1K56   1985   363.7′394′0973   85-11224
ISBN 0-87857-571-5   paperback

2 4 6 8 10 9 7 5 3 1   paperback

Contents

Acknowledgments

In this era of sophisticated high-tech communications, we tend to overlook the tremendous amount of effort that goes into a humble book. Literally hundreds of people took the time and effort to tell their stories, give information, and share their observations. Matt Rothman was more than a researcher for this book; he was also a partner. Ron Selden, Judy Mathewson, Devorah Lanner, Van Metaxas, Susan Hansen, and Lynn Arditi did additional research. Jeffrey Trauberman reviewed the victims' compensation chapter for accuracy. Judy Coburn and Howard Kohn provided valuable editing suggestions.

The Center for Investigative Reporting is an excellent working environment for journalists, largely because of the individuals who work there. I am grateful to the entire staff, especially to Howard Kohn, Mark Schapiro, Connie Matthiessen, David Weir, Judy Coburn, and Douglas Foster, for their constant support and encouragement. I would also like to thank the Joyce Foundation and the Ruth Mott Fund for their crucial financial support.

Many friends shared the inevitable ups and downs of writing this book, none more than Sarah Kidwell, who unflaggingly shared her unique abilities as researcher, editor, and, above all, friend. Her encouragement was vital in times of self-doubt.

Introduction: Poison from the Tap

We live in the most productive nation in history, in terms of goods, food, and armaments. The fruits of our industriousness have been a comfortable and richly varied way of life.

But our wastes are monumental, as well. For too long, we've carelessly disposed of industrial chemicals, pesticides, and radioactive waste with little concern for our lakes and streams and the groundwater that feeds our wells.

We have scattered our waste in several hundred thousand landfills across the country, according to the National Association of Counties;[1] up to 37,000 of these may be contaminating groundwater, says a report by the congressional Office of Technology Assessment, and the cost of cleaning up the mess could total $229 billion.[2] In addition, an estimated 181,000 pits and ponds are used to store wastes; of the roughly 26,000 that contain toxic industrial chemicals, 87 percent lie directly atop vulnerable underground water supplies.[3]

We store gasoline and other petroleum products in more than 2.5 million underground tanks.[4] Constructed of steel, many of these vessels are leaking—perhaps a fourth of them, guesses the Environmental Protection Agency (EPA).[5]

Traditionally, the approach to waste disposal has long been naive: out of sight, out of mind. Each year, the United States injects some 10 billion gallons of sewage, radioactive waste, chemicals, and brine deep into the earth. Now, these poisons are coming back to haunt us, in our groundwater and the thousands of wells it serves.

Water pollution is spreading across this country like a stain. Clearly, the guardians of our supply—the EPA, state and local agencies, and the waterworks themselves—haven't been equal to the task of keeping society's wastes out of its drinking water.

- In its 1982 survey of large public water systems served by groundwater, the EPA found 45 percent of them to be contaminated with organic chemicals.[6]

- According to the EPA's survey of the nation's rural households, two-thirds were drinking water that violated at least one of its health standards.[7]

- In California, pesticides have tainted the drinking water of nearly 1 million people.

- In New Jersey, every major aquifer—or groundwater formation—is affected by chemical contaminants.[8]

We Americans are not accustomed to worrying about our water. Undrinkable tap water is something of a novelty, a problem that we associate with Third World nations. The vast delivery system that serves our taps has been called a magnificent achievement of engineering, and it delivers a seemingly inexhaustible supply of water. But whether you drink chlorinated municipal water or pump your own from a hand-dug, hundred-year-old well, the era is past when you could take water for granted.

Just what is in *your* water? What risks do these contaminants pose? Should you protect the household by investing in a filter of some sort, or is bottled water a better choice? Finally, how did our technologically advanced society allow itself to get into such a vast mess?

This book was written to answer such questions. It suggests what you can do both at the tap and in your community to purify and protect drinking water, a delicate resource on which our lives depend.

The Threat to Groundwater

Chemical contamination of our water supplies has become the most serious environmental problem of our time. "The next great domestic crisis we may face as a nation is a water crisis and . . . its solution may be more expensive and more elusive than the energy crisis," warns Representative Mike Synar of Oklahoma.[9] Most troublesome is pollution affecting groundwater. While streams, rivers, and lakes hold only about 4 percent of the water in the continental United States, the rest lies from a few feet to hundreds of feet below the surface, unseen in vast underground reservoirs called aquifers. These are popularly visualized as subterranean lakes and streams, but most aquifers are porous layers of sand or rock. The water moves slowly—sometimes only a few inches a day—through narrow pathways in the ground.

Groundwater is not isolated from surface water; the two are intimately connected. Groundwater "outcrops" into springs and contributes about 30 percent of the volume of the nation's streams, lakes, and rivers. Rain and surface waters, in turn, seep down through the earth to replenish groundwater.

Perhaps because groundwater is out of sight, most people give it little thought, even though it provides drinking water for half the population of the United States, and more than 90 percent of its rural residents. Our use of groundwater has tripled since 1950, and all indications are that we will become increasingly dependent on it.[10]

Groundwater was once thought of as a pristine resource to be tapped at will. But in the late 1970s, reports of chemically contaminated wells showed how vulnerable groundwater could be. And once chemicals percolate down through the soil and invade an underground water supply, they don't readily disperse, settle out, or degrade. Thus, even a leak of a single gallon of gasoline per day is enough to render the groundwater supply for a town of 50,000 people unfit to drink.[11] In its dark, cool, contained underground environment, groundwater may remain contaminated for hundreds, even thousands, of years. Back in 1950, for example, new wells in Norwich, England, were found to be severely contaminated. The source of the pollution: whale oil that had been dumped in 1815.[12] "For all practical purposes, ground-water contamination is irreversible by natural forces," according to Robert Harris, a hazardous waste expert at Princeton University.[13]

Equally disturbing—and initially surprising to many experts—are the *levels* of contaminants that are now routinely found in groundwater. Because chemicals don't readily break down or disperse in groundwater, their concentrations are often several hundred times greater than the levels found in surface water. Trichlorethylene (TCE), a widely used solvent suspected of causing cancer, was originally not thought to pose much of a threat to drinking water because its concentrations in surface water were usually minute. But that perception has changed dramatically in the past few years. TCE has now been detected in groundwater at concentrations up to 510,000 parts per billion[14]—more than 3,000 times the highest level ever recorded in surface water.[15] (Parts per billion, or ppb, is a standard measurement for concentrations of chemicals in drinking water.)

A myriad of industrial and agricultural chemicals have found their way into groundwater—chemicals from hazardous waste sites, heavy metals and radioactive substances from mining, gasoline from underground storage tanks, pesticides and nitrates from agriculture, salt from road deicing, brine from oil and gas drilling, and nitrates and bacteria from leaky septic tanks.

How much of the nation's groundwater is contaminated? Estimates range from the EPA's 1 percent to as high as 4 percent.[16] But the extent of the problem is not known. The EPA requires public water systems to sample for only a few of the industrial chemicals commonly found in groundwater, and no testing at all is required for the nation's millions of private wells.

One percent—or even 4 percent—may not sound like a lot of polluted water, but these figures don't really describe the gravity of the problem. Every state now reports groundwater contamination. "Our groundwaters, long considered pollution-free, are threatened with ruinous contamination," warned Eckhardt Beck, former EPA assistant administrator for water and waste management, back in 1980.[17]

What Went Wrong?

Ironically, our current groundwater contamination woes have crept up on us during a time of heightened environmental awareness. Visible pollution of our rivers and lakes helped to catalyze the environmental concern that led to the formation of the EPA in 1970. Initially, the EPA focused on problems it could see—the flow of stinking raw sewage into our nation's waterways. As a result, fish returned to many lakes and rivers. Swimming areas were reopened.

But that's not to say these waters were drinkable. Chemical contamination of drinking water burst into the national consciousness in 1974, when the EPA announced that its tests identified 66 different organic chemicals in the drinking water of New Orleans.[18] The city draws its water from the Mississippi River, which serves as the final repository of waste from hundreds of industrial firms that line its banks. Shortly following the EPA's report, the private Environmental Defense Fund released a study linking New Orleans's elevated cancer death rates with the presence of organic cancer-causing chemicals in the city's drinking water. In response, Congress passed the Safe Drinking Water Act, which had been languishing on Capitol Hill for several years. This act gave the EPA the power to set and enforce safe exposure levels for toxic substances in drinking water.

But while the EPA and the nation focused their attention on controlling the discharge of pollution in our surface waters, billions of tons of chemical wastes in landfills, dumps, pits, and ponds were slowly seeping through the ground into the underlying water table. Once there, they could make their way toward nearby drinking water wells. EPA officials have explained the agency's slow reaction to the threat of hazardous waste to groundwater as being based on a lack of knowledge. "Ten years ago, for all practical purposes, we were unaware that there was a hazardous waste problem," said former EPA Administrator William Ruckelshaus in 1984. "Burial, after all, was the symbol of ultimate disposal. Groundwater was the very symbol of purity."[19] It took environmental disasters like Love Canal to force the agency and the nation to notice the threat from land disposal of hazardous chemicals.

Even after Love Canal and other contamination calamities of the late 1970s, our underfunded bureaucracies have moved at a snail's pace. They've failed to mend the damage, much less ensure clean drinking water for the future. The EPA's efforts all but ground to a halt during the early 1980s, when the Reagan administration ushered in a period of environmental retrenchment. The new administration, riding high on its antiregulatory crusade, drastically slashed the EPA budget, which had never been sufficient to do the job in the first place.

Water programs suffered heavily. As a result, the EPA missed deadlines and set no new drinking water safety standards. The agency's existing regulations fell apart because they were no longer enforced. In frustration, Ohio Representative Dennis Eckart remarked, "You can lead the Environmental Protection Agency to water, but you can't make them regulate it."[20] By the time Anne Burford, Reagan's first EPA administrator, resigned from office in 1983, the EPA was a shell of its former self. The damage will take years to repair.

Both the EPA and industry have made the worst of a bad situation by continuing to rely on land disposal of toxic wastes, even though the EPA itself admits there is no known way to prevent these sites from leaking and eventually contaminating water supplies. If there were no alternatives to land disposal, perhaps the EPA's approach would be more understandable. But there are. Waste can be recycled, incinerated, or chemically and physically treated to render it practically harmless. Also, there are proven ways for manufacturers to reduce the amount of waste generated. Only now are we beginning to turn to these alternatives.

The Environmental Debt

Joel Hirschhorn, a hazardous waste management expert at the congressional Office of Technology Assessment (OTA), calls it "the environmental debt":[21] the price we will have to pay for the years of neglect and mismanagement of our water supplies. We will end up paying that debt, either with our money or our health.

Americans already spend more than $2 billion a year on bottled water and home filters.[22] This money must be paid out indefinitely, because groundwater, once contaminated, is extremely difficult and expensive to clean up. Sometimes the job proves impossible. Just determining the extent of groundwater contamination from a single waste site can cost up to $250,000.[23] The price tag for the actual cleanup itself can reach $100 million,[24] as at Love Canal, or even into the billions, as at the U.S. Army's heavily contaminated Rocky Mountain Arsenal outside Denver. Several hundred thousand sites exist around the country. In contrast, the five-year "Superfund" legislation, passed by Congress in 1980 to clean up abandoned hazardous waste sites, amounts to a mere $1.6 billion.

And Superfund won't make the toxins disappear, because the waste is rarely reduced, treated, or destroyed. Rather, it is simply contained or carted off to other waste disposal sites, some of which are now leaking themselves.

One way or another, we will end up paying the costs, through higher water bills, increased taxes, or—if industry is forced to pay a large share of the cleanup costs—through higher prices. We will have to abandon some aquifers as hopelessly polluted and tap deeper, uncontaminated water supplies. Atlantic City, New Jersey, decided to drill new wells instead of trying to clean up toxic chemicals that were moving toward its existing water supply. "We have to write off some groundwater, like under Newark [New Jersey]," says one EPA hazardous waste official. "There are areas where so much crap went—what can you do?"[25]

The other cost is more subtle, more permanent, and more important—our health. From around the country come reports linking toxic chemicals in drinking water with cancer, birth defects, kidney and liver ailments, headaches, rashes, mental depression, and a host of other problems. There is no way to accurately determine the toll, and those exposed to tainted drinking water must live with the uncertainty of not knowing what disease may strike their household or when. "Everybody is just afraid," said one resident of a contaminated New Jersey community.[26]

The Fight for Clean Water

If no one wants dirty drinking water, and we have the knowledge and means to avoid it, then why is pollution so widespread?

The answer is that government and private industry are ill suited to deal with problems before they become crises. Industry has consistently chosen the cheapest (and most dangerous) forms of waste disposal. The EPA has promoted the status quo by managing the problem rather than reducing it. The EPA and industry will actively prevent water contamination only when public pressure becomes great enough. It was this pressure that gave birth to the environmental concern of the 1960s, urged the passage of environmental protection laws in the 1970s, and forced government agencies to enforce these laws. Now, people have found they cannot rely on the judgment of the scientific community, the altruism of polluters, or the industriousness of government regulators to protect their water quality. They have taken matters into their own hands, forming citizens groups to pressure polluters and government regulators. They have lobbied in Congress and their state legislatures. They have become the driving force behind a number of local initiatives designed to protect water quality. Despite the obstacles, many have gone to court to win enforcement of environmental laws and compensation for their injuries.

As one Kansas resident put it, "We have had to become overnight students of chemistry, geology, hydrology, government, law, and politics just to protect ourselves."[27] Such efforts have an impact that reaches far beyond the individual fight or local courtroom decision—an impact that is felt by government and polluters across the country. Ultimately, citizens will be guaranteed clean tap water only when they collectively demand it.

Toxic Waste

1

In the upstate New York town of Fort Edward, Richard and Marion Arlington were about to get ready for bed when the phone rang. As Richard went to answer the phone that December night, four days before Christmas, he had no idea what a profound impact the call would have on their lives.

The voice on the other end of the line was that of Brian Fear, an official from the New York State Board of Health. He warned Arlington to stop using his water immediately. "Mr. Arlington, you have 11,000 ppb of TCE in your water," was the message, recalls Richard, a man in his 70s who is usually jovial. "Now this wasn't anything at all to me. I didn't know what TCE was. I didn't know what 11,000 meant. It had no bearing whatsoever on my life." Brian Fear assured him that he would explain everything.

True to his word, Fear came over to the Arlingtons' house the next day to explain the unfamiliar scientific jargon. TCE, he told them, is a shorthand name for trichlorethylene, a clear, colorless liquid and a known toxin. And ppb, or parts per billion, is a way of measuring the concentration of the chemical in water. TCE is widely used as a solvent and degreaser in industrial processes and consumer products. Because of this ability, the chemical strips away natural skin oils and causes rashes and cracking. In high doses, TCE can cause headaches, nausea, dizziness, and kidney and heart problems. Further, it causes cancer in laboratory animals[1] and is suspected of producing the same effects in humans.

The level of TCE in the Arlingtons' water was more than 200 times the state's recommended safety level of 50 ppb. Because TCE

1

vaporizes into the air, Fear told the couple, even taking showers could pose a danger. Richard recalls that Fear warned them, "Shut your water off. Do not use your bathroom. Do not take a shower. If you go to the bathroom, put the lid down, flush it, and get out." This was not going to be an ordinary holiday season.

Two days after Christmas, health officers returned to test wells in the neighborhood. Four of the 11 homes on the Arlingtons' street were contaminated with TCE. The levels in the Arlingtons' own well had doubled to 21,000 ppb; nevertheless, Richard remembers, "I was one of the lowest. The people across the street were 45,000 ppb. The people two doors up were 50,000."

The day they could no longer simply turn on their tap to get water, the Arlingtons' lives changed. They had to drive 40 miles round-trip to their daughter's house just to take a shower. Richard, who had had two heart attacks, was forced to lug water from friends' houses. They had to wash their clothes at the laundromat. More seriously, the Arlingtons now trace mysterious health problems to the toxins in their water, including rashes and dry skin. "We break out," Richard says. "The skin peels right off our hands." Some of their neighbors, including children, have suffered repeated bladder infections. Others have more serious problems. Across the street, Kay Powers has a ten-year-old with a bleeding ulcer. Residents also contend that the number of people on the Arlingtons' street, Stevens Lane, with high blood pressure is well above normal. Did TCE cause any or all of these problems? The state says there is "no evidence,"[2] and nothing can be proved.

A well-manicured town of stately Victorian houses and quiet tree-lined streets, Fort Edward has the historical aura characteristic of many upstate New York and New England villages. The Arlingtons' house, bordering on a large dairy farm at the end of a little street, hardly seems the kind of place where people have to worry about chemical contamination. But Fort Edward, located on the headwaters of the Hudson River, is also an industrial town, and several large manufacturing plants are located on the edge of residential neighborhoods. Looking out the Arlingtons' kitchen window, across their backyard, you can see the object of their worry: a General Electric (GE) factory that manufactures electrical capacitors. In the plant's 40 years of operation, chemicals from many leaks and spills have soaked and resoaked the ground. Presumably, rainwater has pushed the toxins down through the soil and into the water table. Once there, the contamination may have traveled slowly south toward Stevens Lane. Chemicals first were found along Park Avenue, the street between Stevens Lane and the GE plants. Several months before the health department tested the Arlingtons' well, chemicals were discovered in several Park Avenue wells. GE did not admit it was responsible for the contamination, but it paid $25,000 to hook several houses to the town's water supply. The company said this was simply a neighborly gesture. In return, the Park Avenue residents signed an agreement releasing GE from "all claims" relating to the loss of their water.[3] The company later made the same offer with the same conditions to the households on Stevens Lane. Richard Arlington couldn't believe his eyes when he read the formal written offer. But, says Arlington, he wasn't about to sign away the right to sue, and many of his neighbors had similar feelings. "They'll give you the water for a lousy, rotten $30,000," he says angrily. "But if you die, that's tough. Don't sue."

Too Late, Too Much

From the beginning of time, societies have thrown away their wastes in the cheapest and most convenient manner. Our industrial society has been no different. Chemical wastes were discharged into the nearest body of water, dumped into pits and ponds, or simply thrown out the back door. Until recently, the problem was relatively manageable. At the end of World War II, this country produced only 1 billion pounds of hazardous chemical waste annually,[4] while today we produce several hundred times that amount.

World War II was a turning point. It marked not only the dawn of the nuclear era, but also the beginning of the synthetic chemical age. In the following decades, a virtual explosion of new chemicals found their way into almost every type of industrial and consumer product imaginable. Synthetic fibers have now taken the place of cotton, wool, and silk. Plastic has replaced wood, glass, and metal. Styrofoam is used in place of paper in disposable drinking cups. The "rubber" in tires is now synthetic. Modern agriculture depends on huge amounts of chemical pesticides and fertilizers. Petroleum fuels our transportation systems. Today, more than 60,000 chemicals are used in commerce, but very little is known about the effects of the vast majority of them in the environment or on human health.[5]

Our increasing use of chemicals has been paralleled by an exponential growth of hazardous waste, but disposal techniques have not kept pace. In the early 1970s, the newly created EPA first tackled the most obvious problem, that of controlling industrial and municipal discharges into surface waterways. These wastes flowed downstream into public water systems and poured out of taps in millions of homes. The EPA sampled drinking water from many systems and found low levels of dozens of organic industrial chemicals—many of them toxic and cancer causing. This discovery, coupled with a study linking the high rate of cancer deaths in New Orleans with the city's contaminated drinking water supply, focused national attention on the magnitude of the chemical contamination of our surface waters, and forced Congress to pass legislation to ensure safe drinking water.

The EPA moved hesitantly in these initial years to control the chemical waste pouring into our nation's waterways. But the agency largely ignored the damage that lay beneath the surface of the land, in the vast aquifers under the country. That's because the EPA thought that soil would act as a buffer, filtering out chemicals before they reached the water table. "If you had asked us in 1977, we would have said we're most concerned with surface waters," admits Victor Kimm, director of the EPA's Office of Drinking Water. "We did not expect to find man-made organic chemicals in groundwater based on the limited data we had seen. Obviously, that conventional wisdom was flat wrong." As Representative Toby Moffett of Connecticut pointed out in 1980 congressional hearings on groundwater contamination, "Our Earth is not a bottomless sponge which will soak up poisons and somehow miraculously make them go away."[6]

That myth was exploded in the late 1970s by a series of chemical contamination incidents. The most infamous of these occurred in Niagara Falls, New York; chemicals dumped years before by Hooker Chemical into the Love Canal had seeped into the basements of nearby subdivisions, forcing the evacuation of several hundred residents. And groundwater contamination was showing up around the country. In rural Hardeman County, Tennessee, about 50 miles west of Memphis, health authorities closed several wells after finding extremely high levels of chemical contamination. A study headed by Robert H. Harris, of the Center for Energy and Environmental Studies at Princeton University, traced the source to a site used by Velsicol Chemical Company from 1964 to 1972 to dispose of 16 million gallons of extremely toxic pesticide waste. Over the years, the chemicals percolated down through the soil and traveled a fourth of a mile to nearby wells. The contamination was discovered only after people living near the disposal site complained repeatedly to health officials about the water's terrible odors and taste and about recurring health problems, including children born with birth defects.[7]

The contamination in Hardeman County affected only a few families, but the same year, chemical contamination was discovered in the drinking water wells that supplied 80 percent of the 20,000 residents of Bedford, Massachusetts.[8]

Scientists were surprised by the levels of chemical contamination in groundwater. The concentrations of toxic and cancer-causing chemicals in the drinking water in Bedford and Hardeman County were from 10 to 100 or even 1,000 times the levels typically found in the polluted surface water supplies of New Orleans, Cincinnati, Philadelphia, and Chicago. The reason is this: exposure to sunlight and air dissipates chemicals from surface water, but groundwater simply stores them. In time, the levels in groundwater may increase as more pollution seeps through the soil and enters the aquifer. "A contaminant that penetrates groundwater tends to form a 'plume' of highly contaminated water, moving slowly through the aquifer for years, decades, and even longer," explains Eckhardt Beck, former EPA administrator for water and waste management. "If you should happen to find a contamination plume, what are you going to do about it? In most instances, the answer is 'shut down the water supply wells.' "[9]

As it turned out, incidents like Hardeman County and Bedford were only the beginning; many more wells would be shut down over the next few years.

- In Massachusetts, a special Commission on Water Supply reported in 1979 that the drinking water in at least one-third of the state's 351 communities had suffered some degree of chemical contamination. In 22 towns, private and community wells were closed or their use was restricted.[10]

- In 1979, the Michigan Department of Natural Resources identified 268 sites where the groundwater was known to be contaminated, along with another 361 sites where contamination was suspected.[11]

- In 1978, 36 community wells in Nassau and Suffolk counties on Long Island were closed because of contamination by suspected carcinogens. More than 2 million people were affected.[12]

- An EPA survey of 350 hazardous waste disposal sites, released in 1980, found these had caused 168 cases of groundwater or drinking water contamination in 32 states, forcing the closing of nearly 500 wells.[13]

The EPA's Weak Hammer

The final responsibility for regulating hazardous waste and safeguarding water supplies belongs to the EPA. Congress gave the agency the power to regulate waste when it passed the Resource Conservation and Recovery Act (RCRA) in 1976. Under the RCRA, the EPA had 18 months to develop a system for the safe generation and disposal of hazardous waste. But the EPA was ill prepared for this monumental task. In conjunction with the states, the EPA had to keep track of about 70,000 firms nationwide that handled hazardous waste.[14] Several thousand companies also required detailed permits to store, treat, or dispose of toxic waste. But the EPA had little idea of how much waste was being generated or where it was going. By 1980, the agency estimated the country was producing somewhere between 28 and 54 million tons of hazardous chemical waste each year.[15] In 1983, the EPA revised its estimate drastically upward to about 150 million metric tons.[16] The following year, the EPA almost doubled that guess to 290 million tons[17]—more than 1 ton for each of us—and these figures did not include 6 *billion* tons of municipal garbage, waste products from mining and oil and gas drilling, agricultural waste, and domestic sewage.[18]

The EPA had little idea of where this waste was going. The agency's 1979 estimate of 32,000 to 50,000 potentially hazardous waste sites[19] requiring cleanup clashed with that of the Chemical Manufacturers Association (CMA), the powerful trade organization for the $100-billion-a-year chemical industry, which claimed the nation had only 4,800.[20] Nobody could account for the huge discrepancy in estimates. "We do not know what the dimensions of the problem are," admitted James Moorman, U.S. assistant attorney general for land and natural resources, speaking before a congressional subcommittee in 1979. "We do not know where the millions of tons of stuff is going. We feel that the things that have turned up like Love Canal are simply the tip of the iceberg. We do not have the capacity at this time really to find out what is actually happening. In my view, it is simply a wide-open situation, like the Wild West was in the 1870s, for toxic disposal."[21]

Over the next few years, discoveries of thousands of waste sites proved him right. In 1980, 400 new hazardous sites were being found each month, under parks, schools, and housing developments and in the country, suburbs, and even urban areas.[22] Reports of groundwater contamination were growing also. EPA Region 10, covering Oregon, Washington, Idaho, and Alaska, received 31 reports of groundwater contamination during the 1970s, and 46 in 1981 and 1982 alone.[23] The New Jersey Geological Survey investigated 220 cases of groundwater pollution in 1981. Two years later, that work load had jumped to 350.[24] Since 1971, the state has had to close about 1,100 public and private wells, mainly because of industrial chemical contamination.[25] Not one major aquifer in the state has escaped contamination, and the EPA predicts that over the next several decades 40 to 50 million gallons of the 750 million gallons of groundwater used daily in New Jersey will be lost to pollution.[26] New Jersey is not the only state with such serious contamination problems.

- Since 1980, TCE and other toxic chemicals at levels higher than the state safety standards have been found in more than 100 wells in the San Gabriel Valley, near Los Angeles, California. About 4.5 million suburban residents have been affected.[27]

- In New England, chemicals have contaminated 490 public and private wells, forcing the closing of 38.[28]

- In Indiana, 43 percent of the wells in a recent sampling contained industrial chemicals.[29]

Nationally, the magnitude of the problem is staggering. The EPA says that 881 waste sites have contaminated or now threaten the drinking water supplies for 14.7 million Americans[30] and that nearly 30 percent of 954 public water systems supplied by groundwater contain volatile organic chemicals.[31] The Congressional Research Service estimates that chemical contamination has forced the closing of at least 4,000 public and private drinking water wells.[32]

And that figure is certainly a gross underestimate. There is still no comprehensive survey of the extent of groundwater pollution and no systematic monitoring of drinking water for chemicals. State agencies are usually responsible for enforcing drinking water standards and safeguarding water supplies, but they typically are so understaffed that they can barely respond to citizen complaints and the most obvious problems, much less attempt to gain a complete picture of the extent of contamination. "The majority of information relating to groundwater contamination remains anecdotal, scattered, and poorly organized," remarked the Congressional Research Service.[33]

But this much is known: if you put chemicals in the ground, they will eventually end up in groundwater. All told, some 80 percent of our toxic waste ends up in the ground, where it will remain toxic for decades, even centuries. This country is literally laced with millions of potential contamination sites.[34]

Hazardous Waste Landfills: A False Sense of Security

"Hazardous constituents which are placed in land disposal facilities very likely will migrate from the facility into the broader environment," the EPA states. "Even with the application of best available land disposal technology, it will occur eventually."[35]

In Kansas, the operator of a modern disposal facility that accepted waste from 22 surrounding states claimed the landfill would not leak for 5,000 years. The facility opened in 1977, and in less than 5 years, chemicals leached into the groundwater and showed in springs more than a half mile from the site. The site, now on the EPA's Superfund list, is still closed today, while the operator, the EPA, and the Kansas Department of Health and Environment try to figure out how to clean up the mess.

Although many people probably picture large hazardous waste landfills when they hear of waste disposal operations, these commercial operations account for only about 3 percent of the hazardous waste disposed of in this country.[36] Most of the remainder is dumped into pits and ponds, or injected deep into the ground.

Surface Impoundments

Since the late 1800s, natural sinkholes, excavated pits, ponds, and lagoons—collectively known as surface impoundments—have served as cheap, convenient sites of hazardous waste disposal. Sometimes wastes have been dumped into surface impoundments simply because they've been considered too dangerous to pour directly into surface waters—the other popular disposal method.

Over the years, the number of surface impoundments has rapidly multiplied. According to EPA estimates, there are now more than 180,000 pits and ponds containing liquid waste at approximately 80,000 sites around the United States.[37] Every day, these impoundments receive about 50 billion gallons of liquid waste:[38] including hazardous industrial waste; agricultural by-products; municipal and domestic sewage; water contaminated with heavy metals, radioactivity, and acids from mining operations; and heavily salted brine from oil and gas drilling. Approximately 26,000 of these pits are used for hazardous industrial waste. Taken together, they would cover an area about three-fourths the size of Rhode Island.[39] Their potential threat to groundwater is tremendous.

The liquid waste in these ponds is supposed to evaporate. Some does, in fact, but much of the waste simply soaks down into the ground, its percolation accelerated by the pressure from the liquid on top. About 87 percent of all industrial pits and ponds are located above underground aquifers that could provide drinking water, yet less than a third have any barrier to prevent hazardous chemicals from leaching right down into the groundwater.[40] More than 100 billion gallons of this waste seeps into groundwater each year. That volume could fill a container ten feet deep, 1 mile wide, and 50 miles long.[41] By 1980, the EPA recorded more than 500 cases of groundwater contamination from surface impoundments.[42]

One of the worst cases of groundwater contamination from waste ponds has occurred near Sacramento, California, where Aerojet General Corporation dumped large quantities of hazardous wastes including solvents, herbicides, and arsenic into surface impoundments on the company's 12,000-acre site. In 1979, state health officials found concentrations of trichlorethylene as high as 360 ppb in wells near the Aerojet property. More than a dozen suspected cancer-causing chemicals have been found in the groundwater. Eventually, about 20 private and municipal wells were shut down. It may take as much as $600,000,000 to clean up the chemical mess.[43]

The industrial waste pit is not the only type of surface impoundment that threatens drinking water supplies. Some 65,000 impoundments are used to store brine,[44] the naturally occurring salt water that is produced when oil and gas are pumped to the surface. Brine is not simply ocean water. It can contain up to 300,000 parts per million (ppm), or nearly one part in three, of chloride and 150,000 ppm of sodium—concentrations about ten times higher than those in ordinary seawater. Although chloride and sodium are simply the constituents of ordinary table salt, in high enough concentrations they are dangerous to health. Chronic exposure to high levels in drinking water can increase the risk of high blood pressure, and the EPA allows no more than 250 ppm of chloride in public water supplies. Additionally, brine often contains toxic substances such as lead and radioactive strontium and is contaminated with toxic hydrocarbons. Brine has now contaminated groundwater in 17 states.[45]

In Ohio, the state's 40,000 active oil and gas wells produce between 1 and 2 million gallons of brine each day. Much of it is simply dumped into pits or onto the ground. The Ohio Environmental Protection Agency has documented cases of brine disposal in roadside ditches, in private ponds, in streams, in sanitary sewer manholes, on school grounds, in state parks, and even in a cemetery.

Ohio and EPA investigators call brine ponds "magic pits" because they never fill up; the brine soaks right down to the groundwater. One Ohio investigator reports, "I sat and secretly photographed a truck or two each hour on a continuous basis, 24 hours a day, dumping brine into this disposal pit. We estimate that there was 60,000 to 75,000 gallons of brine dumped into this disposal pit every day. The level of the pit never fluctuated." Hundreds of wells in the state have been contaminated with brine, and livestock and wildlife have died after drinking from streams and springs laced with it.[46]

Several other states have been severely affected by brine contamination from oil and gas drilling. In Oklahoma, 83 of 348 groundwater and surface water sites sampled have shown brine contamination.[47] Contamination from Louisiana's estimated 13,000 waste sludge and brine pits has fouled numerous wells.[48] According to a report in the *Wall Street Journal*, 81 of 84 wells tested in one Louisiana town turned out to be contaminated with heavy metals. In another town, the water is so briny that the drinking fountains have turned white.[49]

Underground Injection:
Out of Sight, Out of Mind?

Each year, this country injects some 10 billion gallons of sewage, radioactive waste, chemicals, and brine deep within the earth—into formations as far down as a mile.[50] Deep well injection is now the most popular method of hazardous waste disposal.[51] It costs only about half as much as putting waste in a secure landfill.

The waste disposal industry, chemical manufacturers, and the EPA generally consider deep well injection to be an acceptable method to get rid of hazardous materials. "If operated properly, deep well injection is a safe and successful disposal technology," says Suellen Pirages, director of the Institute of Chemical Waste Management, formed by waste disposal firms.[52] Injection wells are "technologically, economically, and environmentally preferable to the use of alternate surface treatment technologies," maintains Dupont's Phillip Palmer.[53]

Underground injection may appear to be the perfect "out of sight, out of mind" disposal method, but the EPA's Victor Kimm warns, "This isn't a panacea. Man can screw it up. He can put [them] in the wrong place. There have been a few of those. He can operate [them] improperly."

The problem is that there are still too many unknowns. Most hazardous waste is injected below drinking water sources into confined rock or clay formations. But well operators often know little about the chemical, hydrological, and physical characteristics of the area into which they are injecting the waste. Although the EPA doesn't require monitoring of what happens to the wastes, they can escape, according to a report by the congressional Office of Technical Assessment (OTA). Chemicals can leach through cracks in rocks or migrate up the side of the well casing. Highly corrosive or acidic wastes may dissolve the confining rock or clay or even the walls of the well itself. In December 1983, the Ohio EPA closed five underground injection wells found leaking at a site owned by Waste Management, the nation's largest waste disposal firm. A deep injection well in Colorado is even thought to have set off a series of tremors. There is also concern that waste can escape up through the nation's million-odd unplugged, abandoned wells.[54] In northwestern Pennsylvania, hazardous papermaking wastes were injected 1,600 feet underground, only to reappear more than four miles away through an unplugged gas well.

Problems like these have led several states to ban all underground injection. "Operators of injection wells may know where the wastes are injected," the OTA concluded, but not "where the wastes will end up."[55]

The so-called class IV wells, which inject hazardous waste directly into or above drinking water aquifers, pose the most obvious threat to groundwater. "The class IV wells are a nightmare," Kimm says flatly. "The problem is no matter how you build the damn thing, it's likely to end up in fresh water."

The agency has now banned new class IV wells. It does permit existing ones to continue to operate, as long as they don't inject directly into an aquifer. The EPA believes there may be 120 or fewer still open,[56] but Kimm, for one, thinks there are more: "I believe there are lots of them out there, but no one ever thought of them as a well." For example, "A guy's got a hole in the ground in the back of the plant into which he dumps buckets of stuff they don't know what else to do with."

Leaking Underground Storage Tanks: The Slow Drip

Like Fort Edward in upstate New York, the tiny town of Lee, Maine, seems an unlikely place to be grappling with chemical contamination. But the water supply of one-fourth of the rural community's 600 residents is polluted with gasoline.[57] One resident said that showering in the water caused his hair to turn yellow and fall out.[58] The gasoline has been traced to a local service station's leaking underground storage tank (known in the environmental trade as LUST, one of the more interesting acronyms in the dull alphabet soup of chemicals, agencies, and statutes).

Gasoline may be responsible for as much as 40 percent of the nation's groundwater contamination.[59] The EPA estimates that up to a fourth of our 2.5 million gasoline storage tanks may be leaking.[60]

Whatever the number, the effect is great. Connecticut investigates about 100 incidents of gas contamination every year, according to Michael Harder, a sanitary engineer with the Connecticut Department of Environmental Protection. The reported incidents probably represent at least 25 percent of the contamination cases, Harder adds.[61] In Michigan, a fourth of the state's contaminated wells are polluted with gasoline.[62] In Florida, the Miami airport sits on top of 3 million gallons of jet fuel that is seeping into groundwater and threatening the drinking water supply for nearby communities.[63] A gasoline tank field near Boise, Idaho, has leaked approximately 90 million gallons of gasoline into the ground over the past 30 years; the levels of contamination are so high that the gas vapors in the basements of some nearby homes threaten to explode.[64]

People whose wells are rendered unfit by gasoline have joked about being able to light their water on fire, but gasoline carries other, less obvious dangers. Gasoline's complex formula contains some 225 to 250 distinct chemical compounds, including such known cancer-causing agents as benzene and ethylene dibromide.[65]

The problem is only going to become worse in the coming years. During the late 1950s and early 1960s, thousands upon thousands of steel storage tanks were installed, most with an expected lifespan of 15 to 20 years. That means they could rust and spring leaks at any time now. The American Petroleum Institute figures another 350,000 tanks will become leakers before the end of the decade.[66]

Detecting leaks before the gasoline or chemicals show up in someone's well or basement is a hit-or-miss proposition at best. One method simply involves sticking a pole down into a tank to monitor the level of gas, but this may be inaccurate because gasoline volume increases as its temperature goes up. Additionally, even a serious leak can "appear as only a small percentage of the total volume pumped," points out geologist Marcel Moreau of the Maine Department of Environmental Protection. "For example, a 100 gallon-a-month loss at a station which pumps 30,000 gallons a month represents only a 0.3 percent loss. In addition, many retailers do not keep the kind of detailed inventory records needed to detect leaks."[67] In Lee, Maine, 10,000 gallons had seeped out of a tank before gasoline was discovered in the town's wells.

Several companies have compensated victims of contamination from underground storage tanks, although they haven't necessarily admitted responsibility. Chevron, U.S.A. has spent more than $10 million to purchase 41 homes and relocate residents in the Denver suburb of Northglenn, where groundwater was tainted with gasoline from an underground tank. In Canob Park, Rhode Island, Exxon and Mobil agreed to pay more than $1 million to install a new community water system for homes affected or threatened by a gasoline leak.[68]

The Town Dump:
More Than Just Garbage

Few people want to live next door to the town dump. The stench and the roar of garbage trucks are unpleasant. But town dumps often turn out to be more than just an eyesore. Many contain a lot more than household trash. Until federal regulations went into effect in 1980, it was perfectly legal to dump hazardous chemical wastes in these municipal sites. In fact, as long as a firm produces less than 1,000 kilograms (2,200 pounds) of hazardous waste a month, it still is allowed to simply truck it down to the nearest town dump. When added up, the volume of chemical waste these so-called small generators produce is substantial. The OTA estimates that the total comes to between 3 and 4.5 million tons of hazardous waste each year.[69] Finally, in late 1984, Congress moved to close this loophole, passing legislation that restricts the small generator exemption to firms that produce less than 100 kilograms per month. The new regulations will go into effect in 1986.

Other hazardous materials may escape federal waste regulations and end up in municipal or industrial solid waste landfills. Household wastes, for example, contain hazardous substances such as cleaning fluids, home and garden pesticides, and heavy metals. A recent New York State Assembly report concluded, "The distinction made between hazardous and municipal waste is an artificial one."

The sheer number of landfills dwarfs other potential sources of water contamination. According to the EPA, the United States has 12,000 to 18,000 operating municipal landfills and 75,000 on-site industrial sanitary landfills and open dumps;[70] but the National Association of Counties puts the total at 360,000.[71] Added to these figures is an equal or greater number of closed landfills and dumps.

The OTA concludes that several hundred thousand active and inactive dumps may be threatening groundwater. The pollutants include organic solvents, pesticides, polychlorinated biphenyls (PCBs), heavy metals, acids, radioactive substances, and asbestos. In New York, the state Department of Environmental Conservation estimates that nearly half of the state's 420 operating municipal landfills are already contaminating groundwater.[72] Chemicals from a 185-foot-high, 50-acre landfill near the town of Babylon on Long Island have produced a plume of contaminated groundwater two miles long and several hundred feet wide. In Connecticut, "every landfill produces leachate," says John England, a senior environmental analyst with the state Department of Environment Protection. Twenty-five of the state's 200 landfills have already contaminated drinking water, and another 35 landfills are considered threats.[73] New York and Connecticut may be representative of the national problem—or other states may have it worse. Many states are simply not looking at the problem, through either lack of resources or simple neglect.

Cleaning Up the Mess

The Resource Conservation and Recovery Act did nothing to clean up the hazardous wastes that had already been strewed about the country. When these wastes began to appear in people's wells, backyards, and basements in the late 1970s, Congress realized that it had to act—or risk scores of other Love Canal incidents.

In 1980, after a long debate, Congress passed the landmark Comprehensive Environmental Response, Compensation, and Liability Act (CERCLA). This was hailed as the final piece of legislation necessary to deal with the country's hazardous waste problems. CERCLA authorizes the EPA to quickly clean up releases of hazardous materials from abandoned or inactive waste sites such as Love Canal, and to intervene when it deems there is an imminent threat to public health or to the environment. To pay for these operations, the legislation established a $1.6 billion "Superfund." More than 80 percent of the money for the fund comes from a five-year tax on the chemical industry that expires in 1985. Federal funds provide the remainder.

Because there are so many hazardous waste sites around the country, the EPA has chosen to make only the most serious sites eligible for Superfund cleanup money. By late 1984, the EPA had developed a list of 786 sites that could receive Superfund money. About three-fourths of these sites have leaked into groundwater, and more than half have polluted surface water. The EPA projected in December 1984 that its list would eventually grow to 1,500 to 2,500 sites and that money required for Superfund could reach $22.7 billion.[74] Many observers think that those estimates are conservative.

In the meantime, EPA cleanups have been neither swift nor free of controversy. Certainly, that's been the experience of residents of a Montana lumber town.

Mining the Land, Ruining the Water

Milltown, Montana, is a working-class community of old wood houses located on a triangular spit of land at the confluence of the Clark Fork and Blackfoot rivers. As its name suggests, Milltown's 300 or so residents are almost completely dependent on the nearby Champion International lumber mill for their livelihoods.

Many townspeople were suspicious of their water quality—it had an odd taste and odor and left an unremovable black stain on sinks and bathtubs. In 1981, routine sampling of wells in Milltown found high levels of arsenic, a heavy metal linked to cancer, nerve disorders, and digestive tract ailments. The concentrations were several times the EPA's standard for drinking water. The Montana Department of Health and Environmental Sciences advised 33 Milltown households not to use their tap water for drinking or cooking.

The source of the arsenic lies many miles upstream on the Clark Fork, near Butte, the mining capital of Montana. In and around the city are hundreds of copper, silver, and gold mines that have built many fortunes. Stories abound about how, in past years, the upper Clark Fork ran red for hundreds of miles with mining wastes, causing mass fish kills. Now, long after most of the mines closed and the money was made, poisonous runoff continues to flow into the Clark Fork. Unfortunately for Milltown, a reservoir behind a dam proved to be an ideal trap for the waste. The suspended arsenic settled down to the river bottom and apparently seeped into groundwater that supplies Milltown's wells.

Although the Milltown residents were advised not to use their water for drinking or cooking, no new supply was provided. People had to get their water from outside spigots, connected to another source, or from neighbors. Later, when the state told people it was dangerous to even bathe or water their gardens (high levels of arsenic were discovered in vegetables grown in Milltown), children had to arrange to take showers at school, while adults used whatever facilities were available at neighbors' and relatives' homes.

Finally, in December 1982, it looked as though relief was in sight. Milltown was placed on the EPA's national priority list of the country's worst waste sites, which made it eligible to receive federal funds to clean up the contamination and provide a new supply of water. In May 1983, after waiving the requirement that states pitch in 10 percent of the cleanup costs, the EPA put Milltown on a "fast track" cleanup timetable because the contamination directly involved drinking water.

Still, by August 1984, Milltown had no new source of water. "The response has been real slow," remarks Dan Corti, an environmental health specialist with the Missoula County, Montana, health department. "Thirty-three families in Milltown, Montana, don't carry much weight at the EPA." Agrees resident Bonnie Bush, "The EPA has been terribly slow. We've been hauling water for nearly three years now and we're darn tired of it."

Drilling for new wells was about to begin when another snag developed. Two wells adjacent to the proposed location of the new water supply were found to contain coliform bacteria. Health officials closed the wells, which served another 25 households. "We don't know what to expect now," Bonnie Bush said. Officials still hoped to have the new wells drilled and operating by the beginning of the bitterly cold Montana winter.

Piles of mining waste threaten water quality across the country with heavy metals, radioactivity, and acids. The EPA estimates that contamination from approximately 10,000 inactive mines may require cleanup.[75] In 1980, the Metropolitan Water District of southern California discovered unusually high levels of cancer-causing asbestos in the California Aqueduct, which transports water from the northern part of the state to millions of southern California residents. The fibers were traced to three abandoned asbestos mines in the coastal Diablo mountain range outside the town of Coalinga. Heavy rains wash the asbestos from huge mine waste piles into the aqueduct, which then carries the asbestos to the taps of southern California.

In the East, acid drainage from coal mines has caused severe water quality problems in more than 3,000 miles of streams in Pennsylvania, West Virginia, Maryland, and Virginia.[76]

One of the worst sites of mining waste contamination is in a tri-state area where the Oklahoma, Missouri, and Kansas borders join. There, at the so-called Tar Creek site, wastes running from abandoned zinc and lead mines have dumped cadmium and lead into 40 square miles of shallow groundwater running from northeastern Oklahoma into southwestern Missouri. The pollution also threatens the deeper Roubidoux aquifer, which supplies drinking water to more than 40,000 people in four states. Tar Creek is one of 18 mining sites on the EPA's Superfund list.

Until recently, the EPA was reluctant to use the newly created $1.6 billion Superfund to finance mine cleanups. The fund is largely financed by a tax on the chemical industry, which didn't want to pay to control contamination from mining sites. Further, the mining industry resisted being regulated by the EPA. Rita Lavelle, who was head of the EPA's hazardous waste program at the time, met with both chemical and mining industry representatives on several occasions during 1982 to discuss their objections. The result was an EPA policy to delay spending Superfund money on cleaning up mine waste contamination. In hearings before the Subcommittee on Oversite and Investigations of the House Committee on Energy and Commerce, Lavelle's assistant William Hedeman testified that Lavelle advocated turning over responsibility for cleaning up hazardous mining sites to the Department of the Interior. (She was later fired amid the subcommittee's allegations of mismanagement of the EPA Superfund program and favoritism toward regulated industries.) Such a move would have amounted to a virtual standstill on cleanup.

Then–Interior Secretary James Watt was vehemently opposed to federal intervention in this area, which he regarded as exclusively the domain of the states. Through his department's Office of Surface Mining (OSM), $600 million was available to reclaim land and water resources damaged by surface mining, but the fund was mainly geared toward coal mining, and the OSM's policy was to withhold money to clean up other sites.

Montana already had firsthand knowledge of the OSM's policy. Back in 1980, with no alternative source of money available, the state approached the OSM for funds to clean up Silver Bow Creek, which lies on the outskirts of Butte. For more than a century, ton upon ton of acid mine drainage laced with heavy metals from copper and silver mines had maimed Silver Bow as it flowed into the Clark Fork River. But the OSM turned down the state's request because it could not prove there was any immediate threat to public health—what some state officials call "the floating body proof." The OSM also reiterated it would not provide funds for noncoal sites until Montana's coal sites were taken care of. "They [OSM] don't want to set a national precedent in cleaning up anything other than coal," said one congressional aide.

The fight between Montana and the OSM turned more bitter as time passed. When the EPA designated Silver Bow as the nation's twenty-first worst hazardous waste site, the OSM again refused to provide any funds, claiming that the EPA would then pay for cleanup. Finally, in 1984, following approval of a congressional amendment authored by Montana Senator Max Baucus, the OSM announced it would provide Montana with $1 million to cover "administrative expenses" for mine reclamation. But hard feelings remain. "We've lost a few years on cleanup already and we're still losing it," remarks Victor Andersen of the Montana Solid Waste Management Bureau.

The tentative plan to clean up Silver Bow involves removal of tailings piles. While the EPA continues to study what to do, it is also trying to decide which companies are responsible for contamination of the Silver Bow, and thus who will ultimately pay. In interviews with biologists and government officials, a prime suspect is the Atlantic Richfield Company, which owns Anaconda Minerals Company, the major mine operator in the area. But Anaconda does not seem concerned about possible problems from Silver Bow. "We have two studies . . . which show no damage," says Jim Windorski, Anaconda's manager of health, safety, and environment for Montana operations. "The area looks bad—we'd be the first to admit that—but our studies have shown no significant damage." Windorski even sees improvement. "Silver Bow is making an incredible comeback on its own."

But the EPA says the pollution from the mining operations extends for 43 miles on the Silver Bow and Clark Fork. State health officials are also concerned about the possibility that the mining ponds and tailings piles may contaminate the groundwater. But privately, many scientists say the contamination from Silver Bow extends much further downstream on the Clark Fork and is at least partly responsible for the arsenic at Milltown. "Silver Bow has been no surprise, but Milltown was," Andersen says. "There was no knowledge of any problem [downstream on the Clark Fork] before the [Milltown] arsenic was found." But the EPA still does not acknowledge any connection. "The sites are separate and they are being treated as such," says John Wardell, director of the EPA's Montana office. "There has been no definite link established." But scientists who have studied the area think otherwise. "The contamination is all the way down the river, but they [the

High-Tech Contamination

Even high-tech, light industry may threaten water quality. Near San Jose, California, Fairchild Camera and Instrument somehow managed to lose 58,000 gallons of toxic waste and trichloroethane (TCA), an industrial solvent, from a 5,000-gallon tank over only 18 months. The company claims it reported the leak as soon as it was discovered in late 1981, but by then it was too late. The chemical had already contaminated a community drinking water well, serving thousands of people, with levels several times greater than the state's danger limit. Residents of the neat, modern California subdivisions near the Fairchild electronics plant do not know how long their water was laced with TCA, which can cause damage to the nervous system and birth defects in laboratory animals. But many of them blame the contamination for what a recent state health department study showed is an unusually high rate of birth defects among children born to parents who drank the water. Infants were born with their intestines outside their bodies, heart defects, and missing limbs. Fairchild admits responsibility for contaminating the local drinking water but denies that TCA had anything to do

EPA] don't want to hear about it," says University of Montana botanist Vicki Watson, a participant in a number of studies of the effects of pollution on the Clark Fork.

The cost of cleaning up Silver Bow will be extremely high. The EPA has spent nearly $1 million simply to study what actions to take. "There's not enough money in the Federal Treasury to take care of the whole Silver Bow problem," claims Ben Mundie, a geologist with the Montana Bureau of Abandoned Mine Reclamation. "I don't think they [the EPA] will ever do anything about Silver Bow."

Back at Fort Edward

Given the current pace of cleanup, and the magnitude of the country's hazardous waste problem, it is inevitable that many

with birth defects or miscarriages among people living near the plant. State health officials maintain there is no proof that the contaminated water caused the high rate of birth defects.

The Fairchild leak was the first hint of the widespread groundwater contamination in the Santa Clara Valley (called Silicon Valley because of its heavy concentration of electronics plants). According to the EPA, 300 leaks and spills at high-tech manufacturing plants threaten groundwater in Santa Clara County.[1] In one case, the plume of contaminated groundwater extends more than two miles from an IBM plant in South San Jose. The EPA has placed 19 Silicon Valley sites on its Superfund hazardous waste cleanup list. This gives Santa Clara County, often hailed as a model for future economic development, the dubious distinction of having more Superfund sites than any other county in the United States. Nationally, the EPA estimates that several hundred thousand underground tanks may eventually leak chemicals.[2] Chemical tanks are already responsible for 57 sites on the EPA's Superfund cleanup list.[3]

more people like the Arlingtons and their neighbors on Stevens Lane will find their drinking water contaminated with toxic chemical wastes.

After the Stevens Lane residents refused to sign the agreement with GE, negotiations for providing an alternative water supply dragged on. The company continued to deny responsibility for the contamination, and they refused to pay for the residents' medical exams. "Our understanding is that the department of health has the capability to do the exams, so we didn't consider it appropriate for the company to participate in this evaluation," a GE representative said.[77] The Arlingtons and their neighbors filed a lawsuit against GE asking for $108 million in damages. When no agreement was reached, the New York Department of Environmental Conservation ordered GE to pay to hook up Stevens Lane to the Fort Edward water supply and to pay for health tests. GE threatened to contest the state's order in court. "The order was based on inaccurate data and assumptions," the company claimed. "Even if the data had been accurate, no imminent hazard to human health has been shown."[78] The company's stance did not go over well with the state. "The company was offered several opportunities to negotiate before the order was issued and they chose not to do so," state attorney Marc Pellegrino told a local newspaper.[79]

Finally, on May 11, 1983, after almost four months without water, houses on Stevens Lane were connected to the town water supply. The Arlingtons and their neighbors could turn on their taps and get a drink of water. During that time, Richard Arlington had lugged 1,150 gallons of water into his home.

That didn't end their problems, however. Their house is practically worthless now. Says Richard, "I have nothing to substantiate the fact that none of the realtors will take my property, but I have been given to understand that they do not want a listing on anything on that particular street."[80] The following January, state tests revealed that TCE from another GE dump—the so-called Moreau site, located west of Fort Edward in a wooded area across the Hudson River—was apparently flowing into one of the three reservoirs that supply water to the town's 3,700 residents.[81] The reservoir was closed, but the irony was not lost on state health officer Brian Fear. "They [GE] took it [the waste] from Fort Edward to Moreau and now it's coming back to Fort Edward. It's come full circle."

Now all the Arlingtons and their neighbors can do is wait— for their lawsuit to make its tortuous way through the court process and for any future effect the chemicals might have on their health. But Richard retains his spirit: "We started litigation for the simple reason that everybody said, 'Don't make an attempt. You cannot beat GE.' And I decided that I was going to damn well try. Mostly it's for my children. We've got a lot of kids on this street. It's not for us. We're old. But all these children, in 10 or 20 years, could have all kinds of difficulties."

Despite the obstacles the Arlingtons face, they are lucky in one respect. They can enlist the support of government agencies. But elsewhere in the nation, people often find they cannot turn to the government for help because the government itself is the cause of the contamination.

Military
Contamination
2

The intermittent roar of jets overhead reminds a visitor to Jacksonville, Florida, that this is a navy town. The city has two naval air stations and a combined aircraft carrier port and airfield. The largest of these bases is the Jacksonville Naval Air Station, an immense facility of aircraft hangars, office building complexes, and housing subdivisions, which sprawls over thousands of acres of Jacksonville's south side. Locally known as NAS Jax, the base is largely devoted to maintaining and overhauling navy jet fighters.

The navy has brought prosperity to Jacksonville, where it employs 38,000 military and civilian workers. That's more than the combined employment of the city's next top 12 industries. Its annual payroll is close to $700 million. A navy publication boasts, "Red, green, and blue Department of Defense bumper stickers are visible throughout the business community—at your grocery stores, your shopping centers, your restaurants, at the Gator Bowl, the Coliseum, the Civic Auditorium."

But for some residents the navy's presence has become a mixed blessing. It is northeast Florida's largest generator of hazardous waste. NAS Jax alone produces as much waste as the nine largest companies in the region.[1] The navy now has its hazardous waste hauled to a huge landfill in Alabama, but for years, the waste was either dumped into huge pits on the bases or turned over to private trash haulers. Few records exist of where all this trash ended up. Most likely, it was taken to any number of dumps around Jacksonville. Now, years later, that waste is reappearing in the wells of Jacksonville residents.

Don and Yvonne Woodman live on the western edge of Jacksonville. Their neighborhood along Hipps Road is still semi-rural. Long, straight roads crisscross the flat, sandy, pine-covered countryside so characteristic of northern Florida. When the Woodmans bought their 4.7 acres in 1970, the couple knew the parcel contained 3 acres of a recently closed landfill. During the early 1960s, a local refuse company had simply bulldozed 7 acres of swampy ground and filled the pit with refuse. But the landfill owner assured the Woodmans before they purchased the property that the dump contained only trash and had been supervised by the local sanitation department. The land was cheap, and the young couple was happy to be able to afford the rural lifestyle the neighborhood offered.

It was not until 1979 that the Woodmans' neighbors along Hipps Road noticed anything wrong with the water. Carroll Pittman, a machinist who lives a couple of houses down the road from the Woodmans, recalls that his water "started tasting like oil. It had a bad smell to it. You'd take a shower and you'd open the door of the shower and you could smell it all over the house." When Pittman ran water into a glass, he noticed oil spots on it.

When the county health department tested the Pittmans' well, it checked only for bacteria. The water was fine, the health department told the Pittmans. "But I couldn't drink that water," Pittman says. He purchased a water softener for $300, only to find that the water became worse. The couple next turned to bottled water. But they still had to shower and wash their clothes and dishes with well water. In 1981, after another series of tests showed the water was bacteria-free, the Pittmans shelled out another $1,200 to sink a new well. But one day in the spring of 1983, they returned from a vacation to find a warning from the county health department advising them not to drink their water. The county had retested the water in the neighborhood after complaints from other residents. The tests showed that several wells along Hipps Road were contaminated with low levels of more than a dozen toxic chemicals, many of them cancer causing.

The likely source of the contamination was the landfill in back of the Woodmans' house. There, sandy, barren craters could be seen through a thin screen of pine trees. Rusty cans, old shoes, and discarded tires were scattered about the landfill's moonscape surface. Here and there, a piece of jet fuselage jutted out of the ground.

Although local health officials tried to assure people that the levels of contaminants were too low to cause any immediate health problems, the Woodmans' neighbors Gail and Alvin Speicher weren't so sure. Shortly after the Speichers moved to Hipps Road, their son Wayne was born. They immediately noticed something was wrong with their baby. Wayne was having trouble digesting his food. The Speichers took him to several doctors and finally determined that a rare enzyme deficiency was preventing the infant from processing sugar in his stomach. The Speichers had to monitor his diet carefully. Curiously, after they learned their well was contaminated and began drinking bottled water, Wayne's problem disappeared. Later, after doing some research, the Speichers discovered that ketones, chemical solvents found in their water in relatively high levels, are suspected of interfering with an unborn fetus's ability to form enzymes.

Other residents have suffered from a variety of unexplained health problems, including kidney infections, bladder cancer, hypertension, nausea, dizziness, blackouts and fatigue, muscle spasms, headaches, and learning disabilities among children. Common problems, perhaps, but many residents think their problems are a result of drinking contaminated water, asserts Yvonne Woodman. She herself has suffered prolonged kidney infections, severe headaches, dizziness, and blackouts. Medical testing has not determined the cause of her ailments. "We have some problems here," asserts Mrs. Woodman, a dark-haired woman in her late 30s. "And we have only begun to scratch the surface."

Longtime residents of the neighborhood are pretty sure the navy is the main source of its contamination. Dorothy Johnson, who has lived there for more than 30 years, says trucks filled with navy waste came to the Hipps Road dump "one after another."

Mrs. Woodman agrees. "It was navy trash. Everything was coming from NAS Jacksonville and Cecil Field [the city's other big naval air station]."

When the residents turned to the navy for assistance and information, they were rebuffed—the navy claimed it had no records of any waste having been taken to Hipps Road. "They denied everything, from the very beginning," Mrs. Woodman says angrily.

The Country's Biggest Polluter?

The problem at Hipps Road is just one case of contamination by what may be the country's largest polluter—the military. By its own estimates, the Department of Defense (DOD), which includes the navy, the army, and the air force, generates 1 billion pounds of hazardous material each year, dwarfing the amount produced by most private companies. The navy says that its "ships and shore activities in the United States generate 19 million gallons of liquid hazardous waste and 35 million pounds of hazardous waste solids each year."[2]

Many people don't think of the military as an industry, but it is, and a huge one, employing 4 million people. Its work force is many times larger than that of giant General Motors. Its operations range from munitions manufacturing to ship and aircraft overhauling to on-base dry cleaning. They produce a myriad of toxic substances, including paints and paint removers, solvents and degreasers, hydraulic fluids, heavy metals, by-products of the production of explosives and chemical warfare agents, pesticides, and polychlorinated biphenyls (PCBs). Many of these chemicals are linked to birth defects, cancer, nerve damage, and liver and kidney ailments.

The other major source of military waste is the Department of Energy (DOE). The DOE's principal job is not regulating energy companies or funding research on new sources of energy, but developing and manufacturing nuclear weapons.

The DOE maintains ten nuclear weapon facilities with a combined land area greater than Delaware. Laboratories in New

Mexico and California conduct nuclear weapons research and development. Plants in Ohio, Washington, Idaho, and South Carolina manufacture nuclear material for the warheads. Facilities in a half dozen other states produce components for the nuclear bombs and assemble the weapons. Private industrial contractors—mostly energy and chemical giants such as Rockwell International, Dupont, Exxon, and Bendix—conduct the daily operations of the facilities for the DOE. "The nuclear weapons development and production programs are unique in government in that they constitute an integrated government-owned industry," said the director of the DOE's Office of Military Application, General William Hoover. "We are . . . talking about, in terms of assets and products, what would be a major U.S. industrial corporation—one that would rank in the upper quarter of the Fortune 500."[3]

And, like many private sector industrial corporations, the DOE produces a massive amount of chemical wastes. But unlike most other industries, much of this waste is laced with deadly radioactivity, tiny amounts of which can damage cells and lead to cancer, sterility, and birth defects. There are hundreds of waste sites at 38 DOE facilities around the country. Although the military seeks the most up-to-date technology for weapons and communications, it has used the most primitive methods to dump its billions of pounds of toxic waste. Across the country, military installations are littered with pits and ponds oozing hazardous waste into water supplies. The magnitude of the problem is staggering. The Defense Department has more than 400 facilities handling or storing waste. These installations contain thousands of sites where waste has been deposited. Some of these facilities are huge. The 27-square-mile Rocky Mountain Arsenal near Denver, Colorado, is laced with contaminated land and water. "The magnitude of the problem at some Federal facilities parallels some of the largest hazardous waste dump sites you are going to see anywhere in the country," said Stephen Picco, former assistant commissioner of the New Jersey Department of Environmental Protection.

Many military bases are located in areas where groundwater is extremely vulnerable to contamination. Many air force air fields are located on floodplains, where the land is flat. Such areas are great for runways, but they often have high water tables, which are easy targets for chemicals percolating down through the soil. "Anywhere on an air force base [that] a guy spilled a can of solvents, if you stick enough holes in the ground, you are going to find something," says Lieutenant Colonel Peter Daley, who recently left his position as the Defense Department's director of environmental policy.

The military also has dumped vast quantities of trash and waste into literally thousands of off-base landfills, according to Daley. Some of these sites are now showing up on the EPA's hazardous waste Superfund list. Among the most notorious is the private Stringfellow dump in southern California, which now threatens the drinking water supply for 500,000 people.

The military's most massive contamination problem occurred at the Rocky Mountain Arsenal near Denver, Colorado. The army established the arsenal to manufacture munitions and chemicals for World War II. After the end of the war, the army leased some of the arsenal's facilities to a private chemical concern, which was purchased by Shell Oil in the mid-1950s. The waste from both the army and private operations was discharged into unlined disposal ponds. Before long, the chemicals seeped down to the underlying water table and migrated northward.

The first signs of the contamination occurred in the early 1950s, when farmers northwest of the arsenal noticed that crops irrigated with groundwater were turning yellow and dying. When they complained, the army investigated and determined that the cause of the problem was contaminated groundwater. It had taken the chemicals from the arsenal disposal ponds only a few years to travel three miles. The army compensated the landowners for the damage, and the matter was apparently quietly dropped.

In 1957, the arsenal built a 100-acre asphalt-lined pit to store its waste. Although an improvement over past waste receptacles, the lined pit eventually failed. In 1973 and 1974, there were new claims that tainted groundwater was damaging livestock and crops, and the Colorado Department of Health discovered two chemicals with tongue-twisting names in the groundwater north of the arsenal: di-isopropylmethyposphonate, or simply DIMP, a by-product of the manufacture of toxic chemical warfare agents, and dibromochloropropane (DBCP), a cancer-causing pesticide manufactured by Shell. The state ordered the army and Shell to stop immediately the discharge of DIMP and pesticide wastes into ground and surface water. But ten years later, the waste ponds are still leaking, and the chemicals have spread over 30 square miles of groundwater. Contamination has been detected in irrigation canals, in lakes on arsenal land, and in the nearby South Platte River. At least 12 drinking water wells are tainted.

Rocky Mountain Arsenal was only the first of many such military pollution sites to be discovered. The Defense Department's waste has forced the closing of hundreds of wells from Florida to Washington State. At the pace the cleanup is moving, it will be years before we know the full extent of the damage. As Representative Mike Synar of Oklahoma commented, "We may only be seeing the tip of the iceberg here."[4] Among the worst known cases are these:

- A plume of contamination three miles long and a half mile wide has spread from the army's Cornhusker TNT manufacturing plant near Grand Island, Nebraska. Some 300 wells have been contaminated with TNT, solvents, and RDX, a cancer-causing by-product of explosives manufacturing.

- In 1979, following the discovery of trichlorethylene (TCE) in groundwater near Sacramento, California, officials at nearby McClellan Air Force Base found 11 organic chemicals and toxic heavy metals in nearby wells; one well on the base contained a concentration of the toxic solvent 1,1 dichlorethylene that tested 630,000 times the maximum level recommended by the California Department of Health Services.[5] Four wells on the base and 12 off-site wells have been shut down, and the contamination has spread to a number of others.[6]

- The New Jersey Department of Environmental Protection found concentration of carcinogenic chemicals up to 700 times EPA drinking water standards in groundwater at the Picatinny Arsenal, an army weapons research and development facility in the northwest part of the state. The disposal of chemicals and explosives at Picatinny dates back to the 1920s.

• In early 1983, the seemingly omnipresent TCE was discovered in wells near an army munitions facility in New Brighton, Minnesota. The contamination has spread over an 18-square-mile area. Even though the army denies the facility is the source of the contamination, it has provided bottled water to the affected households.

• Chemicals from an air force missile manufacturing plant operated by Hughes Aircraft Company have infiltrated the aquifer which serves as the primary source of drinking water for the more than 500,000 people in the Tucson, Arizona, metropolitan area, forcing the closing of more than 20 wells, 7 of them municipal.[7]

In a number of cases, the military has been slow to release information or admit responsibility. When the navy denied it dumped waste at Hipps Road, the residents armed themselves with shovels to find out what was actually in the dump. Within a short time they unearthed a dummy artillery shell and an empty can with NAS Jacksonville marking and the label "methyl ethyl ketone," a chemical that also happened to be in their water. Armed with what they considered conclusive evidence of the navy's dumping, the residents turned to their congressman, Charles Bennett, to get some answers.

In his reply to Bennett's inquiries, Captain Salvatore Martinelli, the navy's director of environmental protection, said it was unlikey that the navy ever dumped hazardous waste at Hipps Road, "since NAS Jacksonville had its own hazardous waste disposal sites on base until a few years ago." But the night Martinelli wrote his reply, a retired NAS Jax employee named Henry Foster contacted base officials to tell them the navy had indeed contracted with local refuse companies to remove trash and residual wastes and sludge from the base. Foster also said that, after his retirement from NAS Jax, he had personally dumped navy wastes at Hipps Road. The navy was forced to backtrack. "It is possible that, during this period, the sewage sludge included oils and solvents from the Naval Air Rework Facility at Jacksonville," Martinelli admitted, adding, "We also learned that considerable amounts of wastes from other non-Navy sources were disposed of at the Hipps Road site."

In September 1983, Hipps Road was placed on the EPA's national priority list, making it eligible to receive Superfund cleanup money. The navy has not yet contributed any money, and each household in the affected area has had to pay several hundred dollars to hook up to the city's water system. "You can tell this is not a wealthy neighborhood," Yvonne Woodman says heatedly. "People are on fixed incomes. They cannot afford to plunk out even for a monthly water bill."

Although they blame local officials for failing to heed their earlier warnings, the Hipps Road residents reserve most of their anger for the navy, which they are preparing to sue for damages. "The navy has a responsibility to the citizens in the communities where it is to make sure that it doesn't jeopardize lives from its waste," Mrs. Woodman says.

The Military's Special Status

Ironically, it is more difficult to bring the federal government into compliance with its own environmental regulations than private industry. "We may find that the federal government, which is responsible for ensuring that private companies properly dispose of hazardous waste, is one of the nation's worst violators of our environmental laws," notes Oklahoma Representative Mike Synar.[8] Says Kenneth Kamlet of the National Wildlife Federation, "On matters of hazardous waste [and other pollution control] compliance, federal facilities, most notably Department of Defense installations, have been notoriously recalcitrant in subjecting themselves to supervision by federal and state regulatory authorities."[9]

A major reason for this, Synar explains, is that "DOD, unlike any other federal agency or private company, has been given full authority to determine what constitutes a contamination problem and what action, if any, should be taken to clean it up." The Pentagon's control over its own hazardous waste cleanup dates back to 1975. That year, the army, faced with the discovery of extensive hazardous waste contamination at its Rocky Mountain Arsenal and several other facilities, created the Installation Restoration Program (IRP) to identify and control the migration of hazardous waste from its bases. In 1978, the air force and the navy joined the program.

Then, with the arrival of Superfund in 1980, there was some confusion over whether responsibility for cleaning up military sites rested with the EPA, as it did for private dump sites, or with the DOD. President Reagan decided the question, signing an executive order giving the Defense Department full responsibility to oversee its own cleanup. "We do not have the authority under the law to take corrective action on Federal facilities," stated William Hedeman, head of the EPA's Superfund program, in a 1982 memo.[10] The EPA's enforcement powers are effectively undermined still further by the position of the Department of Justice (DOJ) that it would not sue the DOD or any other federal agency to force it to comply with environmental regulations. The Justice Department declared that suing of an agency of the United States was not among the "enforcement tools . . . necessary or appropriate for one unit of government to use against another."[11] Until 1984, the EPA did not include military sites on its list of the nation's worst hazardous waste dumps.

"The EPA's hands are tied behind its back," contends National Wildlife Federation's Kamlet. "The DOD can basically thumb its nose at the EPA. To make negotiations work, you have to have credibility. There is no credible threat that EPA or DOJ has."

Meanwhile, the military's IRP program has moved extremely slowly. By the end of 1984, the military still had not completed cleanup at a single facility. In fact, according to a November 1984 General Accounting Office (GAO) report, the Defense Department had determined the extent of contamination at only 48 of 200 sites.[12]

Even the assessments that are complete have come under criticism. One EPA regional official said the military's IRP assessments often do not provide enough data for the EPA to tag those DOD facilities which should be placed on the EPA's list of waste sites that pose threats to the environment and public health.

Finally, critics have pointed out an inherent flaw with the IRP: because the Pentagon pays for cleaning up its own mess, there is a built-in conflict of interest. As Synar pointed out, "It is natural the Department of Defense would be reluctant to identify and clean up such sites."[13]

The Department of Energy

Like the Pentagon, DOE has taken the approach of scraping by with the cheapest, most rudimentary waste disposal practices. And the Energy Department enjoys even more autonomy from environmental regulations than the DOD. The DOE sets its own radiation exposure levels, decides how to dispose of its waste, and conducts its own environmental monitoring.

The Energy Department's tightly guarded control over nuclear weapons production is a legacy of the Cold War. Congress was obsessed with the need to closely guard the secret of the atomic bomb and gave the Atomic Energy Commission (AEC), the DOE's predecessor, broad powers to classify information on nuclear weapons production. The AEC used that mandate to create a wall of secrecy around our nuclear weapons program. It would not even release data on what waste its plants produced, arguing that such information could be used to figure out how nuclear weapons were constructed.

Despite growing concern for the environment through the late 1960s and 1970s, the government has been slow to reveal the extent of environmental damage caused by the production of nuclear weapons.

     • In Colorado, the DOE's Rocky Flats facility, which manufactures plutonium triggers for nuclear warheads, has contaminated water supplies in nearby Denver and eight suburban communities with low levels of radioactive plutonium. Although the levels are within federal drinking water standards, one former AEC scientist estimates that levels found periodically in the suburb of Broomfield may increase the risk of developing bone or liver cancer by about 6 percent each year.[14]

• In December 1983, high levels of toxic industrial solvents were found in a domestic well on a farm adjacent to the DOE's nuclear weapons laboratory in Livermore, California, about 50 miles east of San Francisco. A likely source of the contamination was hundreds of leaking chemical storage drums stored at the DOE facility. Lab officials knew about the contamination for more than a year before notifying state authorities, and they excused the delay by claiming it was unclear whether the lab was required to notify the state about the contamination. Martin Kurtovich, an inspector with the state's Regional Water Quality Control Board chalks, it up to a different problem: "I'd call it long-term negligence."

• For more than 30 years, the DOE's Idaho chemical processing plant, operated by Exxon, injected low-level radioactive and chemical waste directly into the Snake River aquifer, which underlies southern Idaho. The radioactive contaminants included strontium-90, cesium, cobalt-60, tritium, plutonium, and iodine-129, which was measured in the groundwater near the injection well at concentrations more than 25 times the recommended EPA drinking water standards.[15] Iodine-129 remains radioactive for millions of years. The tritium in the groundwater has reached the plant's boundary 9 miles away from the injection well and has spread over some 50 square miles.[16] The plant closed its injection well in 1984 and is now discharging the waste into a four-acre, unlined seepage pond. It now takes the tritium in the seepage pond "about a year to reach the groundwater," according to Barney Lewis of the U.S. Geological Survey (USGS).

Probably the most egregious example of the DOE's cover-ups of contamination problems occurred at its nuclear facility in Oak

Ridge, Tennessee. Oak Ridge is one of the nation's oldest atomic plants. In the early 1940s, the government chose the 38,000-acre site to build its first facility for enriching uranium and plutonium for use in nuclear weapons. The rural area was isolated and had access to plentiful electricity. As the Cold War heated up, Oak Ridge grew dramatically. It now employs about 16,000 people and encompasses several large industrial complexes, including the K-25 gaseous diffusion plant, which produces enriched uranium; the Y-12 complex, which manufactures critical components for nuclear weapons; and the Oak Ridge National Laboratory (ORNL).

As Oak Ridge grew, so did its waste problems. The EPA and state health officials knew next to nothing about what chemicals the plant used, how it disposed of its waste, or how Oak Ridge was affecting the surrounding environment. That ignorance changed in the early 1980s, after ORNL biologist Stephen Gough happened to notice "large and unusual" mercury levels in plants while gathering data for a research project.

When his bosses saw his findings, they hit the roof. Gough later said, "Some of the consequences of that reaction included a quashing of further analysis and a request that all material be returned from the USGS without any official recording, the inability by me to pursue this or similar projects, a reprimand for the action, threats aimed at preventing public disclosure of any information, a rapidly deployed follow-up study by Union Carbide [the private contractor that managed Oak Ridge for the DOE] and my removal from consideration for promotion."[17] Gough saw the handwriting on the wall and resigned. It soon became clear why Oak Ridge authorities were so upset by his research.

Around that time, a small local newspaper, the *Appalachian Observer*, got wind that there might be mercury contamination around Oak Ridge and filed a Freedom of Information request to learn what it could. In May 1983, the DOE released a formerly classified 1977 Union Carbide report which revealed that over a 13-year period, from 1953 to 1966, Y-12 had "lost" as much as 2.4 million pounds of toxic mercury to the surrounding environment.[18] An estimated 470,000 pounds of mercury had spilled into the east fork of Poplar Creek. It may be the largest known spill of mercury, a toxic metal that affects the central nervous system to cause paralysis and death.

Oak Ridge had known about the mercury problems since 1976. In 1977, the chief of Oak Ridge's environmental protection branch, Jerry Wing, noted in a memo, "This type of information could reach the public in an aberrant perspective and cause undue concern over non-existent health hazards or relatively insignificant environmental matters." Oak Ridge kept the mercury loss a secret.

Y-12 hasn't used the mercury process for more than 20 years. But each day, from the mercury trapped in springs and sumps beneath the plant, about two ounces leaks out into Poplar Creek.

Health officials say that mercury poses no immediate threat to residents of the area. But the revelation of the lost mercury has opened Oak Ridge to closer scrutiny by the State of Tennessee and the EPA. "Y-12 is a witch's cauldron of environmental problems," says Michael Bruner, assistant commissioner of the Tennessee Department of Health. "Other known pollutants from Y-12 may have an even more significant impact than mercury. Until there is a comprehensive assessment of all the problems at Y-12, it would be premature to focus on mercury and mercury alone."[19]

Nearly 150 pipes pour wastewater contaminated with heavy metals, toxic solvents, and radioactivity into the headwaters of Poplar Creek. Says Tennessee Valley Authority (TVA) director David Freeman, "We do not know the precise pollutants that are being discharged except that DOE has reported to the state that they include such highly toxic items as PCBs and uranium, beryllium, thorium, lead, and plutonium."[20] At the other end of the Y-12 facility, 1.5 million gallons of untreated waste, including plating sludges, acids, solvents, uranium, beryllium, and thorium (the last three elements are radioactive), are discharged into four settling basins known as the S-3 holding ponds. Much of the waste in the S-3 ponds simply leaks into nearby Bear Creek, which flows into the Clinch River or percolates down to the water table. Chemical analyses of groundwater in the vicinity of the ponds have extremely high levels of a number of radioactive and chemical contaminants. The concentration of perchloroethylene, a cancer-causing solvent, has been tested at more than 35,000 times the recommended EPA water quality criterion.[21]

The wastes from the K-25 gaseous diffusion plant and ORNL may pose equally serious water problems. At the state health department, Michael Bruner predicts, "If the antiquated waste handling methods at Y-12 are representative of the Oak Ridge operation, then the surface may have only been scratched in terms of the total magnitude of the problem."[22]

Oak Ridge is also a receptacle for an enormous amount of radioactive waste. About 13 million cubic feet of radioactive debris—enough to fill a large stadium—has been dumped into dozens of burial trenches. The bottoms of many of the trenches are below the water table, and radioactivity at levels up to millions of times higher than federal drinking water standards has contaminated groundwater. Large amounts of radioactive elements have also poured out of the trenches and into nearby streams which flow into the Clinch and Tennessee rivers. No underground drinking water supplies are immediately threatened, but because radioactivity can persist for millions of years, there is concern the contamination may eventually reach some of the 16 public wells within 20 miles of Oak Ridge.

The "Bomb Plant"

The uranium metal fabricated at Oak Ridge is shipped to the DOE's Savannah River plant (SRP) in South Carolina, where it is bombarded with neutrons to make plutonium for nuclear warheads. SRP also manufactures most of the tritium for our nuclear weapons. The amount of radioactivity the SRP handles dwarfs that at all the other DOE facilities; nearly 75 percent of all DOE high-level radioactive waste is stored there, and the plant handles tremendous amounts of low-level radioactive and chemical waste.

The SRP, which is managed for the DOE by Dupont, is located on 300 square miles of countryside along the Savannah River, which forms the South Carolina border with Georgia to the south. There is little to suggest the presence of this huge federal facility on a drive through the small towns on the road leading to the plant. A couple of miles before the SRP, however, the road changes into a newly poured double-lane highway, and the large gates to the plant become visible. Signs along the road to the administration building warn of the need for security.

None of the SRP's huge production facilities is visible from the administration building, but reminders of the SRP's mission are everywhere. Portraits of the president and the DOE secretary adorn the walls of the lobby. A row of urine samples in plastic bottles stands on a shelf in the men's rest room, awaiting analysis for radioactivity. Visitors are not allowed beyond the lobby without special permission. We could not tape any conversation.

A couple of miles to the east is the SRP's main radioactive storage area, which contains 51 double-walled steel tanks located in two "tank farms" called the F and H areas. These tanks contain fission by-products of the manufacture of tritium and plutonium. At least 8 of the tanks have leaked.

In the tanks, the waste eventually separates into a liquid portion and a highly radioactive sludge. The liquid—still radioactive—is decanted and eventually discharged into seven large seepage basins. Like many settling ponds, these leak. Alpha radiation levels more than 1,000 times higher than federal drinking water standards have been measured in nearby monitoring wells. Strontium-90 and tritium have also been migrating into the groundwater.[23]

Located between the F and H areas is a 195-acre low-level radioactive burial ground. For more than 30 years, SRP personnel dumped contaminated equipment, spent reactor parts, used oil, mercury, and tritium waste into trenches. As was the case at Oak Ridge, much of the waste was simply put in cardboard containers or dropped straight into the trenches. The radioactivity migrated into the shallow water table under the burial ground, and radioactive tritium, cobalt, cesium, strontium, and plutonium have all been detected in the groundwater.

This contaminated groundwater flows several hundred yards into Four Mile Creek. The creek, in turn, flows into the Savannah River, which provides drinking water for several thousand people downstream. The DOE contends the levels of radiation in the Savannah River are so dilute that they pose no threat to public health.

But according to one former SRP waste management expert, the plant did not tell the public the full extent of the groundwater contamination problems at its waste storage facilities. William Lawless, an engineer, had been responsible for auditing the effectiveness of Dupont's radioactive waste management program. During his six years as a DOE employee at the SRP, Lawless became aware of what he considered serious deficiencies in the plant's waste operation. He filed reports detailing the problems, but Lawless says his criticisms of the burial ground operations were simply shuffled around by the DOE-Dupont bureaucracy and never published. He was stripped of most of his responsibilities and resigned in 1983.

Lawless charges that Dupont knew the groundwater under the burial ground was contaminated with tritium levels up to 200,000 times the EPA drinking water standard but that they omitted that information in external SRP reports. "So, instead of finding something 200,000 times higher, you might find a level many times lower, just above the drinking water standard." The SRP's director of environment Grover Smithwick does not dispute Lawless's claim, but he contends that comparing the contamination level to EPA drinking water standards is "really inappropriate" because the groundwater is not a source of drinking water. The high levels of tritium contamination were not reported publicly, he adds, simply because the results were not intended for publication in external reports.

Nonradioactive substances discarded from SRP operations, including mercury, TCE, and chromium, have also contaminated groundwater. The worst incident to date affected drinking water for plant employees. In March 1983, it was revealed that wells supplying SRP's administration building were contaminated with cancer-causing solvents, an estimated 100,000 pounds of which had leached into the groundwater from a seepage basin located nearby.[24] It turned out that Dupont's public works department knew about the contamination for more than a year but failed to inform the DOE's environment department. The heavily contaminated wells were closed, and the plant began to pump water out of the ground to strip away the contaminants. But Smithwick, a health physicist who speaks extremely deliberately, doesn't appear concerned. "I am not worried about any of the contamination posing a threat to either the public or the plant workers," he says assuredly.

Lawless doesn't agree. He predicts the area around the plant will be unusable—for centuries.

Uranium Mining and Milling

The threat that nuclear weapons production poses to water quality is not confined to the Department of Energy's nuclear facilities. Uranium mining and processing also have contaminated water in many states in the Southwest, particularly New Mexico and Colorado.

The final product of uranium milling is only a tiny fraction of the amount of ore taken out of the earth. The leftover wastes contain much of the original radioactivity and a variety of toxic substances, primarily heavy metals; they are dumped into waste ponds or piled up in huge mounds called tailings piles.

New Mexico has 5 of the nation's 23 operating uranium mills. All 5 use evaporation ponds to dispose of wastewater, and all have caused contamination of groundwater.[25] In the groundwater below a Homestake Mining Company uranium mill in Milan, New Mexico, concentrations of uranium, nitrate, selenium, and molybdenum exceed the state's standards. Selenium concentrations are high enough to have forced about 200 residents of nearby housing subdivisions to go to bottled water, provided by the company. In July 1983, Homestake reached an out-of-court settlement with residents who had brought a lawsuit, agreeing to pay cash settlements and to foot the bill for water and sewer hookups to a municipal water system. Homestake will also continue to pay the residents' water bills for ten years.[26]

Since 1977, acidic wastes at United Nuclear Corporation's uranium mill in Church Rock, New Mexico, have been leaking out of evaporation ponds, contaminating the underlying aquifer with radioactive thorium-230, arsenic, cadmium, and nitrates. The concentrations of thorium are among the highest found in water anywhere in the world. The contamination has spread to a Navajo Indian reservation located three-fourths of a mile away from the site, so the groundwater there can't be used for livestock or domestic uses. The EPA has placed both the Homestake and the United Nuclear Corporation sites on its Superfund list of the nation's most hazardous waste sites. Both companies have sued the agency over its listing.[27]

Under the 1978 Uranium Mill Tailings Radiation Control Act (UMTRA), the EPA is responsible for establishing groundwater protection requirements. Either the U.S. Nuclear Regulatory Commission or the state then approves the mill operator's plan to control the tailings and prevent seepage into groundwater. The UMTRA also mandates that controls for nonradioactive hazards in tailings be "consistent with" those adopted under the Resource, Conservation, and Recovery Act (RCRA). In December 1983, the EPA issued regulations that require all existing and new tailings piles to have synthetic liners to prevent groundwater contamination. The uranium mining industry has lobbied Congress to repeal the "consistency with" RCRA language, but so far it has been unsuccessful.

Inactive mill tailings sites were supposed to be cleaned up by the mid-1980s, but not a single job is expected to be completed until 1986.[28]

Keeping the Public in the Dark

Even if the military has not, as Peter Daley said, made a "deliberate" attempt to mislead anybody, state officials and citizens around the country feel that the military has used its authority and special status to keep them in the dark about its massive contamination problems. The incident at Jacksonville is not an isolated example. At McClellan Air Force Base, near Sacramento, base officials have been extremely slow to release information about its groundwater contamination to state and local regulatory agencies. In a 1983 report, the GAO concluded that these agencies "have repeatedly been hampered because the Air Force did not respond in a timely manner to requests for data." In Florida, the state Department of Environmental Regulation is locked in a legal battle with the navy over who will pay for the cleanup of groundwater contaminated by navy wastes.

The DOE, hiding behind the cloak of national security, has been even more reticent to divulge information about its environmental problems. "We don't feel we have to comply with state law," says Ed Keheley, chief of the Environmental and Nuclear Branch in the DOE's San Francisco office. When the Tennessee Department of Health and Environment tried in 1979 to obtain information on the chemicals the DOE's Oak Ridge facility was discharging, "What we got was garbage, total garbage," state health official David Kinney told the *Knoxville Journal*.[29]

The EPA shares part of the blame. For years it preferred to leave its fellow federal agencies to their own devices. It did not, for example, challenge the DOE's claim of exemption from environmental regulations because of national security. "Perhaps we were not as aggressive as we could have been," admits Howard Zeller, the EPA's assistant regional administrator for the Southeast.[30] The results of this self-regulation are predictable. "There isn't a DOE site in the system that could pass an environmental test of any sort," Bill Lawless contends. "All of them are really in bad shape."

State regulators are now more apt to enforce environmental laws at DOD and DOE facilities. They finally realize the magnitude of the threat to public health and the environment that these bases pose. In January 1983, South Carolina joined a successful lawsuit brought by the Natural Resources Defense Council (NRDC) to force the DOE to prepare an environmental impact report on its planned start-up of an additional plutonium production reactor at the SRP. In Tennessee, a month later, the state health department responded to the huge mercury releases from the Y-12 facility by conducting its first comprehensive inspection of the plant. The state found many deficiencies in waste disposal practices there, and it later joined a lawsuit filed by NRDC and the Legal Environmental Assistance Foundation charging DOE with improperly dumping tons of chemicals. DOE lawyers argued for dismissal of the suit because "any limitation on the operation of the Y-12 facilities would impair all weapons production." But a U.S. District Court judge ruled that the DOE should not be exempt from any hazardous waste laws. (The DOE still regulates the disposal of radioactive waste, however.)

The EPA, after much prodding, has finally also become more aggressive with the Energy Department. After a 1983 meeting between the DOE, the EPA, and the Tennessee Health Department to discuss cleanup of the Y-12 facility, DOE environmental official Gabriel Marciante noted in a memo, "We can no longer expect EPA to buffer us from the state."[31]

There have been some changes in the relationship between the DOD and the EPA. In August 1983, the EPA and the Pentagon signed an agreement giving the EPA some power to determine whether the DOD is responsible for off-site contamination and to collect reimbursement for the funds expended on cleanup. The DOD is also supposed to share information with the EPA. The military, however, retains control over on-site cleanup. Since the agreement was signed there have been no problems, according to Daley. "Without exception, we have been able to negotiate satisfactory resolutions with the EPA to every problem that has come to my level," he says.

But the Pentagon still refuses to acknowledge responsibility for contamination past its bases' boundaries unless it can be proven conclusively that the military is the sole source of the problem. Says one state health official, the air force has "demonstrated a tremendous reluctance to address the off-base issues in any fashion." "We are fiscally constrained from spending defense money on things that are not defense responsibilities," says Daley. "If the EPA or state or any responsible public agency came to us and said, 'Pick up your share,' we would be glad to enter into discussions."

But the balance of power remains on the side of the Pentagon. "We can't enforce a penalty. We don't have the leverage," says one EPA official. "I guess we're hoping for cooperation."

Suing the Military

The Woodmans are taking a different approach to dealing with the military. They and several dozen of their neighbors are about to file damage claims against the navy. It is likely the military will try to claim some sort of government immunity—in other words, that the contamination occurred while the military was conducting its appointed duty: defending the country. The plaintiffs will have to prove that the navy acted recklessly. Additionally, any suit against the military is decided by a judge, not a jury. Juries tend to be more sympathetic, and less obsessed with minute legal details. "I'd rather argue in front of a jury of peers," says Washington, D.C., attorney Ron Simon, who represents the Hipps Road residents.

One plaintiff against the military who has already met such hurdles is Maud Thomas. She and her husband live on four acres of woods and meadows in Phoenix, Maryland, about 20 miles north of Baltimore. When the Thomases bought the land in 1974, they intended to retire there. "My husband worked every evening and weekends to build this house," says Mrs. Thomas. "We never thought of any water problems." Indeed, looking at the blooming dogwood and azaleas that surround the Thomas house, it's hard to imagine that their well could be less than pure. But shortly after they moved in, Mrs. Thomas noticed the water tasted odd. When they brewed tea, the pot turned black. A greasy scum formed on the top of their coffee. Earlier, county tests had shown no bacteria, so they continued to assume the water was safe.

But in 1981, the Baltimore County Health Department told the Thomases that their water was contaminated with trichlorethylene. Several of their neighbors' wells were also fouled. The apparent source of the TCE was located about a fourth of a mile away—an abandoned army Nike missile base, strangely incongruous in the lightly settled area.

The army refused to acknowledge it was the source of the contamination and did not provide drinking water to the affected households. In frustration, the Thomases appealed to their congressman to intervene, and after nearly two years the army began to deliver bottled water to the houses with tainted wells. But the

Thomas family still had to use well water to shower and wash clothes. After showering in it, the family broke out with skin rashes. Their clothes came out of the washing machine frayed and full of tiny holes. They have thought about moving, but they realize their house would now bring them little money.

Meanwhile, they wait for their day in court. Already their suit has been delayed several times. "We wait on them," says Mrs. Thomas. "It's not fair. The military has its own rules."

The Massive Cleanup

Back in 1981, then–Deputy Assistant Secretary of Defense George Marienthal explained the military's position on cleanup of its bases to a Senate committee: "If we no longer need that particular land, then the best position for the U.S. government to take is to put a very large fence around it and let nature take its course, because there is not enough money in the world to clean up all the sites in light of today's knowledge. . . . So the big fence concept is much more viable than the ultimate cleanup."[32]

This concept hasn't set well with several states. Michigan wants the military to restore an aquifer contaminated by TCE from Wurtsmith Air Force Base. But because the aquifer has only one user, "We feel that it is not economical for us to do that," Daley says. "We would much prefer to give this one user an alternate water supply and let the problem take care of itself."

Perhaps the longest-running battle over cleanup of military contamination has been at the Rocky Mountain Arsenal. Ten years after the Colorado Department of Health ordered the army and Shell Chemical to stop discharging waste into surface and ground-water, the waste disposal basins were still leaking. The army and Shell spent millions of dollars through the end of 1983 to study the problem and stem the spread of the groundwater contamination, but the army has balked at restoring the arsenal's land and water to its original purity.

Instead, along with Shell, it has constructed a series of three barriers on the arsenal's northern and northwestern boundaries, to prevent the chemicals from migrating off the site. The barriers consist of trenches filled with a mixture of clay and sand. Contaminated water is pumped out of the ground inside the boundary, passed through a series of carbon filters to remove the contaminants, and then reinjected into the aquifer.

But three years after the construction of the barriers, "We're still finding DBCP and DIMP in off-site wells," says Colorado public health engineer Mary Cervera. "The waste disposal basins are still there. They're being cleaned up very slowly—in effect not at all." The state has found the Rocky Mountain Arsenal in violation of the federal RCRA and of the state's Hazardous Waste and Solid Waste acts. It has sued the army and Shell, asking for $50 million for each release of a toxic substance that damages natural resources. "The state is very concerned about the potential for those contaminants leaching to deeper aquifers and passing under the barriers," says Thomas Looby of the Colorado Health Department.

Cervera thinks the most optimistic estimate is "probably partial clean-up over the next ten years. That's if they figure out why the barrier systems are either seeping through or leaking." The money already spent on cleanup at the arsenal is a drop in the bucket; estimates of the eventual cost of restoring the site range up to several billion dollars.

All told, the Defense Department had spent only $202 million on cleanup from 1975 to 1983.[33] In 1984, the Pentagon estimated it would have to spend another $1.6 billion through 1993. But that figure is "probably not even in the ballpark," said Representative Vic Fazio of California at that time. Added Representative James Florio of New Jersey, "This estimate drastically understates the scope of the problem and it reflects the military's unwillingness to take an aggressive and honest approach to facing the cleanup needs it will inevitably face." Sure enough, in early 1985 the military increased its estimate of clean-up costs to $5 to $10 billion.

The price of cleaning up the TCE-contaminated aquifer beneath Tucson, for example, is now estimated to be $79 million, up from an earlier guess of $20 million.[34] In 1982, the DOD thought it would cost $5 million to clean up the contamination at McClellan. In 1984, its projection was $81.9 million,[35] while an unofficial contractor estimated costs of $106 million.[36] These figures do not anticipate the cost of numerous lawsuits against the DOD by private citizens whose wells have been fouled by military waste.

Cleanup at Energy Department nuclear weapons plants will also prove extensive. According to the DOE, the Savannah River plant alone has 145 individual waste sites with the potential to contaminate groundwater.[37] At Oak Ridge, the DOE estimates it will cost $800 million simply to comply with state and federal hazardous waste and water pollution laws.[38] One Tennessee health official thinks it will take ten years to clean up Oak Ridge. That's an optimistic guess. Clearly, restoring groundwater will probably cost much more. The only alternative is to let nature purify itself at its own pace, a process that will take hundreds, even thousands of years.

Whatever is done, the American public will end up paying for the pollution generated in the name of defending the country, both in dollars and in threatened health, for decades to come.

The Pesticide Trickle-Down

3

"I love this country," said Florida Highway Patrolman Lawrence Gladieux, looking out over the gently rolling landscape and orange trees surrounding his house. When Gladieux and his family moved there a few years ago, he was ready to settle permanently. The two-and-a-half acres he owns sits in the middle of the state's vast citrus area. It provides enough pleasant space for his three young children to roam and play and for him to raise geese and chickens. But all that changed in September 1983.

One day that month, a man in a white hat walked up to Gladieux's driveway and said he wanted to sample Gladieux's well. He explained he was an employee of the Florida Department of Agriculture Pest Eradication Branch, which was testing wells near areas where the pesticide ethylene dibromide (EDB) had been injected into the soil. Gladieux knew EDB had been applied several hundred feet from his house, but the official assured him that the department's experts felt sure the tests would confirm that Gladieux's well was safe.

Greatly relieved, Gladieux told the state official to go right ahead and sample his well. "If you can't trust a guy in a white hat, who can you trust?" Gladieux says, his boyish features breaking into a grin.

Soon after the state took samples from his well, Gladieux received a call from a local TV reporter. The reporter wanted to get Gladieux's reaction to the news that his water was contaminated with EDB. Gladieux was caught completely by surprise; he had never heard back from the state about the results of the tests. He hung up on the reporter. But sure enough, a couple of days later, he got a letter from the Florida Department of Health and Rehabilitative Services telling him to discontinue the use of his water because it contained low levels of EDB. The letter gave him a telephone number to call for more information.

Gladieux immediately picked up the phone. The voice on the other end referred him to another number. The second call produced another referral. Finally, he reached a state official willing to talk to him but unable to answer any of his questions. Exasperated, Gladieux asked him what he did know about the EDB in his water. "Boy, if it was me, I wouldn't drink it," the man replied.

"I panicked," recalls Gladieux. "The first thing my wife and I did was call the in-laws and ask them if they could keep the kids."

Now Gladieux and his wife must take time out of busy work schedules to drive six miles round-trip to pick up water from the town of Mineola. The contamination has changed the Gladieux family's lives. "It dwells on my wife and me," Gladieux says. "Every time we wash our hands, every time we have to put my little baby boy in the tub and give him a bath, we wonder, What are we doing to this child? We have to break the children of the habit of thinking you can go to the faucet and get water."[1]

A National Problem

Gladieux's well is 1 of more than 700 Florida wells contaminated with EDB; some 60,000 people are affected.[2] EDB has also been found in drinking water in Hawaii, California, Virginia, Massachusetts, South Carolina, Washington, Connecticut, and Arizona.

According to the EPA, pesticides have been found in groundwater in more than 20 states.[3] Thousands of wells have been closed from Maine to Hawaii. The drinking water of millions of Americans is now tainted with chemical poisons used to kill bothersome insects, fungi, and weeds. "Groundwater contamination by pesticides or pesticides residues is probably the single biggest environmental issue of the next decade," said EPA scientific advisory panel member Dr. Christopher Wilkinson.[4]

- In California, traces of dibromochloropropane (DBCP), a cancer-causing pesticide similar to EDB, have tainted 3,500 wells.[5] Additionally, the California Water Resources Board has reported that 50 other pesticides have been found in groundwater in 23 of the state's counties.[6]

- In Wisconsin, 11 different pesticides have been detected in nearly 250 wells. Seven of the pesticides have exceeded recommended drinking water standards.[7]

- On Long Island, more than 4,000 wells are tainted with Temik, one of the most potent pesticides on the market. Tests also detected the presence of two other pesticides: carbofuran, which has contaminated more than 1,000 wells, and Vydate, which has been found in about 100 wells.[8] None of the three pesticides is used any longer on Long Island.

- Pesticides have also contaminated groundwater in several of the midwestern farm belt states. Generally the levels have been low, and they have not led to well closings. But tests have found that following heavy rains, the pesticide concentrations in the groundwater can increase dramatically.

As with other pollutants, the extent of pesticide contamination of drinking water is not known. There is no systematic testing for pesticides. Water suppliers are required to test for only six of the thousands of pesticides on the market.

But the hazards of pesticides have been known to us for some time. We can't say we haven't been warned. Rachel Carson sounded the alarm about the unrestricted use of pesticides more than 20 years ago in *Silent Spring*. Carson's eloquent appeal had a profound impact. Both her reputation and her book survived vicious attacks by the chemical industry, and *Silent Spring* went on to galvanize the growing environmental concern of the 1960s. It also led to comprehensive studies of the effects of pesticides in the environment, to greater awareness of the dangers of pesticide use, and eventually to extensive reforms of the government's regulation of pesticides.

Silent Spring pointed out a simple truth. Pesticides, which are by definition chemical poisons, are usually indiscriminate killers. They not only destroy the target pest, but may also affect fish, birds, and mammals, including humans. Despite the impact of *Silent Spring*, the use of pesticides continues to soar. The U.S. Department of Agriculture (USDA) estimates that 2.5 billion pounds of pesticides are applied annually to American soil, a 1,800 percent increase since 1947.[9] Sales of pesticides in 1982 totaled more than $4 billion.[10] David Pimental, a Cornell University professor of entomology and agricultural sciences, told the *New York Times*, "We're treating more acres and using more pesticides than ever before. Even after Rachel Carson, we haven't gained a whole lot."[11]

The EPA, which is responsible for making sure of the safety of pesticides before approving them for marketing, is not equal to the task. Its understaffed pesticide program can barely deal with the thousands of pesticide products already on the market. The agency also finds itself overwhelmed by the chemical industry's well-financed scientific and legal staffs. Furthermore, the EPA depends on data generated by the manufacturers themselves to determine the safety of pesticides, and it is handicapped by loopholes in the pesticide laws. The result: the EPA's attempts to regulate pesticides have been inconsistent, hesitant, and fraught with delays.

On top of that, the EPA was slow to discover the impact of pesticides on groundwater. As was the case with toxic waste, the agency focused on pesticides in our rivers, streams, and lakes. Groundwater was until recently assumed to be relatively immune to the threat of pesticides. In 1972, the highly regarded Stanford Research Institute in California concluded, "The incidence of pesticides in groundwater is low and not a significant environmental contamination factor."[12] Many experts thought that pesticides could not move very far through the layer of soil that separates the surface of the ground from the underlying aquifer. They were wrong. They had not considered the role of rainfall.

We think of rain as a cleansing force. A gentle spring shower clears the air, strips away grit and oil from streets and buildings, and brings a sparkle to plants and trees. But while rain cleans our immediate, visible environment of accumulated oil, dirt, pesticides, chemical fertilizers, and bacteria, these substances don't simply vanish. They run into our streams, rivers, and lakes. Less obviously, they are carried through the ground to the underlying water. Substances such as pesticides that are carried by storm runoff into surface water or groundwater are called nonpoint pollution. That term came about because the contamination is not discharged purposely from a specific source—known as a point source—such as a factory or municipal sewage plant. Nonpoint pollution includes runoff from farms, city streets, and roadways; erosion from construction sites and logging operations; acids and heavy metals draining from abandoned mines; and wastes leaking from an unknown number of septic tanks. Pollutants that rain carries down from the atmosphere are also considered nonpoint.

Because it is so diffuse and the source of the contamination is not obvious, nonpoint pollution is much less dramatic than a large factory's wastes spewing directly into a river. But while the threat that pesticides pose to groundwater was initially easier to ignore, by 1979 scientists and government regulators were forced to take notice. That year, two massive pesticide contamination incidents, some 3,000 miles apart, forced a drastic change in attitudes toward pesticide contamination.

Pesticide Contamination, East and West

In 1979, the Suffolk County, New York, health department began to sample wells on the eastern end of Long Island for a powerful pesticide used by local potato farmers. The tests revealed that aldicarb, manufactured by Union Carbide under the brand name of Temik, had seeped through the ground and contaminated an aquifer that provided drinking water for more than a million people.

The discovery of Temik in groundwater was disturbing, to put it mildly. Temik was one of the most toxic pesticides on the market. If, on your way down a staircase, you picked up the product with wet hands, "you wouldn't make it to the bottom of the stairs," says Howard Rhodes of Florida's Department of Environmental Regulation. The chemical's long-term health problems aren't known: "Temik is so toxic, it cannot be tested at high levels in small animals," one scientist told CBS News.

Temik has contaminated more than 4,400 wells on Long Island alone and has been found from California to Maine, where it was detected in two-thirds of the wells sampled. At least 12 states have banned Temik, although the EPA has so far not done so.[13]

While health officials were uncovering the Temik contamination on Long Island, California was confronted with groundwater pollution from another pesticide. In the summer of 1977, sperm tests confirmed what many workers at a Lathrop, California, pesticide plant had feared. Some 35 of the factory's 114 male employees were sterile.[14] The low sperm counts were traced to a pesticide called dibromochloropropane, or DBCP for short. A month after learning of the sterility among the Lathrop workers, the state suspended the use of DBCP. The EPA, although it prohibited the use of DBCP on several crops, did not ban the pesticide until more than two years later.

Ironically, just as California was considering reintroducing DBCP for some uses, it discovered another problem. DBCP, which, like EDB, was injected into the soil to kill nematodes, was getting into groundwater. This might never have been discovered if it hadn't been for a totally unrelated event.

In 1978, Occidental Petroleum was forced to release internal company documents in the course of a lawsuit stemming from its unfriendly takeover attempt of the Ohio-based Mead Corporation. The Occidental memos detailed how pesticide waste dumped at Lathrop by its subsidiary, OxyChem, had seeped down to the groundwater and infiltrated drinking water wells near the plant. It was clear that OxyChem had known about the contamination for several years but had failed to inform the state's Regional Water Quality Control Board.

When the state found out about the contamination, it tested wells near the facility. The concentration of DBCP in one ground-water sample was 1,240 parts per billion (ppb), more than 1,000 times higher than the 1 ppb limit California would eventually adopt as its drinking water exposure standard. Tests also revealed the presence of 20 other pesticides in groundwater near the plant.[15] Late in 1979, California and the EPA sued Occidental to pay for the cleanup. The evidence was stacked against the oil company. In the settlement, Occidental agreed to clean up the contamination and make payments to California until the year 2000.

After the OxyChem contamination was discovered, the state was spurred to look farther for DBCP in groundwater. The findings were alarming. The California Department of Food and Agriculture (CDFA) found that some 20 percent of the 262 wells it initially sampled in the state's Central Valley region contained more than 1 ppb of DBCP,[16] a level the state health department said would cause one additional cancer in every 5,000 people drinking the water. The extent of the contamination caught health officials by surprise. "Until DBCP, we never thought to check the groundwater," admitted Gunter Redlin, supervising sanitary engineer of the state health department.[17]

To date, DBCP has been found in more than 3,500 wells in ten California counties stretching from Sacramento to Los Angeles. More than 20 large public systems, including the water supply for Disneyland, that bastion of childhood innocence and fantasy, have been tainted. The area of DBCP contamination stretches for 7,000 square miles and affects the drinking water of close to a million Californians.

In 1982, the state health department released an unsettling health study that indicated a link between DBCP in the water and cancer. This survey of more than 1,200 Fresno County cancer deaths from 1970 to 1979 revealed a higher rate of stomach cancer where the water supply had been contaminated with higher levels of DBCP.[18] Although the study was far from conclusive, it was difficult to overlook a disturbing coincidence: laboratory rats and mice fed DBCP also developed stomach cancer.

DBCP was later found in dozens of wells in Arizona, South Carolina, and Hawaii. But when the EPA banned DBCP in October 1979, then–EPA Administrator Douglas Costle granted one exception for this effective nematode killer. He allowed its continued use in Hawaii in the mistaken belief that it would not contaminate the islands' water supply. This proved to be a very unfortunate decision for that state.

The Politics of Pesticide Regulation

With DBCP banned, farmers turned to a number of replacements. Among the most common was EDB—a poor choice, because it is more carcinogenic than DBCP. The federal government knew for several years that EDB was dangerous but failed to restrict its use until September 1983, after EDB caused widespread groundwater contamination. The delay was primarily caused by "economic and political considerations, as well as bureaucratic footdragging and inefficiencies," according to a House Government Operations Committee report, "rather than [by] legitimate scientific disputes about the dangers of EDB."[19]

The pesticide was formulated in the 1920s by scientists at Dow Chemical. Its first use was as an additive in leaded gasoline, to prevent lead from collecting in car engines. This remains its primary purpose today. EDB's pesticidal power wasn't discovered until the 1940s, a period when industry and government scientists were testing chemical after chemical for their effectiveness against agricultural pests. Impressed with the chemical's success as a nematode killer, the USDA registered it as a pesticide in 1951 and set out to promote its use on farms across the country. One target area was Florida, where citrus groves were suffering from a disease known as spreading decline, caused by nematodes.

But questions about EDB's effects on health surfaced in the early 1970s. The National Cancer Institute's tests of commonly used chemicals revealed that EDB caused an extremely high rate of cancer in laboratory animals. Exposure to the pesticide could also lead to sterility. In 1977, the EPA began a review of EDB to determine whether to remove it from the market. Three years later, in December 1980, the agency proposed banning many of the chemical's uses but recommended the continued use of EDB as a soil fumigant against nematodes—provided certain safety measures were implemented and that the manufacturers conducted studies to determine whether the pesticide could leach into groundwater. The EPA was worried because EDB was chemically so similar to DBCP, already found to be responsible for contaminating hundreds of wells in California and Arizona.

Any EPA action to restrict the use of EDB ground to a halt with the Reagan administration's arrival in Washington. The new administration ushered in a different approach to environmental regulation. The new regulatory relief task force, under the direction of Vice-President George Bush, announced its intention to make it easier and faster to register pesticides. The regulation of EDB was one of the first casualties of that new philosophy.

In spring 1981, an EPA advisory panel of expert scientists agreed with the decision to restrict EDB. But, in response, the EPA, now under a new administration, put regulatory action on hold. In fact, it went one step further: it expanded EDB use. That summer the USDA decided to *require* the use of EDB on fruit exported from California to Japan. The Japanese had threatened to refuse imports of unfumigated California fruit because of the possibility it had been infected with larvae of the Mediterranean fruit fly.

EPA Assistant Administrator for Pesticides and Toxic Substances John Todhunter recommended the use of EDB on exported fruit over the objections of his own staff. Dr. Adrian Gross, chief scientist of the EPA's hazards evaluation division, criticized Todhunter's decision, calling EDB "probably the most potent and carcinogenic substance used as a pesticide today."[20]

Anxious to save one of its most effective chemicals, the citrus industry also brought pressure. James Lake, a lobbyist who would later become communications director for President Reagan's reelection committee, arranged a series of meetings between representatives of the citrus industry and officials from various federal agencies, including the EPA and USDA.[21] From fall 1981 through the next spring, the citrus industry conferred with government regulatory staffs. Meanwhile, Todhunter's staff prepared an order that would have immediately banned the use of EDB as a postharvest fumigant on grain and fruit. They presented the order to him in June 1982, but Todhunter delayed signing it. In July, Florida Congressman Andy Ireland wrote Todhunter thanking him for "your assurances that there is no 'rush' to ban EDB, either in 1983 or 1985."[22]

John Todhunter resigned in March 1983 amid charges of undue industry influence over the agency. Two months later, the National Agricultural Chemicals Association—the pesticide manufacturers trade organization—hired Todhunter as a consultant on pesticide safety studies. He denied that industry influenced his decision to delay regulation of EDB. Lake claimed nothing was improper about the government-industry conferences. "We had an industry in trouble and we worked to solve its problems," Lake told the *New York Times*.[23]

As the EPA went back and forth on EDB, the chemical was showing up in groundwater around the country. In 1980, relatively high levels of EDB were found in a well on the Hawaiian island of Maui. In 1982, Dow Chemical, EDB's inventor and a major manufacturer of the pesticide, reported to the EPA's Office of Pesticide Programs that it has found EDB in three irrigation wells in Georgia. The concentrations ranged from 30 to 100 ppb. And that year in California, EDB was found in several wells at levels up to 5 ppb.

Florida's first knowledge of EDB's ability to leach into groundwater, Florida Agriculture Department attorney Frank Graham says, came in 1983, when a California Department of Food and Agriculture scientist happened to mention over the phone to a Florida agriculture official that EDB was showing up in wells in California.

Soon, Florida Agriculture personnel began to sample wells where the state had applied EDB to citrus groves. Sure enough, many of the wells contained EDB. Florida Agriculture Secretary Doyle Conner ordered suspension of his own department's use of EDB. In two months of testing, unsafe levels of EDB were found in more than 100 wells, including 4 municipal systems serving a total of 10,000 people.[24] One well contained 700 ppb of EDB, 35,000 times higher than the state's current drinking water exposure standard.

Florida's EDB problems are exacerbated by the state's sandy soil and high water table, which make its aquifers extremely vulnerable to contamination. Nobody, however, took this into account until it was too late. Although thousands of pesticides are registered for use in Florida, no state agency even tested for the presence of pesticides in groundwater until August 1982.

Faced with this mounting crisis and news from Washington that the EPA was finally going to suspend many uses of EDB, Conner announced a statewide ban on EDB as a soil fumigant. Two weeks later, on September 30, the EPA announced a national ban—only the second emergency suspension in its history.

But for Doyle Conner and the victims of EDB contamination, the trouble was far from over. Two days before the EPA banned EDB, it was revealed that Florida Department of Agriculture employees had for the past 20 years systematically used two-and-a-half times the amount of EDB allowed by federal law and recommended by the manufacturers' label instructions. Conner claimed his department had simply been following the dosages recommended by the USDA, which had failed to inform Florida that the allowable EDB dose had been reduced. The EPA, after reviewing the evidence, finally cleared the Florida Department of Agriculture of blame "because we have no evidence that the state of Florida was adequately notified."[25] "They should have used a little common sense," says EPA pesticide expert Stuart Cohen, shaking his head in bafflement. "If you are putting hundreds of pounds of EDB in the ground, you might contaminate groundwater. Didn't anybody think about that?"

Florida legislators were incensed at the state Agriculture Department's lack of awareness of the dangers posed by EDB and its failure to monitor groundwater. "The Department of Agriculture should have tested. They never should have put out anything before they tested," says Sidney Martin, a state representative from central Florida. "That's the awful thing—putting EDB out all over Florida, and people who had nothing to do with it finding it in their wells."[26]

The regulation of EDB is a particularly telling example of how the federal and state governments fail to protect the public from dangerous pesticides—and of how chemical and agricultural interests exert influence on government agencies. Unfortunately, the handling of EDB is not exceptional.

EDB: Not an Isolated Case

When the EPA was created in December 1970, it assumed responsibility from the USDA for ensuring the safe use of pesticides. This was a significant victory for the burgeoning environmental movement, which had seen the USDA as a captive of the pesticide manufacturers it was supposed to regulate. Too often, critics charged, the USDA officials responsible for deciding the safety of pesticides had routinely approved dangerous products for marketing. In 1969, the House Government Operations Committee charged, "The USDA pesticides regulation division has failed almost completely to carry out its responsibility . . . to protect the public from hazardous and ineffective pesticide products."[27]

To remedy this failure, Congress amended the 1947 Federal Insecticide, Fungicide, and Rodenticide Act in 1972 to give the EPA broader powers to ensure pesticide safety. In particular, the amendment required the EPA to approve all new pesticides and all new uses of existing pesticides; that is, each time a manufacturer wished to use its product on a new crop, it had to apply to the EPA. The EPA was also given the responsibility to review and reregister (or ban) all pesticides that had been approved for use before 1972, and thus were already on the market. To reregister a pesticide product, the manufacturers were required by the EPA to provide data showing whether their products caused cancer, birth defects, or other health problems in laboratory animals.

But in 1972, there were some 50,000 pesticide products on the market.[28] Faced with the monumental task of reregistering all these thousands of pesticides, the EPA decided to narrow its concern to 600 active ingredients; but by mid-1984, the agency had reviewed only 76 of them. Consequently, the EPA had reregistered less than 1 percent of the 50,000 pesticides. At that pace, the review of all 600 ingredients will not be completed until the year 2005, according to the House Government Operations Committee. The vast majority of these chemicals have not been adequately tested for their potential to cause cancer, birth defects, or genetic damage.

To add to the EPA's woes, about 15 percent of the pesticide ingredients on the market turned out to be registered on the basis of fraudulent or faulty animal tests by Industrial Biotest Laboratories, formerly the nation's largest private testing lab, according to Senator William Proxmire. The tests, which involved products from dozens of companies, were conducted to supposedly determine if the chemicals might cause cancer, birth defects, or other health problems. Now the EPA is involved in the time-consuming process of obtaining new, valid data from the manufacturers. The process could take decades at the pace the EPA is moving. Meanwhile, the products remain on the market, where Americans may be exposed daily to them. "All we have now are question marks," an EPA official admitted to the *New York Times*.

To cancel or restrict the use of a pesticide, the EPA must gather considerable data indicating that the chemical's potential health risks outweigh its economic benefits. From 1976 to 1981, the EPA slated 68 pesticides for these special reviews, which are also known in EPA jargon as rebuttable presumptions against registration (RPARs). However, from 1981 to March 1984 the EPA had not begun a single RPAR.[29] Part of the reason for this inactivity was a drastic reduction in the RPAR staff under the Reagan administration—from up to 100 in 1980, to only 22 in 1984.[30] RPARs also often take several years to complete, and there was a backlog from earlier years. For example, the EPA spent five years studying toxaphene, a cancer-causing pesticide chemically similar to DDT, before restricting its use in late 1982. By that time, toxaphene was largely ineffective because insects had built a resistance to it. "Consistent and timely are not words often associated with the Office of Pesticide and Toxic Substances," Todhunter's successor at EPA, John Moore, acknowledged to the *Washington Post*.[31]

But there have been more-serious problems in the EPA's pesticide regulation program than simply timeliness. Although at the end of the Carter administration the EPA was in the midst of canceling or restricting 11 pesticides it considered dangerous, the EPA under Reagan allowed their continued use. A lawsuit brought by the Natural Resources Defense Council (NRDC) and the AFL-CIO revealed that the EPA was holding closed-door meetings with the pesticide manufacturers "to evaluate the risks and benefits of suspect pesticides and decide what ought to be done about them," according to NRDC attorney Jacqueline Warren.[32] In September 1984, the EPA agreed not to hold any secret meetings with the chemical manufacturers it regulates and to reevaluate the decision to leave the controversial pesticides on the market.

Banned But Not Gone

But even when the EPA "bans" a pesticide, there are a number of ways it can make a reappearance. Take DBCP. When the EPA banned its use in October 1979, then–EPA Administrator Douglas Costle decided to allow the use of DBCP on 43,000 acres of pineapple fields in Hawaii, reasoning "the risk of exposure to DBCP in Hawaii through ingestion of contaminated drinking water is controlled in large part by subsoil geological and hydrological considerations that are unique to Hawaii."[33]

The previous summer, EPA scientists, in a cursory check of 16 wells on the islands, had found no contamination. But a separate sampling by the pineapple industry revealed low levels of DBCP in several springs and in an abandoned well at a school on the island of Maui. The pineapple growers claimed that up to 25 percent of Hawaii's pineapple crop would be lost if DBCP were banned and were quick to point out that the contamination didn't affect any existing drinking water source. "The use of DBCP in Hawaii is not resulting in contamination of public drinking water," claimed John Mink, a hydrogeologist who served as a consultant to the Pineapple Growers Association.[34]

The pineapple growers and the EPA were wrong. In 1980, the Hawaii Department of Health found DBCP and EDB in a well serving about 500 people on the Del Monte plantation on the island of Oahu. The well contained 10 ppb of DBCP and 300 ppb of EDB; it was quickly shut down. The contamination was Hawaii's first reported incident of pesticide-tainted drinking water. Also disturbing was the fact that Del Monte had known about the DBCP contamination for a couple of years and had failed to inform the state health department.

Early in 1981, when the EPA was considering extending the approval to use DBCP on Hawaii's pineapples, EPA chemist Stuart Cohen prepared a memo pointing out that DBCP had shown up in 10 of 68 sites sampled in Hawaii since 1979. "It has been demonstrated that irrigation water from cultivated fields in Hawaii reaches groundwater," Cohen noted. "Thus there is a possible path for DBCP to contaminate groundwater in Hawaii."[35]

But the EPA, at the urging of the Pineapple Growers Association and the state, decided to allow the continued use of the pesticide on the island, arguing that the frequency and levels of DBCP contamination in Hawaii were much lower than on the mainland. The Legal Aid Society of Hawaii argued against the continued use of DBCP, saying the decision amounted to "second-class protection" for Hawaii.[36]

It seemed almost inevitable, given the course of events, that DBCP would turn up in the drinking water somewhere else in Hawaii; and it did. In October 1982, the state health department closed a well that served 25,000 residents of the town of Mililani on Oahu because of DBCP contamination. In summer 1983, additional sampling revealed low levels of EDB and DBCP contamination in wells on Oahu and Maui. In all, the state closed ten wells that summer.

In January 1984, almost five years after DBCP was first found in groundwater in California, the EPA finally banned it completely. The EPA did, however, permit the use of existing stocks on Maui until 1987.

The EPA's decision to allow the continued use of DBCP on the Hawaii pineapple crop despite such undisputed and pervasive water contamination is but one example of how banned or unregistered pesticide products can survive at the state level. State and local governments are allowed to petition the EPA to grant an emergency exemption for the use of a banned or unregistered pesticide for up to one year. The EPA is supposed to grant such an exemption only if there are no existing alternatives. The number of emergency exemptions granted by the EPA has skyrocketed, from 165 in 1978, to 727 in 1982.[37] The EPA has approved the use of banned pesticides such as DDT, heptachlor (another carcinogen), and strychnine. It was under such provisions that the EPA in 1982 allowed Clemson University to use DBCP on 20,000 acres of peaches in South Carolina. Clemson claimed the use of DBCP was necessary because nematodes had destroyed about 72,000 South Carolina peach trees since the pesticide was banned in 1979.

State Commissioner of Health Robert Jackson, however, attacked the EPA's approval of the exemption, calling it "a total reversal in policy."[38] Jackson was particularly incensed that the EPA had not bothered to inform him about the exemption. He angrily told the EPA that the state health department could not guarantee that the use of DBCP would not contaminate groundwater, and he blocked its use. A local environmental organization also won a court-ordered ban on DBCP, effectively killing any hope of using it in South Carolina.

State governments, also, can permit local communities to apply pesticides for unregistered uses. The number of these so-called special local need exemptions (SLNs) has also increased rapidly, from 440 in 1976, to 1,656 in 1982.[39] Jay Feldman of the National Coalition Against the Misuse of Pesticides charges that pesticide manufacturers are using SLNs as a way to avoid testing requirements for unregistered uses of pesticides. A study by the National Sharecroppers Fund found that chemical manufacturers, not farmers, obtained 90 percent of more than 2,000 SLNs granted in 25 states during 1981 and 1982.[40] "In some cases," the EPA noted in its own 1983 audit of the emergency exemptions and SLN programs, "the involved company provides the information needed to support the state's request for an emergency exemption. . . . Moreover, there have been some cases where more than one state had submitted a virtually identical request, the only differences being in the number of acres to be treated and the number of pounds of pesticide to be used."[41]

Although the EPA has the power to veto SLNs, it rarely does so. In 1981, for example, it turned down only 10 of 1,324 requests for such permits.[42] Despite the agency's qualms about EDB, it permitted 104 SLNs for the potent nematicide through July 1982.[43] In one case, an SLN was granted for the use of a herbicide called Bolero on rice fields north of Sacramento, California. Its use resulted in low levels of contamination of the city's drinking water. Although Bolero gave the water a bitter taste, state health authorities claimed there was no evidence it would cause any long-term health problems.

An Uncertain Future

Some states are now responding to the problem of pesticide contamination. In Florida, which failed to test its groundwater for any pesticides until 1982, there has been a remarkable turnaround. Sid Martin's state House Community Affairs Committee has succeeded in passing a package of legislation aimed at shifting responsibility for regulation and monitoring of pesticides in water from Florida's Department of Agriculture to the state Department of Environmental Regulation. The Department of Agriculture's conflicting roles as pesticide promoter and regulator cannot be reconciled, Martin argues. Not surprisingly, the department's counsel Frank Graham disagrees. "We haven't done a bad job. I don't go along with Sid Martin's fox-in-the-hen-house theory."

Martin is adament. "To safeguard the environment, there ought to be an independent agency," he maintains. Martin has also authored a bill to establish a state research program to investigate safer, nonchemical methods of controlling pesticides. For example, an alternative means of preventing nematode infestation is to construct a physical barrier around the infected area to prevent the spread of the tiny creatures.

The EPA is proceeding with a program to check dozens of pesticides for their ability to travel through the soil and contaminate underground aquifers. Cohen actually proposed conducting such an evaluation back in 1979, when widespread pesticide contamination of groundwater was first discovered. But, says Cohen, "Management made no initiative to support this. Nothing was ever done."

"The potential for groundwater contamination is high," Cohen concludes in a scientific paper. "It is clear that much more groundwater monitoring must be done."[44] But because we currently have so little data, we really have no way of knowing if another pesticide contamination problem the magnitude of EDB or DBCP is lurking a few years down the road.

Center Pivot

Another area threatened by pesticides is the midwestern farm belt, where modern agricultural techniques are compounding already existing groundwater contamination. In the last decade, a technique called center pivot irrigation has become widely popular in Nebraska, Kansas, Iowa, and Wisconsin. Flying over the country's farm belt, one can see the work of the center pivots: large green circles of crops that are rapidly replacing the patchwork quilt of traditional farming.

The center pivot irrigator is essentially a giant sprinkler attached to a well that draws directly from the underground aquifer. The water is pumped up and mixed in an irrigation line with pesticides and fertilizers from a "nurse" tank. A giant sprinkler, slowly rotating in a circle, sprays the chemical mixture over an enormous area. In a 18-hour revolution, a single irrigator can cover 130 to 220 acres of cropland. This center pivot "chemigation" system has proved to be a much cheaper, more effective method of applying agricultural chemicals than those used in the past. *Nebraska Farmers Magazine* conservatively estimates that in Nebraska alone, 200,000 acres are under this type of irrigation.

But for some farmers, the happy relationship with the center pivot is ending. In Nebraska, farmers and ranchers have complained to both the state Department of Environmental Control and the EPA that center pivot chemigation techniques are ruining groundwater. Faulty safety valves allow chemicals to flow back down the irrigation line into the well, tainting the groundwater. In addition, when the system shuts down, reverse pressure created by the water flowing back down the irrigation line can siphon the pesticides and fertilizers out of the nurse tank and into the well. According to internal EPA documents, the director of the EPA's Region VII air and waste management division in Kansas City, Missouri, notified EPA headquarters in 1982 that "while most systems presently have certain anti-siphon and check valves, it has been conservatively estimated that up to 75 percent of these devices are not in working order."[45] Comments one EPA official, "It is only a matter of time before significant groundwater contamination is going to occur."[46] The EPA's Office of Pesticide Programs has not investigated the valves' failure, choosing instead only to issue a warning not to use pesticides in systems that have safety valves—whether these are working or not. Nebraska, however, is considering a ban on the use of chemicals in center pivots altogether.

Center pivot irrigation is adding its chemical burden to the huge Ogallala aquifer, a source of drinking and irrigation water for eight states stretching from South Dakota to Texas that has been contaminated by nitrates.

Nitrates

The main source of nitrates in groundwater is nitrogen-based fertilizer that leaches through the soil into the water table. Since 1950, the use of chemical fertilizer in this country has increased more than 600 percent.[47] According to USDA estimates, plants take up little more than a third of it.[48] The remainder either runs off the land into surface waters or filters down through the ground to the water table.

High levels of nitrates can cause oxygen depletion in infants. This leads to a condition known as methemoglobinemia, or blue baby syndrome. Since 1945, there have been 278 reported cases of blue baby syndrome linked to nitrates in drinking water. The syndrome can be fatal; 39 infants have died, although not in recent years.[49] The syndrome can also affect adults, but only at much higher levels of exposure.

Nitrates carry another potential danger. Once ingested, they may be converted to cancer-causing chemicals called nitrosamines. Several studies have linked nitrates to a high incidence of stomach cancer, although the evidence is far from comprehensive.

Nationally, more than 500,000 households are drinking water that contains potentially unsafe levels of nitrates.[50] The problem is particularly serious in midwestern farm states such as Nebraska, Iowa, and Minnesota. More than 700 of 4,300 private wells tested in Nebraska from 1976 to 1980 contained nitrates in excess of EPA guidelines.[51] According to Cliff Summers, director of the Nebraska state health department's environmental engineering department, the state also has 45 to 50 public systems that have excessive levels of nitrates. One town's water contains three times the federal standard. Filtering nitrates is too expensive for most water suppliers, so once a water system is contaminated with nitrates, drilling a new well is usually the only realistic alternative. There is no guarantee, of course, that a new well will remain uncontaminated.

The Aftermath

But for Lawrence Gladieux in Florida's citrus region, the problems are more immediate. Pesticide contamination of his well has destroyed the value of his house and land, into which he sunk most of his life savings. Although he wants to move, he can't. Six months after the state first found EDB in his well, new samples determined the level was almost four times higher than the initial concentration. He is obviously pained by risks to his children. And he knows that eventual health problems can't conclusively be traced to EDB.

"My children could be killed as sure as they were shot down by a criminal and there is nobody to point the finger at. There is no way to prove which finger is on the trigger," he says with the merest hint of bitterness.

Scientists estimate the EDB could remain in Gladieux's water for up to 14 years. Thus, like millions of other Americans whose drinking water is contaminated with potentially dangerous chemicals, he has three alternatives: clean his water with a filter, which must be changed often to prevent higher levels of contamination; drill a new well; or hook up to an existing supply of clean water.

Gladieux is lucky in one respect. Because the Florida Department of Agriculture is responsible for contaminating his well, it will pay for an alternative source of water. In California, people with contaminated wells who want an alternative water supply must pay for it themselves. There, DBCP contamination has spawned multi-billion-dollar lawsuits demanding that the pesticide's manufacturers pay to clean up the water. In the meantime, those who can't afford bottled water or filters have little choice but to drink the tainted water. "Water is very precious," Gladieux reflects. "But not until you are deprived of it do you realize that."

The Treatment Plant and Beyond

4

Since the 1960s, concern about water pollution has focused on industrial and agricultural poisons that turn up in the nation's drinking water. But little attention has been given to contamination of our drinking water on its way from the treatment plant to the kitchen sink. Now, a growing body of evidence suggests the way we treat and transport our drinking water also may pose serious health problems.

Just as trees depend on intricate root systems extending far into the ground to tap moisture in the soil below, most Americans rely on a maze of underground lifelines to provide water. Beneath our feet and under skyscrapers, sidewalks, streets, and subdivisions runs a snaking, subterranean network of pipeline totaling perhaps a million miles nationwide and delivering more than 30 billion gallons of water each year.

This network is run by 50,000 public and private water companies. Some cities, such as Chicago, St. Louis, and Pittsburgh, obtain their water from nearby rivers. Other cities, particularly in the more arid western United States, pump water from up to hundreds of miles away. San Francisco obtains its water from the Sierra Nevada Mountains more than 200 miles to the east. Some of the drinking water for Los Angeles comes from the Colorado River, which never enters the state. Many cities, including San Antonio, Miami, and Honolulu, rely entirely on groundwater pumped to the surface.

Whatever the source, when water comes out of the tap, it has been transformed—passed through screens to keep out debris and fish, mechanically mixed with chemicals to destroy bad tastes and odors and to kill bacteria, run past a series of baffles to give the chemicals more time to act, gathered in ponds to allow sediment to settle out, and then pumped under tremendous pressure to consumers.

Processed Water

In the 1850s, British physician John Snow showed that polluted water could cause the spread of the deadly disease cholera. By the late 1800s, it was common knowledge that many disease-causing germs (now known to be bacteria and viruses) were spread by drinking water contaminated with raw sewage. At that time, several of the leading causes of death in this country, including typhoid fever, were waterborne diseases.

By 1930, however, typhoid had become a relatively insignificant problem, ranking as only the twenty-sixth leading cause of death in the United States. This dramatic turnabout was brought about by treatment of drinking water with chlorine and filters to kill bacteria. Chlorine was first added to combat the typhoid bacterium in public water supplies in England and Belgium at the turn of the century. In this country, chlorination dates back to 1908, when a small amount of bleaching powder was added to a reservoir serving Jersey City, New Jersey. Two years later, a cheaper, liquid form of chlorine was added to Philadelphia's water supply. Not only was chlorine effective in small amounts, but the quantities utilized apparently had no adverse effect on human health. Soon, the use of chlorine as a disinfectant for drinking water had spread around the country. (Ironically, about the time that chlorine was rapidly gaining popularity in this country, Europeans were abandoning its use. Europeans, who had seen hundreds of thousands of their young men killed and maimed by chlorine gas during World War I, were repelled by the thought of it in their water.)

The advent of water filtration and disinfection was one of the most important public health revolutions of our century. But it also ushered in an era of complacency among public health officials, water supply professionals, and the public. Sanitary engineers came to rely heavily on chlorination, thinking that if a little chlorine was good, more must be better. Public health officials, in turn, put their faith in residual levels of chlorine in "finished" drinking water to assure safety.

By the end of the 1970s, the quality of many rivers and lakes had improved dramatically. Fish had returned to numbers of rivers. Levels of so-called conventional pollutants—dissolved and suspended solids, oil, and grease—had decreased. Ohio's Cuyahoga River and the Buffalo River in New York no longer threatened to burst into flames, as they had during the 1960s. In 1984, the Environmental Protection Agency (EPA) Assistant Administrator for Water Jack Ravan called the Clean Water Act "one of EPA's true success stories." But the EPA did not score so well on controlling the pollutants that, by the late 1970s, had become the nation's major water-quality problem.

In the mid-1970s, EPA researchers in a Cincinnati drinking water laboratory discovered that chlorination seems to spawn new, possibly carcinogenic, contaminants, called trihalomethanes (or THMs).

In 1975, then–EPA Administrator Russell Train ordered a national survey of 80 municipal drinking water supplies. When the water tests came in, one THM, chloroform, was found in the tap water of *all 80 cities*. Also common in the samples were three other THMs that are formed as by-products of chlorination. "This was a startling finding," remarks Victor Kimm, director of the EPA's Office of Drinking Water. "To our surprise, the organic contamination that we found the most frequently was this group called THMs." These chemicals are created when chlorine reacts with organic matter, such as rotting leaves, already in the water supply.

The possible health effects of THMs alarm many scientists. Chloroform is known to cause cancer in laboratory animals. The EPA, in fact, estimates that the level of chloroform in Miami's drinking water might "account for up to 40 percent of the observed liver cancer incidence rate."[1]

In November 1979, the EPA adopted a drinking water standard of 100 parts per billion (ppb) for THMs. It noted that

Fluoridation

Although fluoride is added to much of the nation's drinking water for its beneficial effect on health, it has caused a tremendous amount of controversy. About 60 percent of the American population now drinks artificially fluoridated water. Fluoride is a compound found in almost all soils, plants, and water, both fresh and salt. In the United States, natural fluoride concentrations in drinking water range from 0.05 to 8 parts per million (ppm).

Much evidence suggests that fluoride, when added to water in concentrations around 1 ppm, significantly reduces dental cavities; from 1970 to 1979, the prevalence of cavities among school children declined about 50 percent.[1] Proponents claim fluoridation is one of the most cost-effective public health programs of all time. The annual cost to consumers is only a few cents each; according to one estimate, every $1 spent on fluoridation saves $50 in treatment later on.[2] Thus, the main beneficiaries of fluoridation, supporters argue, are poor people who can't afford dental care.

Antifluoridationists, however, claim that long-term exposure to fluoridated drinking water can weaken the immune system and can cause genetic damage, birth defects, heart disease, and cancer. Fluoride supporters respond that there is no evidence that low levels of fluoride produce these effects.

The U.S. Public Health Service recommends an "optimum" intake of 1 milligram (mg) of fluoride per day, but

"THMs are the most ubiquitous synthetic organic chemicals found in drinking water in the U.S., and are generally found at the highest concentrations of any such chemicals." At the time, the EPA estimated that a lifelong exposure to 100 ppb of THMs might result in 200 extra cancer deaths a year nationwide.[2] (The regulations apply only to those water systems serving more than 10,000 people, leaving some 46 million people unprotected by the standard. The EPA reasons that the levels of THMs in most smaller

many people consume far more fluoride than that because fluoridated water is used in processed foods and beverages. "Fluoride ingested daily in foods and beverages by adults living in fluoridated communities ranges from 3.5 to 5.5 mg," according to a 1977 report of the National Research Council.[3]

No one really knows the long-term effects of consuming fluoride at these levels. But a 1979 report by the Quebec Ministry of the Environment stated, "Fluorides are highly toxic for humans and a narrow margin separates an 'acceptable level' from a toxic level."[4] It is known that at levels higher than about 3 ppm, fluoride can cause dental fluorosis, a condition in which the teeth turn yellow, brown, or black and the tips break off. At higher levels, fluoride can damage bones and kidneys. In some individuals, signs of fluorosis appear after exposure at much lower levels.

Many water supplies exceed the EPA's fluoride drinking water standard of 0.7 to 1.2 ppm because of naturally occurring fluoride, so the EPA is considering raising the current standard. Whatever the EPA's decision, the fluoridation issue is sure to remain charged. Even though the vast majority of the medical establishment continues to vehemently support fluoridation, opponents of the additive continue to win victories at the ballot box. In recent years, a number of communities have voted to either prohibit or repeal the use of fluoride in their water supplies.

systems may be relatively low because those systems draw on groundwater, which contains less organic matter.)

The EPA encouraged water system operators to control THMs by a series of "relatively simple and inexpensive . . . changes in the existing treatment processes," Kimm said. These steps include using a different disinfectant or changing the point of chlorination, reducing THMs after they are formed, and reducing organic matter in the water before treatment.

Water suppliers immediately resisted the new regulations. The American Water Works Association (AWWA) filed a court challenge to the THM rules. Articles appeared in the AWWA's journal downplaying any link between cancer and THMs in drinking water. "There have been trihalomethanes in the water ever since we've been chlorinating," the association's executive director Eric Johnson asserted. "We can't see it as suddenly becoming an imminent danger. The reason it's been brought to public attention is they've designed sophisticated lab equipment to detect it. The best solution seems to me is to get rid of that lab equipment and we wouldn't have a problem."[3]

The water system operators' reaction was predictable. For years, their practices had rarely been questioned. Now, suddenly, they were under fire, and they were unprepared. The water suppliers "had never dealt with trace contaminants because no one could ever measure them before," says Victor Kimm. "They had dealt with a technology that had been stable most of their professional careers." The water utilities "went from essentially an industry that had no public scrutiny to being under a microscope," adds Nancy Wentworth, who manages state programs for the EPA's Office of Water.

Soon after the THM standard was issued, scientific studies confirmed a link between elevated cancer rates and chlorinated drinking water. In 1980, the President's Council on Environmental Quality reviewed five studies covering more than 11,000 deaths from gastrointestinal and urinary tract cancer in New York state, Louisiana, Illinois, Wisconsin, and North Carolina. The conclusion: people drinking chlorinated water ran a 13 to 93 percent greater risk of developing rectal cancer and a 53 percent greater chance of colon cancer than people supplied with untreated water.[4]

The council did note that the data fell somewhat short of establishing a "causal relationship" between chlorination and cancer. "Increased risks of rectal, bladder, and colon cancer of the magnitudes suggested by these studies are large enough to be of concern," the report noted, "yet small enough to be very difficult to separate from . . . risks associated with other environmental factors."[5]

The EPA and the American Water Works Association finally agreed on a settlement of the suit over the THM standard in March 1982. The settlement grants some suppliers a variance from meeting the THM maximum contaminant level but requires them to get as close to the standard as feasible. Although Kimm says the 100-ppb limit has been "fairly easy" to meet, the EPA recently estimated that as many as 200 of the 3,000 affected systems may be unable to comply with the standard.[6]

But as it turns out, the problems of chemical contamination do not end when drinking water leaves the treatment plant. In recent years, evidence has surfaced that the very systems we use to transport water to our homes may pose unforeseen problems.

The Battle over Plastic Pipe

Back in 1980, Dr. Marc Lappe was head of the California State Department of Health's hazard alert section. The job of Lappe's small department was to study the health effects of chemicals in the environment and workplace. In May, Lappe was contacted by Sacramento attorney Raymond Leonardini, who represented the California Pipe Trades Council, a union of plumbers and pipe fitters. Leonardini wanted Lappe to investigate reports he'd been receiving that pipe fitters who installed plastic pipe had a high rate of a rare form of lymphatic cancer, as well as blood in the urine, kidney infections, rashes, nausea, and dizziness.

Lappe conducted a search of the scientific literature that turned up some disturbing findings about plastic pipe used in household plumbing and about the solvent-glues used to join the sections of pipe. He found that these glues contained dimethyl-formamide, a chemical linked to lymphoma and birth defects in lab animals. Lappe also came across a study sponsored by the U.S. National Institute for Occupational Safety and Health that uncovered a "significant excess" of cancers of the esophagus, lymphatic system, larynx, and lungs among pipe fitters and plumbers.

Lappe became still more concerned when he read a scientific article describing high levels of two chemicals found in water stored in polyvinyl chloride (PVC) plastic pipe, commonly used to transport drinking water. He managed to prod a reluctant state health department to commission a series of tests to determine exactly what substances could migrate into water as it flowed through PVC pipe and chemically similar chlorinated (CPVC) pipe.

The laboratory results surprised Lappe; organic chemicals had leached into the water at concentrations higher than the recommended federal government safety levels. After the water was allowed to sit for two weeks in a section of CPVC pipe, the THM levels were 150 ppb. The tests also detected several other suspected carcinogens, including DEHP, a plasticizer used to make the pipe more flexible.

The plastics industry downplayed the results of the study, claiming that flushing the pipes after they were newly installed would remove a lot of the chemicals and that other contaminants were the result of sloppy laboratory procedures. But a month after the test results were released, in November 1980, the California Housing Commission decided against extending approval of PVC and CPVC pipe for use in homes and high rises. (Their use was still allowed outside of buildings.) But the battle over plastic pipe in California wasn't over. In fact, it was just heating up.

At its November meeting, the housing commission did approve another type of plastic pipe, polybutylene (PB), for use in plumbing inside buildings. Lappe had excluded PB pipe from the health department tests because Shell, the sole manufacturer of polybutylene, had assured him its product was a pure polymer, thoroughly tested by the U.S. Food and Drug Administration. Furthermore, installation of PB pipe did not involve the use of solvent-glues, as PVC pipe did. But Leonardini had become suspicious of PB pipe and hired a Sacramento laboratory to look at what was in the pipe itself. In December 1980, the laboratory reported to Leonardini that the samples of pipe contained DEHP, the same suspected carcinogen the state had found in its leaching tests with PVC and CPVC pipe.

When word of these results got out, Shell bristled, categorically denying that its product contained DEHP. The company produced its own study showing no detectable levels of DEHP. But in April 1981, the housing commission reversed its approval of

PB pipe. Shell continued to maintain that its product had no problems.

The issue goes beyond safety, however. "Basically, this is an economic fight," says John Stolton, an attorney representing the Society of Plastics Industries (SPI), the largest industry trade association. Pipe fitters have traditionally opposed the introduction of plastic pipes because they are easier to install, a quality that translates into fewer jobs. So far, plastic pipe has been winning the fight. Sales of plastic pipe grew from 60 million pounds in 1960 to 2.8 billion in 1980. By 1985, sales are expected to more than double to 6.2 billion pounds. The value of the market is more than $8 billion annually.[7] With so much at stake, plastics manufacturers don't hesitate to react strongly to a study that questions their product's safety. Four months after the housing commission retracted its approval of PB pipe, Shell Oil sued Ray Leonardini over the laboratory study he commissioned. The company accused him of publishing and communicating the results "in reckless disregard of the truth." Essentially, Shell was asking the courts to shut Leonardini up fast by ordering him to stop talking about the disturbing findings.

Even though Leonardini was confronted by the huge, well-financed legal department of one of the world's largest corporations, he was not intimidated. "I felt they were trying to divert our meager resources," he said. (The laboratory work in question had cost just $125.) He fought Shell's suit.

A year later, he was successful; the suit was thrown out of court. The presiding judge commented that the suit "reeks of corporations with great economic power in this country seeking to silence political debates. It is a very, very serious matter." In December 1983, Leonardini turned around and filed a $102 million lawsuit alleging that Shell's legal maneuver was an "abusive use of the legal process in a political debate."

Further Plastic Problems

In fall 1982, Leonardini said a "much more important" discovery was made about possible contamination associated with plastic pipe. A study funded by the California Pipe Trades

Council found that gasoline, chlorinated solvents, and several pesticides penetrated PB and polyethylene (PE) pipe with surprising ease. The study, conducted by Anlab, a Sacramento testing firm, raised the possibility that hazardous chemicals in soil could pass *through* plastic pipe and contaminate drinking water. This was a problem that had previously received scant attention, and it raised another storm.

The study found that water inside PB and PE pipes immersed in gasoline for a week contained 100 ppb of benzene, a known human carcinogen. Massive amounts of cancer-causing solvents also quickly penetrated the pipes. "Some of this pipe appears to act like a sponge, sucking these toxics into water," said Richard Spohn, then-director of the California Department of Consumer Affairs. By comparison, copper pipe showed almost no permeation. Spohn asked the state legislature to fund further research on the problem of plastic pipe permeation. "We may be unwittingly polluting drinking water by putting plastic pipe in soils contaminated with hazardous chemicals," Spohn told the legislators.

Again the plastics manufacturers were quick to discount the importance of the Anlab study. SPI's John Stolton pointed out that plastic pipe would never be totally immersed in toxic chemicals in the course of normal use, as it was under test conditions. "You've got to look at the real world situation." Marc Lappe, now a professor of public health at the University of California, agrees the contamination levels in the study would almost never occur during actual use. But he adds that the study was "very short-term" and that levels of chemicals found in the water were up to a million times higher than the safety levels recommended by the EPA.

Spohn and Lappe were concerned because there were already reports of drinking water contaminated by chemicals permeating through plastic pipe. As far back as 1975, in fact, the East Bay Municipal Utility District (EBMUD), which provides water to more than a million people in Oakland, California, and neighboring cities, began to receive complaints of gasoline in drinking water. The problem turned out to be permeation of PB and PE pipes. According to an EBMUD water quality supervisor, from 1975 to 1982, the utility had to replace at least 15 plastic service lines with copper pipes after customers tasted and smelled gasoline in their water. The EBMUD supervisor stated that the gasoline had not gotten into the water through breaks in the line. "It diffused through the pipe itself," he said. Another case of permeation occurred in Michigan, when gasoline penetrated a PB water service line for a house built on the site of an old gas station.

Because of the permeation problems, EBMUD conducted laboratory tests on permeation in 1978. The utility found that gasoline did indeed penetrate PE and PB pipe, within one to three weeks, and recommended that the state Department of Health Services require the use of copper pipe in conditions "where it may be exposed to gasoline, solvents, or other petroleum distillates." The health department adopted the recommendation in 1979 but took little action to enforce it. Many water system operators were, in fact, unaware that the regulation existed. For its part, EBMUD, which has installed approximately 60,000 plastic service lines, did little to publicize the problem and continued to champion the use of plastic pipe. "They were aware of these problems . . . and they proceeded to do nothing about it," Spohn said.

Although reports of penetration are scattered, Lappe, Spohn, and others point out that the potential for problems is great because of the extent of chemical contamination of soil across the country. Several commonly used pesticides can permeate plastic pipe. In 1980, Dutch authorities found small amounts of a pesticide called methyl bromide in drinking water. This commonly used soil fumigant apparently had seeped through PVC water service pipe. It causes cancer in lab animals and yet is a widely applied substitute for the recently restricted EDB in this country. Lappe recommends that the state Department of Food and Agriculture in California monitor agricultural soils for methyl bromide and other residual contaminants which can penetrate plastic pipe.

The plastics industry does not deny that organic chemicals penetrate their products. "It's no big deal to have proved that plastic pipe is permeable to organics," says Alan Olson, manager of industry affairs for the B. F. Goodrich Company, a major manufacturer of PVC plastic. In fact, a recent study by the Vinyl Institute, a trade organization of companies that manufacture PVC products, found that organic solvents penetrated three types of water pipe systems: PVC, ductile iron, and most permeable, asbestos cement.

The study found that most of the permeation occurred through the joints or gaskets used to join sections of pipe, not through the pipe itself. "Because gasketed joints are permeable, neither plastic pipe nor any other present piping system can prevent permeation from major spills or from chemical dump sites," Olson contends.[8]

Like Stolton, Olson condemns the Anlab study for subjecting the pipe to "pretty outrageous conditions. To use [the test] for regulatory purposes seems unconscionable unless you can prove that this is a common occurrence."

In the meantime, the AWWA, which is usually reluctant to take action without massive amounts of proof, has advised utilities to make sure plastic pipe is not used where contamination has already occurred or may occur—for example, land close to underground fuel storage tanks or industrial facilities.

Other Pipes, Other Problems

Although the potential contamination problems associated with plastic pipe are a relatively new discovery, it has been known for years that several other types of water pipe materials also pose potential health problems.

After the end of World War II, many water utilities around the country switched from cast-iron to asbestos cement (AC) pipe. Asbestos cement pipe had two big advantages over iron: it was cheaper and lighter. But when asbestos was linked with cancer, the popularity of asbestos cement pipe declined rapidly.

Much of the country's estimated 200,000 miles of asbestos cement pipe is now decaying and releasing asbestos fibers into drinking water. The levels of asbestos are especially high where the water is acidic. Although an EPA study concluded that "erosion of asbestos fibers from the walls of asbestos cement pipe may endanger community water supplies,"[9] the evidence of a link between cancer and asbestos ingested with water is mixed. A survey of cancer incidence in 169 Connecticut towns, 82 of which received water "delivered either partly or wholly through AC pipe," found no association between cancer mortality and asbestos exposure from drinking water. But studies of cancer mortality in Quebec, Canada, and five California counties have shown a link between cancer of the digestive tract and asbestos in drinking water.[10]

Lead water service lines also pose potentially serious dangers to health. The ill effects of lead have long been known. It has been theorized that the decline of the Roman empire was caused by lead the citizens ingested from pipes and drinking vessels. An 1845 report to the City Council of Boston advised, "Considering the deadly nature of lead poison, and the fact that so many natural waters dissolve this metal, it's certainly the cause of safety to avoid, as far as possible, the use of lead pipe for carrying water which is to be used for drinking."[11]

Despite such warnings, the use of lead pipe was widespread until the 1920s, when its popularity began to decline as copper pipes became widely available. During the last few decades, very few new lead water service lines have been installed. An exception is in Chicago, where the city building code still calls for the use of lead in water service lines. Many observers attribute this anomaly to the power of the city's plumbers union. Elsewhere in the United States, lead service lines are still in use simply because they have not been replaced. According to a recent EPA survey of 153 water suppliers, most serving more than 100,000 people, about two-thirds still have a few lead services. Some utilities continue to rely heavily on lead. An estimated 75 percent of the water service lines in Newark, New Jersey, for example, are lead.[12]

Acute lead poisoning can cause sharp abdominal pain, anemia, tremors, and even death. Long-term ingestion of lower levels of lead can lead to hypertension and nerve and brain damage. Children, with their low body weights and growing organs, are particularly vulnerable to the effects of lead. In concentrations higher than the EPA's drinking water standard of 0.05 milligrams/liter (mg/l), or 50 ppb, lead can cause learning disabilities and mental retardation.

Several European and American studies found high levels of lead in the blood of children who scored lower on intelligence tests. Because of children's vulnerability to lead, the National Academy of Sciences concluded that the current maximum lead contamination level of 0.05 mg/l "may not provide the margin of safety to safeguard the high risk population in urban areas."[13] The academy recommends reducing the drinking water standard to 0.025 mg/l, but the EPA has not changed the standard.

It is difficult to estimate the extent of contamination caused by lead water pipes, but the "principal source of [dietary] lead is from lead used in water supply distribution systems," according to Peter Lassovszky of the EPA's Office of Drinking Water.[14] Concentrations are greatest when water has been sitting in the pipe for a prolonged period of time. Water drawn from the tap after a vacation or even after standing in pipes overnight may contain a relatively large dose of lead.

A 1981 EPA survey of 580 cities found 2.5 percent of the water samples exceeded its 50-ppb lead standard.[15] An earlier study of 383 homes in the Boston metropolitan area found that more than 15 percent had tap water that exceeded the lead standard.[16] More recently, in August 1984, children and pregnant women in Harrisburg, Pennsylvania, were cautioned about high levels of lead in the city's drinking water. The state Department of Environmental Resources (DER) discovered the problem earlier in the year, ironically right in its Harrisburg office. Further testing confirmed the contamination was spread throughout the city. One sample contained lead levels more than 20 times the EPA drinking water standard. The city water utility, which served about 50,000 customers, added lime to the water to reduce the acidity which corrodes old lead pipes, but that didn't solve the problem. Although the DER requested the city to take further measures to reduce the lead levels and to warn residents, it refused. "They think it is not a problem," says DER representative David Mashek. But DER disagrees and has taken out newspaper ads warning about the contamination. The state is also considering bringing suit to force the city into complying with drinking water standards.

Acidic water has caused lead contamination problems in other Pennsylvania communities. In a 1982 test of about 300 children up to age 12 in Mahanoy City, 79 were found to have elevated blood lead levels. The state DER subsequently sampled the water in the homes of the affected children and found high lead levels in every household but one.

Coincidently, Pennsylvania is an area afflicted by acid rain. This occurs when sulfur dioxide and nitrogen oxides, from the combustion of fossil fuels, circulate high in the atmosphere, undergo a chemical conversion, and fall back to earth as sulfuric and nitric acids. Acid rain can render lakes and streams so acidic that fish and other aquatic life cannot survive. There is evidence that it is also affecting drinking water.

A recent EPA study found that 18 of 34 water sources monitored in Massachusetts had become more acidic over the past several decades, while another 14 had remained relatively constant.[17] Although there is speculation that acid precipitation has worsened the problem of corrosion of old lead pipes, there is as yet no consensus. The Metropolitan District Commission (MDC), which supplies water to more than 2 million people in the greater Boston area, has had to treat its water to reduce acidity since the mid-1970s, when high levels of lead were discovered coming out of the city's taps. But MDC representative Guy Foss refuses to blame acid precipitation. "We'd have to adjust the pH here, no matter what," he says. "We just don't know what acid rain is responsible for."

Most lead contamination problems can be solved simply by replacing the lead pipe. But that's costly, and copper pipe, joined together with a 50 percent lead solder, may contribute lead as well. In one survey in Carroll County, Maryland, 78 of 350 households with copper pipes had lead levels higher than 50 ppb in tap water left standing in the plumbing overnight.[18]

Other, more viable options are to reduce the acidity—and thus the corrosiveness—of the water or to coat the pipe so it is no longer in contact with the water. The MDC reduced excessive lead concentrations in its water simply by treating the water to reduce its acidity. The treatment cost each customer 59 cents in 1981.

"Really there is no excuse for any community water system to be delivering corrosive water," contends Princeton University's Robert Harris.[19]

Permeation through plastic pipe, however, presents a different problem, Harris points out. While water suppliers can treat water to prevent most corrosion, there is little they can do to prevent permeation, short of ripping up the water service lines. Prevention—not putting the plastic pipe in areas where contamination can occur—is the only sensible approach. But because permeation is such a recent concern and there is little data about its frequency, many water suppliers probably won't confront the problem unless serious contamination occurs.

The States:
On the Front Line

5

Because water is so essential to industry, agriculture, recreation, and our very survival, it is not surprising that dozens of laws govern its use and quality. Every level of government—local, state, regional, and federal—has a role in ensuring that we have a safe source of drinking water.

Ideally, anyone ought to be able to remedy a water contamination problem by contacting the government agency responsible for enforcing water quality laws. This sounds simple enough, but unfortunately that initial phone call or letter can start an unsuspecting person on a bewildering, frustrating, and time-consuming journey through a labyrinth of government bureaucracies.

Consider the case of people living near Benton, Kansas, a small town a few miles north of Wichita. It's a quiet farming area. Crimes are too few to keep a newspaper in business. It's a good place for families, or so thought Sharilyn Dienst and her husband when they bought their dream house there in 1972. But within a few years, the neighborhood was anything but peaceful. The Diensts and their neighbors became embroiled in a battle with the state health department and a large waste disposal firm.

In 1976, a short item in a local newspaper announced that an 80-acre plot of farmland about four miles east of the Dienst house was to be converted into a waste disposal site. Sharilyn Dienst and a few nearby residents, concerned about the site, contacted the

Kansas Department of Health and Environment (KDHE). In response, KDHE officials had a series of public meetings at which they explained that the site was necessary because other states would no longer accept waste from Kansas.

To obtain a permit, the landfill owners had submitted a hydrogeological study to the state. The study purported to show no danger of contamination because no groundwater existed close to the site. According to the report, it would take at least 5,000 years for waste to seep through 90 feet of underlying clay into the water table. State health officials apparently accepted the report at face value—despite warnings from local residents, who told them the report was wrong. (One longtime farmer stood up in a public meeting and said he knew water existed close to the surface because his cows had been drinking from springs there for 40 years.) State officials also brushed aside the warnings of a Wichita State University geology professor, Robert Berg, who insisted the site was completely unsuitable for waste disposal.

In early 1977, the Diensts and their neighbors decided to take their case to the governor. They journeyed to Topeka and met with him, but they might as well not have gone: upon returning home, they learned that the state health department had approved the landfill before they had even set foot in the state capitol.

For the next two years, Sharilyn Dienst watched as truckloads of toxic solvents, acids, heavy metals, pesticides, and polychlorinated biphenyls (PCBs) were buried in the so-called Furley landfill. Business was so good that by 1979, the landfill was filled close to capacity. The operators requested permission from the KDHE to double the size of the facility by adding an 80-acre chunk of land to the south. Another optimistic engineering report was submitted, claiming the expansion site was as good for a landfill, if not better, than the original plot of land.

The original site had been hard to fight, says Dienst, because "it wasn't a reality at the time." Now it was operating in full bloom, and the site stank. Children living nearby slept with pillows over their heads to hide from the smell. Worse, a heavy rainfall had caused a dam to break, flooding the adjacent pasture and a nearby creek with large amounts of chemical-laced water. Still, the Kansas state health department seemed intent on ignoring public requests for independent testing of the site, and a state official informed Dienst that the decision to approve the expansion site was all but certain.

In frustration, she and some neighbors took their case to the state attorney general's office, pointing out that the site was in violation of several state regulations and that there had been no independent tests to determine if any of the waste barrels buried there were slowly leaking. They were fortunate. In Kansas Attorney General Robert Stephan, they finally found a state official who took them seriously. Not only did Stephan go out to look at the site himself, but he also telephoned then–KDHE Secretary Joseph Harkins and threatened legal action if the health department approved the expansion plant without a new evaluation of the site's geology. Harkins agreed to ask the Kansas Geological Survey to conduct a study. It was assigned to Frank Wilson, a senior geologist who had a reputation as a direct, no-nonsense scientist.

Wilson and his crew began their tests in the spring of 1981. When they drilled toward bedrock, they kept hitting water, far closer to the surface than claimed in the original engineering reports. Some of the waste trenches were barely five feet above the groundwater level. The report of Wilson's crew concluded that chemicals could very likely leach from the trenches into the groundwater.

The report forced the health department's hand. In August 1981, Harkins met with Sharilyn Dienst and several other residents and agreed to test for possible chemical contamination. In October, the KDHE finally took groundwater samples from 13 locations on and near the site. For the next two months, Sharilyn Dienst kept calling and writing to the health department for the test results. As the new year rolled around, no information was forthcoming. By the first week of January, she was so fed up that she filed a Freedom of Information request with the regional office of the federal EPA. Shortly after that, the state health department released the information.

The results confirmed the worst fears of Dienst and her neighbors. One well and the water below an evaporation pond were contaminated. Several chemicals, some of them cancer-causing, were detected in Prairie Creek, a half mile to the north.

Tracking Down Polluters

If you suspect that your water is threatened, the first step is to gather as much information as you can about the potential sources of contamination in your community—underground storage tanks, municipal landfills, industrial facilities, and agricultural activities, to name a few. Many are not obvious; an old gas station down the street with an abandoned, rusting storage tank can pose as serious a threat to your water as a hazardous waste pit next to your backyard.

Government records are a good place to start. Often, facilities that handle large amounts of hazardous materials are required to have permits to store or dispose of chemicals. These permits should be on file with the appropriate state or local regulatory agency. If a company is required to have a permit, then there is a good chance the government agency will also have an inspection file on that firm, containing reports of violations and whether they have been corrected. The file may also give you a good idea of whether the company is a consistent violator of pollution laws and of what types of chemicals it is handling. In California, for example, the regional water quality control boards keep files on companies that discharge wastes, and they have records of reported chemical leaks and spills into groundwater.

You can often find out who owns a particular facility or waste site by checking the records at the registrar of deeds or tax assessor's office. If you suspect that the potential polluter is a large firm, you might ask the local librarian to help you find out how large the firm is, who owns it, and if it has operations in other states. If the company is large enough, its shares may be traded publicly on the stock exchange. That

Governor John Carlin ordered the landfill closed until the contamination had been cleaned up.

KDHE Secretary Harkins said he felt "fortunate" the problem had been found "quickly."[1] He predicted the problem would be corrected and the site soon reopened. He was wrong. In March 1982, further testing revealed that the contamination was spread-

means the firm is required to file a 10-K report with the federal Securities and Exchange Commission. The 10-K, which should be available at a major branch of the public library, will give you a quick profile of the company and may contain information on whether it is involved in any major legal problems.

While the EPA's regional offices may also have information, they may not release information you feel is important. If that is the case, you can file a Freedom of Information (FOI) request. Federal agencies are required to release a wide range of information in response to FOI requests, but certain categories of information are exempt from this, include trade secrets, data that could affect national security, documents concerning ongoing litigation, or anything that would clearly be an unwarranted invasion of an individual's privacy.

To file an FOI request, call the appropriate agency to find out to whom to address the letter, and begin by stating that you are writing "a request under the Freedom of Information Act, 5 U.S.C. 522." Try to be as specific as possible about what documents you want.

You don't have to start from scratch or go at it alone. Try to enlist the support of neighbors. If the threat is real, they may be willing to help. There are also many national environmental organizations that can give you help on a range of problems—legal, technical, and organizational. The better prepared you are, the easier it will be to embark on whatever course of action you or your organization decides is best.

ing southward into the expansion site. Although state health officials again downplayed the significance of these findings, there was by now widespread skepticism about the credibility of the KDHE. The *Wichita Eagle-Beacon* editorialized, "It should come as no surprise that people are suspicious of after-the-fact explanations that are largely theories."[2]

In May, a consulting firm hired by Waste Management Incorporated—the nation's largest waste disposal firm, which had purchased the site in August 1980—reported that chemicals were continuing to leak into groundwater. That revelation effectively disposed of any notion that the site would reopen for a long time to come—in September 1984, the EPA placed Furley on its Superfund cleanup list. The site that was supposed to be secure for 5,000 years had lasted less than 5.

Although residents cheer the news that the Furley site is now slated for cleanup under Superfund, some are bitter they had to battle the very public agencies which are supposed to protect their health. "We don't know who or what to believe anymore, and we are angry," Sharilyn Dienst says. Referring to the Furley site, the state attorney general's office said, "There have been problems concerning the State's ability to make independent decisions. . . . All too often, the State has found itself deferring to the judgment of those individuals who have a direct interest in the continued operation of the facility."[3]

Continuing Problems

Traditionally, state and local agencies have had the primary responsibility of providing safe drinking water. However, by the late 1960s, it became painfully obvious they were not doing the job, and public dissatisfaction helped encourage Congress to create the U.S. Environmental Protection Agency. The EPA was designed to succeed where the states had failed. As a federal agency, it can set nationwide standards and back them up by imposing stiff financial penalties and putting violators in the dock.

Another important aspect of the EPA's duties is to help states develop their own environmental programs. The EPA can return authority to a state that it considers capable of running a regulatory program that meets federal standards. Over the past decade, states have assumed much of the EPA's enforcement and permitting duties for federal environmental regulations. Almost every state now enforces federal pesticide regulations; almost all states now are responsible for enforcing EPA safe drinking water standards; 35 states now enforce and permit industrial and municipal waste discharges under the Clean Water Act; and many states have some responsibility for controlling the disposal of hazardous waste.

But what the feds can give, they can also take away. The EPA is supposed to monitor how state agencies are performing, and if they are not doing a satisfactory job, then the EPA can withdraw authority and take over the program.

The system sounds great in theory, but the experience of Sharilyn Dienst and her neighbors is not uncommon: state and local agencies are often unable or unwilling to do an adequate job. "It has become obvious that the half-hearted attempts by government to protect people from the dangers of chemical exposure have failed," the New York State Assembly noted in a recent report on the state's environmental program. "The widely held belief that government, now aware of the threat of industrial poisons, has taken effective action to control them is a myth."[4]

An EPA survey of 28,000 of the nation's 65,000 community water systems found more than 146,000 violations of the federal Safe Drinking Water Act during 1980.

One reason for this widespread noncompliance was the states' failure to perform required tests of water quality; from 1978 to 1980, for example, the state of West Virginia tested only 83 of 504 water systems for levels of radioactivity and inorganic chemicals.[5]

Many states now have the responsibility of inspecting hazardous waste facilities for compliance with waste disposal regulations. But several studies have shown that many states have been doing a poor job here, too. The General Accounting Office (GAO) found that 51 of 65 hazardous waste facilities in Illinois and North Carolina were not in compliance with federal groundwater monitoring requirements. Two other states—Massachusetts and California—did not "know the extent of non-compliance because most of their facilities have not been inspected," the GAO reported.[6]

Some states also display a lackadaisical approach to correcting violations once they are discovered. The GAO, for example, found that Tennessee notified facilities of violations and then waited for up to 18 months before pursuing further enforcement action.[7]

In California, the state health department "does not have an effective enforcement program" for hazardous waste facilities that pose potential threats to groundwater and "does not consistently resolve violations," concluded a 1983 California Assembly Office of Research report. Of the 380 known hazardous waste violations in the health department's files at the time, only 52 had been resolved.[8]

A 1983 GAO report found that during an 18-month period, 82 percent of 531 municipal and industrial wastewater dischargers violated the amount of pollutants they were permitted to dump directly into surface waterways.[9] In four of the six states the GAO surveyed, the state is responsible for enforcing these discharge limits. Enforcement of clean water regulations is so poor in nine states that, by late 1984, the EPA was reportedly considering retracting their authority to run waste discharge programs.[10]

Why States Fail

In 1983, the potent, carcinogenic pesticide ethylene dibromide (EDB) was discovered in wells in central Florida. By November 1984, more than 700 contaminated wells had been found across the state, and the testing was still continuing. The Florida Department of Agriculture bore much of the responsibility for the contamination because it had used the pesticide as part of a state-run program to control pests in the citrus groves—at a level two-and-a-half times that permitted by federal standards and recommended on the label.

The Department of Agriculture's role is particularly ironic because it is supposed to ensure that pesticides are used safely. Cliff Thaell, director of the Coalition Against the Misuse of Pesticides in Florida, calls this situation "a systemic problem. The state Department of Agriculture had two roles: one, promotion of agriculture, and two, regulation of pesticides. It's a built-in conflict."

Health and safety often take a back seat to pesticide promotion when state agriculture officials are making the decisions. In

Florida, each year about 23,000 licensed pesticide applicators spread thousands of different pesticide mixtures over nearly 13 million acres.[11] Even though more than 90 percent of all Floridians draw their water from groundwater, much of it contained in shallow aquifers vulnerable to pesticide contamination, Florida's health and agriculture agencies did not sample groundwater for pesticides until 1982. (In fact, Secretary of Agriculture Doyle Conner later said he never before realized that most Floridians relied on groundwater.) "I don't know whether it was a matter of naivete," says Stephen King, an official of the Florida Department of Health and Rehabilitative Services. "I suspect that might have been the case in our agency." But by that time it was widely known that pesticides could foul groundwater; large-scale pesticide contamination had already been discovered in Long Island and California.

In fact, aldicarb (Temik) contamination of thousands of Long Island wells prompted the pesticide's manufacturer, Union Carbide, to conduct its own tests of Florida groundwater. Union Carbide found traces of Temik in about 10 percent of the wells it sampled in five Florida citrus-growing counties. But the state apparently didn't become concerned until August 1982, when it received inquiries from a national television news network. The state's own tests for Temik confirmed the bad news: the pesticide had indeed seeped into the state's groundwater. But while Union Carbide's tests showed Temik levels to be below recommended EPA safety standards, the state detected excessive levels of Temik.

With this information in hand, the state Department of Agriculture did next to nothing. A coalition of environmental and farm worker organizations petitioned the department to suspend the use of Temik, but department secretary Conner ducked the issue and instead appointed a task force, heavily populated by agribusiness interests. Predictably, the task force rejected the idea of a ban. The secretary didn't ban Temik until he was convinced that Temik was in drinking water supplies.

As it turned out, Florida had not seen the last of Temik. When Conner suspended the use of EDB, he announced the state was lifting the ban on Temik for 850,000 acres in 1984.

Conner contended that his decision on Temik was not a trade-off for the ban on EDB. "It was done scientifically, it was done professionally," he said. "It was not done politically."[12] But when Conner lifted the ban on Temik, he ignored the state DER's recommendation that the pesticide not be used within 600 feet of drinking wells. DER Secretary Victoria Tschinkel fired off an angry letter telling Conner that his decision was "not fulfilling the highest regulatory goals of public health protection."[13]

The Florida Agriculture Department's failure to protect groundwater from pesticides isn't surprising. The state's citrus industry—the major user of both Temik and EDB—rings up $2.4 billion in annual sales. Because of its size, the industry was able to influence the EPA's decision to delay regulation of EDB.

In Hawaii, too, agricultural interests have been a dominant economic and political force for years. One of the state's major crops is pineapples, and the pineapple growers, who are dominated by large companies such as Del Monte and Castle & Cooke, didn't hesitate to use economic threats when the EPA decided to ban the use of the widely used pesticide dibromochloropropane (DBCP). The pineapple growers argued that they simply could not grow pineapples in Hawaii if they could not use DBCP. The state, fearful of such a tremendous blow to its economy, supported the pineapple industry. The EPA granted an exemption to allow the pineapple growers to continue to use DBCP, even though it was banned in the other 49 states. Not long thereafter, DBCP was discovered in several wells on the islands of Maui and Oahu.

Faced with the near certainty that the EPA would suspend use of EDB, the state again rushed to the aid of the pineapple corporations. With the full knowledge that EDB had already shown up in his state's groundwater, Governor George Ariyoshi asked then–EPA Administrator William Ruckelshaus to again exempt Hawaii's pineapple growers from the suspension. Ariyoshi's request was prompted by the Pineapple Growers Association which, according to one corporate president, had given the governor a draft letter containing "the points we thought were pertinent."[14] This time, however, the EPA did not grant an exemption.

In Hawaii, the pineapple industry effectively has used the threat of job loss to enlist the cooperation of state officials, at the expense of public health. In considering this trade-off between public health and economic growth, state officials fear that if antipollution laws are too strictly enforced, then businesses will close up shop and give their state an antibusiness reputation that hampers economic growth.

But there is evidence that the health-versus-jobs argument is specious: strict enforcement apparently does not lose jobs. A five-year study by the Washington-based Conservation Foundation shows that highly polluting "smokestack" industries such as steel, rubber, oil refining, and chemical manufacturing are just as likely to set up shop in states with strong environmental records. The study found no evidence of a migration of industry from one state to another in search of "pollution havens."[15]

Lax enforcement is often simply a product of a business-as-usual attitude among state officials, who don't want to rock any boats by disrupting the "old boys network" that binds the regulators and the regulated. Officials can become reluctant to let the public in on the network; in a perverse way, ordinary citizens come to be viewed as a nuisance, an intrusion, even a threat. Public involvement can translate into public scrutiny, which is not welcome when government performance leaves something to be desired.

The Biggest Obstacle: Too Little Money

A failure of will may result in lax enforcement in some states, but a much greater problem is simply a lack of personnel, equipment, training, and funds to do the job.

When people suspect their water is contaminated, they often turn first to their local health department or water supplier. But local authorities are often ill equipped to deal with chemical contamination. When Carroll Pittman complained in 1979 to the

Jacksonville City Health Department about a strong odor and taste in his water, the department tested his water for bacteria, not for chemicals. It found none and told Pittman that his water was satisfactory. Not until 1983 was chemical contamination discovered in the Pittmans' well. The city health department's failure to test for chemicals when Pittman first complained meant that the family and several of their neighbors continued to drink contaminated water for several years longer. Even after the city declared an emergency because of the contamination, the health department could only conduct ten samples a week because of a lack of lab space.

Local health officials are trained primarily to respond to the traditional problems of bacteriological contamination; consequently, they may be unaccustomed to dealing with chemical contamination. "Officials in rural areas are likely to be sanitary engineers who view water problems from an exclusively sanitary perspective, which is no longer appropriate for interpreting [chemical] problems," points out Stephen Lester of the Citizens Clearinghouse for Hazardous Wastes.

States are also hampered by a serious lack of resources in dealing with their growing responsibilities, including hazardous waste regulation and cleanup. Many states have been forced to cut back on already understaffed environmental agencies to cope with a financial crunch. In 1983, 41 states reduced or limited their spending, and 23 cut the size of their work force, according to former Massachusetts Lieutenant Governor (now U.S. Senator) John Kerry.[16]

The EPA's policy has been to delegate authority to implement and enforce hazardous waste programs to the states as quickly as possible, but the agency admits that most of the states have been ill prepared to do so. According to a recent EPA draft report, "most states have severe technical staffing problems due to insufficient fiscal resources and an inability to attract experienced personnel." By 1984, state agencies had only 30 percent of the personnel needed to implement the country's hazardous waste program, according to Donald Lazarchek, director of the Pennsylvania Bureau of Solid Waste Management.[17] Massachusetts had only one staff person with groundwater expertise to evaluate all the state's hazardous waste facilities and cleanup work.[18] In Illinois, salaries have been so low that the state hasn't been able to attract and keep qualified staff. The situation became so bad that in 1983, Illinois tried to return the responsibility of running its hazardous waste program to the EPA.[19] In New York, no funds were available during 1983 and 1984 to conduct annual inspections of the state's 2,500 hazardous waste generators.[20]

The federal Superfund cannot clean up more than a fraction of the hazardous waste sites known, which leaves the states either to collect funds for remedial action from responsible parties or to pay for the cleanup themselves. Many states have established their own superfunds to finance these cleanups, but these are usually much too small to deal with the problem. To clean up its hundreds of known or suspected waste sites, the state of New York estimates it will need a minimum of $500 million, but it is collecting only about $3 million a year to finance its state superfund. New York, however, is lucky; some states have no hazardous substance cleanup funds at all.

"A Dangerous Trend"

Although the EPA acknowledges that the states cannot adequately enforce the federal laws entrusted to them, it has sharply reduced its grants to help the states to do so. From 1975 to 1985, there has been a 61 percent reduction in real terms in EPA grants to states. Most of the budget slashing has occurred under the Reagan administration. Massachusetts had 234 EPA-funded position in 1980. By 1985, the number was reduced to 120.[21] In New York, cuts in federal and state funding caused the loss of 100 staff persons from the state Department of Environmental Conservation (DEC) water quality program from 1979 to 1983. The state's program to control discharges of pollutants into the state's rivers and lakes was "so impoverished that DEC . . . had to focus its limited resources on a mere 25 percent of the permitted dischargers," according to a New York Assembly report.[22] Of all the state programs, efforts to regulate municipal and sanitary landfills have suffered the greatest damage from EPA cutbacks. In 1982, the

EPA eliminated all funding to states to regulate these facilities. Under federal hazardous waste laws, these landfills are no longer supposed to receive large quantities of hazardous waste. But they did in the past, and many continue to receive significant amounts of hazardous waste from small generators and even home owners. Consequently, they pose a substantial—and largely unquantified—threat to groundwater and surface water.

Most states depended heavily on federal grants to run their municipal waste programs. When this money dried up, many state efforts were devastated. A survey of state solid waste programs found that 32 states lost more than 200 positions in these programs because of the loss of federal funds.[23] In New York, where 15 million tons of municipal waste is dumped into more than 400 landfills, the loss of federal funds caused an 80 percent reduction in the state's municipal waste staff.[24] The result is that most of these landfills aren't permitted, and monitoring and enforcement activities have been sharply curtailed. Groundwater pollution from these municipal landfills "is massive and growing," according to state DEC Commissioner Henry Williams. The DEC estimates that as many as 200 municipal landfills may be leaking into groundwater.[25]

In Massachusetts, the state has identified 96 landfills as potential threats to groundwater, but Fifi Nesson of the state Department of Environmental Quality Engineering says, "We don't have the resources to go out in the field and check to see if they are leaking. We also find illegal dumping going on at landfills and we don't have the staff to stop it. Which means compliance slips." Again, New York and Massachusetts are probably in better shape than most states; "Seventeen states no longer consider their solid waste programs to be active," says Pennsylvania's Donald Lazarchek.[26]

The damage caused by these funding cutbacks extends beyond the people laid off, the inspections not done, and the permits not written. As John Kerry of Massachusetts points out, "Every time the federal government cuts back on some of those funds they send a message to the state saying, 'We don't think that it is important and, therefore, you don't have to fund it either.' It is a dangerous trend."[27]

Two Success Stories

Some states have not bought that message. One of those is Florida, which recently developed one of the nation's most farsighted environmental programs.

The dramatic change did not come a moment too soon for the Sunshine State, where groundwater contamination was a disaster waiting to happen. More than nine out of ten Floridians obtain their drinking water from underground aquifers, many of which are separated from the surface by only a few feet of sandy soil. For example, the high productive Biscayne aquifer, encased in limestone only five feet below the surface, supplies 7 billion gallons of water each day to more than 1 million people in southern Florida.

The potential sources of contamination in this fast-growing state (its population increased 43 percent from 1970 to 1980) are staggering. In addition to widespread pesticide contamination, Florida has:

● Nearly 400 hazardous waste sites, 98 of which are known to have contaminated groundwater. And 35 of these are on the federal Superfund cleanup list. The state recently has had to close or limit the use of more than 50 municipal wells in the Miami area because of chemical contamination.

● Some 40,000 underground gasoline and chemical storage tanks, many of them sitting in groundwater. There have been nearly 200 known leaks.

● More than 6,000 pits and ponds, many of which are leaking toxic chemicals in the groundwater.

● More than 9,000 drainage wells used to discharge industrial and municipal waste directly into the water table.

The gravity of the problem forced the state to act. In 1983, the state assembly issued a comprehensive report on Florida's water problems that concluded the state had not confronted the threats to Florida's water quality "in a direct or effective manner.

As a result, we have no defenses against the contamination." Later that year, the state legislature passed the Water Quality Assurance Act, which created a waste management plan and a groundwater protection program. The act bans hazardous landfills, requires municipalities to identify all hazardous waste producers, limits the density of septic tanks, and eliminates the small-quantity generators' exemption from hazardous waste disposal requirements. The act also directed the state Department of Environmental Regulation (DER) to set up a groundwater monitoring network consisting of thousands of wells to keep track of the state's water quality. An interagency pesticide review council was established to review the use of restricted pesticides in the state; this was a significant step because it gave state agencies other than the Department of Agriculture a voice in pesticide use. So that the DER could carry out these new responsibilities, the legislature funded 100 new positions in that department.

In 1984, the DER approved regulations that require public water systems to test for 118 chemicals every three years. It also set drinking water standards for 8 chemicals. The standards and testing requirements are the toughest of any state in the country. Even the EPA has yet to set standards for any of the 8 contaminants.

The DER has also started an "amnesty days" program, which will run through 1987, to allow residents and small businesses to turn in small amounts of hazardous chemicals to the state, free of charge. During each amnesty period, SCA Services, a waste disposal firm hired by the state, sets up collection centers in designated metropolitan areas, where waste can be dropped off. SCA then transports the waste to an EPA-permitted waste disposal or treatment facility. So far, SCA has collected more than 500,000 pounds of hazardous materials, an amount which is "just the tip of the iceberg," says amnesty days project administrator Frank Walper. This waste, which includes solvents; paints; banned pesticides such as DDT, EDB, and Temik; and even explosives, might otherwise have been poured down the sink or taken to the dump, which it could have soaked down into the groundwater. State legislator Sid Martin sums up the reason for the tremendous amount of environmental activity in his state: "It doesn't take a genius to realize that we must take action *before* the water becomes polluted, not after."[28]

Three thousand miles away, in Los Angeles, where the landscape is also dotted with palm trees, local authorities are not talking about amnesty. Disdaining negotiations to get companies to comply voluntarily with hazardous waste laws, the city has formed a toxic waste strike force to create "the incentive for industry to police itself," says strike force chief and Los Angeles Deputy City Attorney Barry Groveman. That incentive is the threat of jail. Simply relying on fines won't do the trick, Groveman points out. "Penalties will always be the cost of doing business. Jail is not."

The strike force was formed in 1982 of representatives from five local agencies—the Los Angeles city attorney's office, county health department, city police and fire departments, and city bureau of sanitation. The state health department is also actively involved. Acting on tips from company employees, public complaints, or its own field surveillance, the strike force has made nearly two dozen busts, according to Groveman. Before any raids or arrests are made, the strike force conducts extensive surveillance and scientifically monitors illegal waste discharges and other activities. Then, during a raid on a facility or disposal site, the strike force leaves nothing unturned in its search for incriminating evidence. "We build airtight cases," says Groveman confidently. Apparently so. As of November 1984, nine strike force cases had gone to trial, and all resulted in convictions with prison terms ranging from 1 to 17 months in the Los Angeles County Jail. The convictions have also resulted in more than $1.5 million in fines.[29]

All the prosecutions have involved executive officers. "We go after the people who run the companies," says lead investigator Jim McNally of the state health department. "Ninety-five percent wear white collars and very nice suits." They include David Peairs, president of a Hollywood franchise of Culligan Water Service, who became the first person to be jailed for violating the state's hazardous waste laws. Peairs's company picked up waste from a number of industrial companies and simply dumped it into the city's sewers. The city attorney's office estimates that Peairs's operation was dumping up to 12 tons of hazardous materials, including hexavalent chromium, a known carcinogen, down the drain each year.[30] Other "midnight" dumpers have been caught pouring waste directly on the ground.

Is the strike force having an effect? "The word is definitely out," McNally says. "Every time there's a big raid, [legitimate] waste disposal companies say their phones ring off the hook." Groveman says his office has "gotten calls from all over the place" asking for advice or information about the strike force.

For Groveman, the strike force's success depends on a desire to combat illegal waste disposal, which he calls "violent crime against the community." The young attorney contends that the EPA, with a much larger budget, has been less effective because it is a bureaucracy with "a sluggish look-the-other-way attitude."

Can the States Do It Alone?

Los Angeles and Florida are not alone. Several states have recently enacted stringent controls on potential sources of water contamination, in many cases going beyond the EPA's requirements. New Jersey has passed a law requiring water suppliers to test for 25 organic chemicals in addition to those regulated by the Safe Drinking Water Act. A number of states have eliminated or restricted the federal small-waste-generator exemptions. Illinois has banned the landfilling of several hazardous chemicals by 1987. California has enacted legislation that requires closure by 1988 of leaking hazardous waste pits and ponds, if they are within a half mile of drinking water supplies. California also requires double containment systems of new underground chemical storage tanks, to prevent leakage; but in the face of opposition from the petroleum and electronics industries, the state legislature exempted petroleum and existing chemical storage tanks.

A number of local jurisdictions also have taken steps to safeguard their water supplies. Dade County, Florida (where Miami is located), has forbidden most industrial development on a 90-square mile area surrounding one of its well fields. In 1982, California's Santa Clara County, the hub of the electronics industry and host to hundreds of leaking underground storage tanks, enacted an especially tough ordinance to protect against leaks from underground storage tanks. Sine its passage, 79 cities and counties have adopted similar ordinances. Dozens of states, counties, and cities have passed "right-to-know" measures designed to give residents and workers access to information about hazardous materials used and stored in their communities and workplaces. Such information helps trace the origin of pollution once it is discovered.

Many aggressive and innovative state and local initiatives came about because ordinary citizens got mad and decided to do something—including countless meetings, petitions, letters, and, on occasion, confrontational tactics with polluters or reluctant government regulators.

The Santa Clara ordinance, the first of its kind in the nation, was the direct result of the effects of a coalition of labor unions, local residents, and the local chapter of Citizens for a Better Environment, a national environmental organization. Many of the citizens involved had already seen their wells contaminated with toxic chemicals leaking out of these underground storage tanks. This alliance, known as the Silicon Valley Toxics Coalition, brought dozens of people to hearings on the proposed ordinance, drawn up by local fire chiefs. Eventually the coalition's efforts succeeded in greatly strengthening the final version of the ordinance.

Unfortunately, residents were forced to act; a major leak from an underground storage tank at a Fairchild Instruments plant contaminated the drinking water of thousands of county residents. Many of those people blame the chemicals for birth defects and other ills. "What happened could not have happened if not for a really significant disaster with immediate significant health hazards," said Ted Smith of the Silicon Valley Toxics Coalition. "It became real for everyone, [not] just a bunch of crazies."

The EPA:
A Failed Mission

6

"You win very few victories, it's just varying degrees of defeat." So said former EPA Administrator Douglas Costle, talking to an interviewer in December 1980, just before the end of his tenure at the helm of the federal government's largest regulatory agency.[1]

Costle's statement may seem odd. During the 1970s, the EPA made significant progress toward cleaning up the nation's waterways and air. The agency was beginning to regulate the disposal of hazardous waste. A strategy to protect groundwater was in the works. Congress had just that month created Superfund to clean up the nation's thousands of hazardous waste sites, a move that supposedly closed the last gap in the laws necessary to protect the nation's water supplies.

But upon closer scrutiny, it becomes clear that the bloom of optimism which greeted the EPA did indeed fade. The EPA was a product of the 1960s, a decade in which many legislators shared the feeling that if we simply committed enough resources to a problem, we could solve it. Supporting this optimism were technological achievements such as the space program's successful moon landing in 1969.

But unlike putting a man on the moon, cleaning up the nation's drinking water is not simply a technological problem. Few people anticipated the magnitude and complexity of controlling water contamination, and although it is popular to portray the

EPA as a regulatory "big brother," it has never had nearly the resources necessary to accomplish its mission. Even though it is the largest federal regulatory agency, with a $1.3-billion budget in 1984, its duties are immense. Most other regulatory agencies have to deal with only a specific industry or activity. The Federal Aviation Administration, for example, regulates only air travel. The Securities and Exchange Commission deals primarily with financial markets. But the EPA is supposed to conduct research, set standards, and administer several complex environmental laws that regulate literally millions of sources of pollution that affect everybody living in this country. Clearly, the agency doesn't have nearly enough money to do its job.

At almost every turn, it confronted a thicket of economic and political forces—industry, environmentalists, the public, Congress, even state regulators. With its insufficient resources continually stretched to the breaking point, the agency became a cautious bureaucracy, unwilling to take decisive action. In the more than ten years since the Safe Drinking Water Act was passed, for example, the EPA referred only 21 cases of violation to the Justice Department for prosecution, although tens of thousands of violations of the act occurred each year.[2] Time and again, it missed deadlines to promulgate and enforce regulations. (Ohio Congressman Dennis Eckart told ABC News that by 1983, the EPA had accumulated more than 121 years of "missed deadlines.")[3] When it did act, the agency often found itself buffeted by lawsuits. Another former EPA administrator, William Ruckelshaus, claimed that 80 percent of all the regulations the agency set ended up in court, challenged by industry, by environmental organizations, or by citizens groups.[4] The result was more delays. EPA employees found themselves spending more and more time in court, and it became a common joke in the nation's capital that lawyers were running the agency.

Worse still, the end of Costle's administration marked the end of much of the progress the agency made during the 1970s. The next administration, under Ronald Reagan, tried its best to dismantle the existing EPA. One major casualty was the EPA's effort to clean up the nation's waterways.

Attacking the Clean Water Act

To control the pollution entering our nation's lakes, rivers, and coastal waters, Congress passed amendments to the Clean Water Act (CWA) in 1972—overriding a presidential veto to do so. The CWA's goal was to make the nation's waters fishable and swimmable by 1983 and to end the discharge of toxic chemicals into surface waters by 1985.

To accomplish this task, the EPA established the national pollutant discharge elimination system. Under this system, the 65,000 industries and public sewage treatment plants that discharge waste products into waterways must have permits. It is illegal to discharge without one. These permits, which are supposed to be renewed every five years, specify discharge limits for pollutants and how and when these limits are to be met. Initially, enforcement and permit writing were the EPA's responsibility, but as with other regulatory programs, these activities were turned over to the states as their own programs met federal standards. By the early 1980s, more than 35 states had assumed these duties under the CWA.

Because of CWA, the quality of many rivers and lakes has improved dramatically. Fish have returned to numbers of rivers. Levels of so-called conventional pollutants—dissolved and suspended solids, oil, and grease—have decreased. Ohio's Cuyahoga River and the Buffalo River in New York no longer threaten to burst into flames, as they did during the 1960s. In this sense, the Clean Water Act is one of the EPA's most successful programs.

But the EPA did not score so well on controlling the chemical pollutants that, by the late 1970s, had become the nation's major water quality problem. News of chemical contamination of our waterways surfaced in the 1960s. An early focal point of public concern was the lower Mississippi River. It had become so tainted with toxic chemicals from hundreds of industrial dischargers that New Orleans residents complained of foul-smelling and foul-tasting water, and commercial fishermen were unable to sell their catch because the fish tasted so bad. In 1967, the federal government began to analyze the quality of the Mississippi's water. In

1972, the EPA finally released the results of the study: the water contained 48 different organic chemicals. Among these were three known or suspected cancer-causing compounds—chloroform, benzene, and carbon tetrachloride. The EPA concluded that "the trace organics in the Mississippi River drinking water supplies are a potential threat to the health of 1.5 million people who consume this water, particularly the elderly, those that are ill, and children."[5]

Concerned about chemicals in its drinking water, the New Orleans City Council asked the Environmental Defense Fund (EDF), an environmental organization based in Washington, D.C., to investigate the possible effects of the city's water on the health of its residents. EDF's study revealed a strong correlation between New Orleans's drinking water and its high incidence of deaths from cancer, particularly of the gastrointestinal and urinary systems. The day after the EDF released its study, the EPA announced that its improved chemical detection techniques had found a total of 66 different organic chemicals in the city's drinking water. The two studies, coming one on top of another, caught the national media's attention. Bacteria and infectious diseases were no longer considered the main threat to water quality. Suddenly, cancer was the big issue.

That concern came as no surprise to some scientists. Back in the early 1960s, Wilhelm Hueper, then–head of the National Cancer Institute's environmental cancer section, had warned, "The rapidly increasing pollution of many bodies of fresh and salt water with carcinogenic agents and the inabilities of the presently used filtration equipment to remove such contaminants from the drinking water supply have created conditions that may result in serious cancer hazards to the general population."[6]

Nevertheless, it was the publicity surrounding the EDF and EPA studies that spurred congressional action on drinking water legislation that had long lain dormant. In December 1974, more than four years after it was first introduced, the Safe Drinking Water Act finally was signed into law, giving the EPA power to set and enforce standards for hazardous substances that occur in drinking water.

The agency was required by the CWA to set limits on the discharge of toxic organic chemicals by the spring of 1974. When it failed to meet that deadline, it was sued repeatedly by several environmental organizations. In 1976, the EPA reached an agreement in U.S. District Court in Washington with one of these organizations, the Natural Resources Defense Council (NRDC). The EPA said that by 1980 it would establish standards for the discharge of 65 chemicals, called priority pollutants. The standards would force dischargers to use the so-called best available technology (BAT) in controlling toxic pollutants.

But more delays ensued. By March 1979, the EPA had not proposed a single new BAT guideline and asked for more time. The NRDC agreed to give the agency until 1981 to complete the BAT standards, and industrial dischargers were given until July 1984 to meet the more stringent guidelines. By the end of 1980, the agency had issued standards for the timber industry, and was about to do so for several other industries, when the political climate in Washington changed abruptly. The Regan administration rode into town, vowing to get the government regulators off the backs of industry. Environmental regulations were sure to be a prime target. The Clean Water Act was in trouble.

In April 1981, three months after Reagan because president, the EPA abruptly suspended regulations requiring industries to remove the 250 million pounds of toxic chemicals and heavy metals that poured into public sewers each year.[7] These "pretreatment" regulations, which had gone into effect just a few days before, were reinstated by federal court order in July 1982. But the Reagan administration's assault on the CWA was only beginning.

In July 1981, the EPA, under the leadership of Anne Burford,° again asked the court for an extension of the BAT deadlines. By the agency's own estimates, every year the BAT guidelines were delayed, more than 100 million pounds of toxic chemicals were discharged into the nation's waterways.[8] The court ruled against the EPA's request, and the agency again failed to

°When Burford became EPA administrator, her name was Anne Gorsuch. She later married Robert Burford, director of the Bureau of Land Management in the Interior Department.

meet its deadlines. It will not issue the final BAT guidelines until 1985, and these will not go into effect until 1988.

Because of both these delays and a lack of state and EPA resources, tens of thousands of industrial dischargers and municipal treatment plants have been operating either with expired permits or simply without permits. The result is that most waste dischargers have been granted a reprieve. The EPA estimates that by October 1985, there will be nearly 30,000 expired permits in need of renewal.[9]

Enforcement of the CWA disintegrated under Burford. Of the 531 major industrial and municipal dischargers surveyed by the congressional General Accounting Office (GAO) in six states, 82 percent had dumped illegal amounts of pollutants at least once between October 1980 and March 1982.[10] But the full extent of the violations was not known—nearly half of the dischargers either provided incomplete discharge information or simply submitted no data at all.[11]

Drastic budget cuts were partly to blame for the delays and lack of enforcement. Funds for EPA water quality enforcement were slashed by nearly one-third from 1981 to 1983.[12] Overall, the agency's water quality budget was reduced by nearly half during Reagan's first term.[13] But the EPA's failure to enforce regulations under Burford went beyond scarcity of funds and resources. In 1982, EPA headquarters in Washington advised its regional offices to "settle enforcement cases in a nonconfrontational manner," according to the GAO.[14] Despite rampant noncompliance with the CWA, the EPA's formal enforcement actions against violators dropped 41 percent from 1980 to 1982.[15] NRDC attorney James Banks pointed out that the budget cuts were simply the result of a desire to unravel the CWA. "What we have is an administration determined to reverse Congressional policy by blocking or delaying regulations, ducking legal commitments, and generally creating a situation in which mandatory, statutory programs cannot work."[16]

Top EPA officials made it clear how they viewed the nation's clean water goals. In a 1982 speech to the National Association of Manufacturers, then–Deputy EPA Administrator John Hernandez said the CWA's goal of eliminating toxic discharges into the nation's waterways "just isn't realistic." He told the business group that the EPA would try to modify the act.[17] True to its promise, the EPA proposed several times during 1982 to allow more "flexibility" in setting water quality standards. In the end, the administration was not successful in its attempts to weaken the act, and the courts later reversed most of the EPA's suspensions of clean water regulations.

The bottom line is that 400 million pounds of toxic chemicals still pour into our nation's waters each year. An NRDC review of New York State Department of Environmental Conservation files shows what this means for the quality of our rivers and lakes in just a single state. More than 2,500 pounds of heavy metals are disgorged into the Hudson and Mohawk rivers each day.[18] According to a 1984 New York State Assembly report, 23 companies discharge up to 3,000 pounds of toxic chemicals a day into the Niagara River, which provides drinking water to 380,000 people; scientific analyses of the river and its sediments have detected more than 100 toxic substances, including solvents, plasticizing chemicals, and heavy metals.[19] In recent years, biologists have also found extremely high rates of cancer among fish in a number of rivers and lakes badly contaminated with industrial chemicals.

In 1984, the EPA's Jack Ravan acknowledged that this enforcement performance had "created serious credibility problems for the agency," and he promised, "We are doing everything in our power to regain our reputation as a strong enforcer."[20] Ravan said that the permit backlog would be cleared up by 1987 and claimed that the EPA and the states had made substantial progress in their enforcement programs, bringing hundreds of major violators into compliance and starting enforcement actions against hundreds of others.

But a follow-up survey by the GAO of dischargers on the lower Mississippi River produced findings at odds with the EPA's claims: all of the 33 companies it investigated violated their permit guidelines during the 27-month period from April 1982 to June 1984. Most of these polluters "were extensively and frequently exceeding their permits," the GAO noted.[21]

The EPA is seriously understaffed; one of its regional offices can only "take formal enforcement action against 20 percent of major industrial dischargers," according to a GAO official. "The remaining 80 percent receive either a phone call or a form letter for reported violations."[22]

Ravan responds that the GAO's survey was too small and narrow geographically to draw any broad conclusions. But Representative Elliott Levitas of Georgia, who chairs a congressional subcommittee investigating the EPA's administration of the CWA, is not impressed: "The record suggests to me that perhaps the real problem lies not just in the lack of resources and not in the absence of adequate statutory enforcement tools, but rather it suggests that what is truly lacking is a commitment to strong enforcement. The proof of a true commitment to enforcing the Clean Water Act . . . would be in the record of results. Those results do not exist."[23]

Because the Clean Water Act is not adequately enforced, private citizens and environmental organizations are taking legal action on their own. In 1982, they began searching EPA files for persistent violators. If the EPA or the states had failed to take any enforcement action, they filed suit to bring the dischargers back into compliance. Under the CWA, as with most environmental regulations, the public can bring legal action against violators. "To the aristocrat, it's mob rule," says Vance Hughes, a former Justice Department attorney who is helping citizens groups form their suits. "But let's face it. All of this was built in by those who formed the laws to make sure that citizens participated." By mid-1984, there were more than 200 such suits nationwide. Says James Thornton, an NRDC attorney working on citizens suits, "We find ourselves in the peculiar business of teaching EPA how to do its enforcement. It's sad."

Gutting the EPA

When the Reagan administration took control of the EPA in January 1981, it had two major goals: to drastically slash the agency's budget and to open its doors to regulated industries. Over the new administration's first term, the budget for drinking water programs was cut 31 percent, hazardous waste programs were cut 16 percent, and money for pesticide regulation was reduced 32 percent.[24] The EPA, under its new administrator, Anne Burford, embraced with open arms the industries it was supposed to regulate. Cooperation, not confrontation, became the new policy. What that really meant was that EPA attempted to roll back regulations unpopular with industry. If that didn't succeed because of public or congressional pressure, the EPA simply stopped enforcing the law.

On top of that, the cuts came just as the agency was taking on a whole new generation of water quality and hazardous waste regulations. It was a time, as Vance Hughes puts it, when the EPA was "just barely hanging on." New Resource Conservation and Recovery Act (RCRA) regulations required the monitoring of 70,000 firms that handled hazardous waste. The agency also was supposed to implement the newly created Superfund hazardous waste cleanup program. Finally, pressure was mounting for the EPA to develop drinking water standards for organic chemicals appearing frequently in groundwater.

A cozy relationship with regulated industries was not unique to Burford's EPA. The agency often has had close ties with those it was supposed to regulate. Industry and EPA staffs are in close contact with each other in the course of promulgating and then enforcing regulations: EPA scientists deal with their counterparts in industry; agency lawyers talk with industry attorneys. The result can be a measure of professional camaraderie. In addition, the EPA must also depend on industry to provide much of the scientific data upon which it bases its regulatory decisions. Perhaps most damaging to the EPA's independence, many staffers come from industry, and many more leave the government to take jobs in the private sector. Thus, it's not surprising that industry influences regulatory decision making. Burford and many of her assistants allowed this influence to go unchecked. As EPA hazardous waste official Hugh Kaufman told NBC News, "The Carter administration listened to the polluters with one ear; this administration listens with both ears."[25]

The EPA's record under Burford's leadership was characterized by closed meetings with industry, conflicts of interest, rollbacks of existing regulations industry didn't like, lax enforcement, and regulatory delays. The controversy surrounding such actions forced Burford and more than 20 members of her staff to resign in the spring of 1983. But by that time, much of the EPA was already gutted.

Failing to Protect Groundwater

Burford's policies were most damaging to the efforts to control hazardous waste and groundwater contamination. Groundwater quality had been a major concern behind the passage of the 1976 Resource Conservation and Recovery Act, which gave the EPA until April 1978 to establish a "cradle to grave" system of handling and disposing of hazardous waste. It proved to be an impossible task. Former EPA Administrator William Ruckelshaus admitted, "When we began to write regulations for the control of hazardous waste disposal required by RCRA, we didn't know where the generators were; we didn't know what was in their waste streams, or how much there was of it or how hazardous it might be; and we didn't know where it was going."[26] Recalls Penny Hansen, chief of the EPA's hazardous waste treatment branch, "We didn't know what hazardous waste was, let alone where it should go. It was laughable."

Not surprisingly, the agency didn't come close to meeting its April 1978 deadline. In December 1978, four out of the ten EPA regions reported they could not even keep track of the wastes currently disposed of.[27] In September 1979, three years after the RCRA was enacted, a House committee reported, "We are still awaiting the promulgation of the first hazardous waste disposal regulations."[28] Finally, in May 1980, the EPA issued a partial set of regulations, specifying that most hazardous waste should be disposed of in registered facilities. But there were still no comprehensive guidelines on what measures disposal sites should take to protect against contamination.

Under Burford, even this halting progress would come to a virtual standstill. As soon as she assumed the reins of the EPA in May 1981, she began to dismantle those EPA regulations most unpopular with industry. In June, she suspended three hazardous waste rules. The following February, the EPA made one of its most controversial moves—it lifted a ban on the disposal of liquid

R&D Cuts: The Long-Term Damage

The damage the Reagan administration has wreaked on the EPA goes beyond enforcement and permitting. According to figures compiled by Environmental Safety, a private organization that monitors the EPA's performance, the EPA budget for scientific research and development was slashed by nearly 50 percent from 1980 to 1984.[1] The resources now devoted to the agency's Office of Research and Development are at their lowest level ever.

Research is vital to the agency's regulatory decisions. It's difficult to set safe drinking water standards without knowing whether or not a chemical causes cancer or birth defects. And the EPA may not know if a standard is even practical unless it first determines whether technoology is available to achieve it.

In April 1984, people driving by the EPA's environmental research laboratory along Highway 61 in Duluth, Minnesota, might have seen the lab's director himself raking leaves and laying sod. The lab didn't have enough money to hire a maintenance crew. But the real toll was taken on research inside the building. In 1982, there were "two dozen people working with me," said an EPA scientist working on a five-year acid rain study of more than a thousand lakes in Minnesota, Wisconsin, and Michigan. "Six months ago, 15 people. Two months ago, 8 people. Today, 3 people. Two more months from now, no one."[2]

Why was EPA headquarters opposed to the five-year project? "I don't have a satisfactory answer," the scientist said, "except that the policy changed from the Carter Administration to the present one." The EPA was opposed to congressional attempts to limit emissions from coal-fired power plants, thought to be a major contributor to acid rain; perhaps the agency didn't want its own scientists producing evidence that acid rain was damaging lakes. "We were delivering the product too soon. It was determined that we wouldn't know the answers before a certain time," the EPA researcher said. "They didn't like the message, so they shot the messenger."[3]

waste in landfills. Liquid wastes easily soak through the landfill into the ground and continue down to the underlying water table. Confronted by a storm of protest, the EPA retracted the ban less than a month later. But during that time, thousands of 55-gallon drums of liquid hazardous waste were dumped into the ground around the country. One company alone, Waste Mangement, disposed of nearly 2,500 drums of liquid hazardous waste in its Denver, Colorado, hazardous waste facility,[29] a site that was already known to be leaking into groundwater.

As was the case with the Clean Water Act, enforcement of the new hazardous waste regulations was also lax. An RCRA regulation, promulgated by the previous EPA administration, required some 1,500 waste management facilities to institute groundwater monitoring programs by November 1981 to detect contamination. This consisted mainly of sinking groundwater monitoring wells, conducting periodic sampling, and reporting the results of the sampling to the EPA and appropriate state agencies. But in March 1983, the EPA found that 109 of 171 hazardous waste facilities it surveyed failed to comply with groundwater monitoring requirements.[30] About 70 percent of the noncomplying facilities had received no enforcement action. Subsequent GAO studies showed even higher rates of violations.

For an environmental regulation to work, firms must voluntarily comply. But compliance costs money: it consumes employee time, requires new equipment, and often means hiring new personnel with expertise in pollution control. Companies aren't inclined to bother unless they know that violators are punished or forced to comply. "No regulatory program can function without an extremely high level of voluntary compliance," contends William Drayton, former EPA assistant administrator for policy and management. "The two—enforcement and voluntary compliance—are inseparable." But, says Drayton, "In the last three years we've lost voluntary compliance. All our laws are semi-meaningless."

Under the Reagan administration, there have been tremendous delays in issuing final permits for the nation's 5,200 hazardous waste treatment, storage, and disposal facilities. By October

1984—eight years after the RCRA was enacted—the EPA had issued only 240 operating final permits.[31] The agency estimated that it would take until 1993 to complete the final permitting process.

But the worst abuses under Burford occurred in the EPA's handling of Superfund, responsible for cleanups of thousands of hazardous waste sites nationwide. Superfund got off to an extremely slow start and by 1983 had cleaned up only 5 of the 419 sites it was to handle and had spent but a fraction of the available funds.[32] Even if used up, the $1.6-billion fund could take care of only 170 sites at most, according to an internal EPA report.[33]

Impatient over this lack of progress, Congress investigated the conduct of several top EPA officials, including Burford and Rita Lavelle, head of the EPA's hazardous waste program. The investigation revealed that EPA officials had delayed cleanup of several sites in western states where Republican congressional campaigns stood to benefit by not publicizing the issue. And there was another reason for the inaction: the administration did not want an extension of Superfund. If there were a lot of money left in the fund at its expiration date in 1985, the administration could argue that additional money was not required. "There was a hidden agenda . . . not to set in motion events that could lead to what is referred to as 'Son of Superfund' or the extension of the tax or reenactment of the law beyond the 1985 cutoff," said William Hedeman, head of the EPA's Superfund program, in sworn congressional testimony.[34] The chemical industry, whose fees have paid for more than 80 percent of Superfund, may have had some influence; Rita Lavelle, who was formerly a public relations officer with Aerojet General, a major polluter, met with representatives of the chemical and mining industries on at least 47 occasions in 1982.[35]

The congressional investigation led to the downfall of Burford's administration. Lavelle was the first to go, in February 1983. The following month, Burford and many of her top aides resigned.

Burford was gone, but the Reagan administration officials who had picked her remained in power.

OMB: The Shadow Government

During his 1980 presidential campaign, Ronald Reagan had said, "There are tens of thousands of . . . regulations I would like to see eliminated."[36] As soon as he was elected, he wasted little time getting on with his antiregulation crusade. By the time of inauguration, Reagan's transition team had already picked out many of the regulations slated for extinction or revision. "We hit the ground running," said James Miller, a key player in the antiregulation drive and later head of the Federal Trade Commission. "All the work was done in the transition period. We knew what we were doing the minute we came in."[37] On January 22, 1981, two days after assuming the presidency, Reagan announced that the presidential taskforce on regulatory relief had been formed to scrutinize federal regulations.

Vice-President George Bush was named as chairman of the taskforce. Its members included David Stockman, director of the powerful Office of Management and Budget (OMB), and Vice-Presidential Counsel C. Boyden Gray. Gray encouraged business to come to the taskforce with its gripes. "If you go to an agency first, don't be too pessimistic if they can't solve the problem there," Gray told the U.S. Chamber of Commerce. "That's what the taskforce is for."[38]

On January 29, Reagan announced a 60-day freeze on all new regulations, many of which were passed in the last days of the Carter administration. On February 17, 1981, the president put the most important piece of his deregulation plan into place by signing the now-famous Executive Order 12291. This gave the OMB the power to approve each agency's regulations based on a cost-benefit evaluation. The OMB seemed heavily biased toward considering the short-term financial costs, while ignoring the long-term benefits.

The regulatory relief task force and the OMB quickly became well-traveled routes for industry executives annoyed with costly EPA regulations. In March 1981, the Chemical Manufacturers Association asked the regulatory taskforce to persuade the EPA to drop its chemical pretreatment rule, scheduled to go into effect at the end of the month. Industry had opposed the pretreatment rule for years. The association got its wish; the EPA suspended the rule.

Industry was also working with the OMB to undermine environmental regulations. Of the 31 EPA regulations OMB rejected during Burford's administration, the agency eventually withdrew 22.[39] According to John Daniel, EPA chief of staff under Burford, industry influence was a large factor in the OMB's decisions. Under sworn oath, he told a congressional investigations subcommittee that "there were a number of instances" when the OMB's opinion of proposed EPA regulations was based more on "analysis from the intended regulatee than from OMB staff."[40]

At one point, when the EPA was considering waste water discharge guidelines for the iron and steel industries, the agency received comments from the OMB that were so technical that they could not possibly have come from the budget office, Daniel testified.

Tennessee Representative Albert Gore said, "I am shocked to find that OMB has been ordering EPA to take actions that it felt were not in the best interests of the environment or the public simply because of back-door communications with industries."[41]

Even Burford, who arrived in Washington as a confirmed antiregulatory advocate, increasingly found herself at odds with the OMB. When she proposed a 1983 EPA budget of $975 million—nearly 30 percent less than the agency's budget before Reagan assumed office—she was flabbergasted that the OMB demanded even deeper cuts.

Burford's successor, William Ruckelshaus, had to battle the OMB constantly over his modest requests for increases in the EPA's budget. In spring 1984, the OMB rejected the EPA's request for $10 million to fund a joint program with the U.S. Department of Agriculture to control agricultural runoff, a major source of water pollution. The OMB also drastically reduced funds to conduct health studies among people exposed to chemicals from hazardous waste sites. Observed Representative Guy Molinari of New York, "OMB, in previous years, used funding levels to weaken policy, often in tandem with EPA. Now with policy tightening up in some areas of EPA, OMB is using its control over the budget to restrict the EPA itself."[42]

On top of that, the OMB appears to be gearing up for a renewed attack on key water quality protection laws during Reagan's second term. Just before the 1984 presidential election, the OMB asked the EPA to study the possibility of repealing the Safe Drinking Water Act. Given that kind of opposition, the post-Burford EPA has had very little room to operate.[43]

The EPA under Ruckelshaus

When William Ruckelshaus again became head of the EPA in May 1983 (he was the EPA's first administrator), the agency was in shambles. Its reputation was badly damaged by the scandals of the previous two years, and there was widespread public and congressional distrust of the EPA. The morale of the remaining staff was extremely low. But the appointment of Ruckelshaus was a smart political move. Untinged by scandal, he was remarkably successful in sprucing up the agency's image and turning morale around. He promised stepped-up enforcement and an end to closed-door meetings with regulated industries and quickly earned the nickname "Mr. Clean." In November 1984, Ruckelshaus resigned, claiming the EPA's course was righted. However, still hampered by a continuing scarcity of resources and the setbacks under Burford, the agency is merely conducting a holding action in many areas.

Take hazardous waste regulation. Lee Thomas, Rita Lavelle's successor, contends the EPA "made significant progress" in controlling hazardous waste. "I think you'll probably see the majority of the work completed within ten years," Thomas said in a recent interview.[44] But according to a draft EPA report released in October 1984, the vast majority of hazardous waste facilities subject to groundwater monitoring requirements were still not in compliance, more than eight years after the RCRA was passed by Congress.[45]

To Thomas's credit, the EPA has picked up speed in its Superfund program in the past couple of years. While only 6 sites were completely cleaned up by the end of 1984, the agency was starting about 125 cleanups a year. That may sound impressive, but not when compared with the magnitude of the problem. Many cleanups will take several decades, and the EPA now estimates that 1,500 to 2,500 waste sites nationwide may eventually end up on its Superfund list. Although some of the costs will be recovered from responsible parties, the EPA predicts that Superfund will require from $7.6 to $22.7 billion.[46] These figures are probably far too low. The EPA itself acknowledges that there are hundreds of thousands of municipal and industrial landfills, more than 10,000 inactive mining sites,[47] and up to 187,500 leaking underground chemical storage tanks that pose potential threats to the environment.[48] (By law, Superfund cannot be used to clean up the nation's hundreds of thousands of leaking gasoline storage tanks, which constitute the most widespread threat to groundwater quality.) The EPA admitted in a recent report on Superfund that "if even a small fraction of these sites require Superfund response, the funding needed to address them would overwhelm the central estimates currently projected for the Superfund program.[49] A recent report by state waste management officials says that, given the current pace of the program, it will be nearly a century before Superfund can clean up the 7,000 sites that require attention.[50]

The costs will be huge. According to a draft report by the Congressional Office of Technology Assessment, as many as 37,000 sanitary landfills and open dumps may be contaminating groundwater, and the cost of handling them alone could go as high as $229 billion.[51] In 1985, Congress will consider extending Superfund for another five years. The extension will probably not be for more than $10 billion, and it could be considerably less. "The $229 billion figure does not shock me," said Congressman William Carney of New York. "It's a laudable goal. It's also a goal that would bankrupt the nation in five years.[52]

Leaking Liners

Even if the EPA had the resources and desire to enforce total compliance with its hazardous waste regulations, our groundwater would still receive a steady flow of toxic chemicals. "No amount of regulation or enforcement can eliminate the problem of toxic waste leaking out of landfills and polluting groundwater because there is no known or proven technology for doing so," observes outspoken EPA waste policy analyst William Sanjour.[53]

To protect against contamination from hazardous waste disposal, the EPA requires facility operators to put in liners that prevent the waste from leaking into the underlying water table. It also requires installation of groundwater monitoring systems to detect failure of the liners. But both systems are far from foolproof.

Most of the liners at hazardous waste sites leak eventually. A typical "impermeable" clay liner leaks at a rate of "90 gallons per acre of landfill per day," according to Texas A&M soil scientist Kirk Brown, who has studied the problem extensively. "Ninety gallons is 32,000 gallons per acre per year and it is possible that many of our landfills would meet present day standards with clay liners, but would, in fact, be leaking at such rates." Worse still, organic chemicals usually found in hazardous waste sites "alter the physical structure of the clay liner so that the permeability would be 10, 100 or 1,000 times greater than when measured with water . . . so now 90 gallons a day looks like 900 or 9,000 gallons."[54]

The EPA's solution has been to turn to synthetic plastic liners. But these leak, too. Hazardous waste engineer Peter Montague looked at four "secure" chemical landfills equipped with these synthetic liners and found they all leaked within one year. At Texas A&M, Brown's research showed that 11 of 12 plastic liners tested under field conditions leaked within six months.[55] Many factors can cause the failure of these liners. They may be ripped or punctured during installation or maintenance. Exposure to sunlight can cause deterioration. Chemical solvents dissolve the plastic. Burrowing animals can rip holes in the liner.

In other words, most of the liners in use today provide protection for a few years from wastes that can remain toxic for centuries. The EPA has simply "shifted from one unproven technology to another in an attempt to prevent landfills from leaking into groundwater," Brown observes.[56] The EPA itself admits a leakproof landfill does not exist. "They leak," former

EPA Administrator Ruckelshaus says flatly.[57] Sanjour, who often clashes with his superiors at EPA, takes a dimmer and more cynical view of liners. "Liners really don't prevent leakage. They slow it down," he says. "When you slow it down you are not really doing the community that lives there any great favor. . . . It is better for them to leak sooner than later, because then there will be responsible parties that they can get to clean it up. Liners don't protect the community. They protect the people who put the waste there and the politicians who let them put the waste there, because they are long since gone when the problem comes up."[58]

As further protection, the agency requires hazardous waste facility operators to monitor for groundwater contamination. These monitoring systems consist of three wells located in the direction that the contamination is expected to flow. Because an operator, under federal standards, need install only three monitoring wells no matter how large the facility or how many people are threatened, some states require additional wells. These monitoring wells are sampled and compared to water from a "background" well that is supposedly unaffected by the facility.

Critics of the existing groundwater monitoring requirements contend there is no guarantee they will detect leakage before groundwater contamination is widespread, at which time it is already too late. "From my experience, very few monitoring systems today on existing disposal sites are adequately monitoring the site," says Kero Cartwright, head of the hydrogeology and geophysics section of the Illinois State Geological Survey. "The most common reason we have [for monitoring] is simply a cosmetic procedure to reassure the public."[59]

After a site is closed, the operator is required to maintain it and clean up any contamination for a period of 30 years. From then on, a "post closure liability fund," financed by a tax on waste disposal, is to asssume these costs. Moreover, an operator can turn over liability for maintenance and cleanup costs to the fund after only 5 years if the facility is closed in accordance with RCRA regulations and there is no evidence of leakage.

The closure fund is supposed to total $200 million, but as of mid–1984 it had collected only $3.8 million.[60] Even the full $200 million would be inadequate to cover all but a fraction of the eventual costs, given that these can run up to tens of millions of dollars per site. The upshot is that cleanup costs will probably come from elsewhere—namely Superfund. Already, more than 50 facilities operating under RCRA interim permits are on the EPA's Superfund cleanup list, and an unknown number of additional sites may be added in the future. The result will be an even greater burden on the already overtaxed $1.6-billion Superfund.

Even at those sites that are cleaned up, the toxic wastes may simply be transferred from one leaking site to another in what has been called the Superfund merry-go-round. The Cecos International facility in Niagara Falls, New York, which has received waste from several sites, including nearby Love Canal, is suspected of leaking. Another leaking site, near West Covina, California, was entrusted with 6.1 million gallons of waste from a Superfund cleanup operation near Riverside. "Waste removal actions have transferred risks to other communities," concluded an OTA report on attempts to clean up the Riverside site.[61]

After Waste Management, Incorporated, trucked hazardous waste from the Superfund site in Seymour, Indiana, to its Vickery, Ohio, waste facility, the state of Ohio closed five of Vickery's six injection wells because they had leaked millions of gallons of waste. Ironically, Waste Management was one of the firms that had dumped waste at the Seymour Superfund site. "Thus, Waste Management, Inc., has been paid to dump the same wastes twice in succession in two different leaking sites," Sanjour wrote in a memo quoted in the *Washington Post*.[62]

A Lesson Not Learned

Even though the inadequacy of land disposal is now well known, the EPA still chooses to favor this method. Caught between an alarmed public and powerful industrial forces that want to continue to dispose of their wastes in the cheapest manner, the EPA favors the latter party. This decision means that safer technologies will remain more expensive for the disposer, so there is little incentive to develop them.

Alternatives are at hand. We could replace toxic substances, such as persistent pesticides and chlorinated solvents, with less-deadly substitutes. Many industrial wastes can be recycled or destroyed in a way that renders them less dangerous. As far back as 1974, the EPA's "philosophy" according to John Lehman, director of the agency's hazardous waste management division, was "to minimize hazardous waste disposal to the land. . . . We strongly support waste recycling or detoxification treatment prior to land disposal wherever possible."[63]

Today, roughly 80 percent of hazardous wastes are still dumped into the ground, where they will threaten water supplies for decades, possibly centuries. In the end, the public pays. As Sanjour points out, "The real cost of dumping is not borne by the producer of the waste or the disposer, but by the people whose health and property values are destroyed when the wastes migrate onto their property and by the taxpayers who pay to clean it up."[64]

This was made clear to a delegation of people who live near toxic waste sites when they visited William Ruckelshaus in 1984. They went to Washington to ask him to support an extension of Superfund that was on the congressional legislative agenda at the time. Ruckelshaus told the victims of toxic exposure he supported the idea of extending Superfund. But he could not support an extension of the cleanup law at that time because more study was necessary. "I looked him in the face and I told Mr. Ruckelshaus that I had had a miscarriage and a child who died two days after birth," said Cathy Hinds, a member of the delegation, to a press conference after the meeting. "It is beyond me how a man can sit and listen to stories like this and still say no [to the Superfund extension]." Hinds and her family had drunk water fouled by benzene, trichlorethylene, and other toxic chemicals from a waste site in East Gray, Maine.[65]

Sadly, the EPA cannot be expected to act on its own. Time and again, the agency has reacted only when it has come under public and congressional pressure. People "realize that the existing technology and regulation will not protect their health or environment," says former Love Canal residents leader Lois Gibbs, who now runs the Citizens Clearinghouse for Hazardous Wastes. "Consequently, toxic waste issues and problems have catalyzed the birth of many citizens groups who are taking action to protect their families, their homes, and their land."[66] Without this citizen pressure, there is little doubt that government inaction would be the rule. Without this action, in the words of the citizens delegation that visited former Administrator Ruckelshaus, "more people will be exposed to toxic hazards, cleanups will cost more, and more tears will be shed."[67]

The Suffering
Behind the Statistics

7

There was something wrong in James McCarthy's neighborhood. His nine-month-old child had died of a rare form of cancer. He himself had had an operation on his kidneys, and several of his neighbors were suffering from serious kidney problems. In addition, McCarthy told a Senate committee chaired by Edward Kennedy of Massachusetts, "In the neighborhood, there are seven to eight known miscarriages, there is another unknown baby death. . . . We have an abnormally large amount of six- to nine-year-old females with vaginal problems, which is, from what I am told, unheard of at this stage and this age."[1]

At the time of the hearings, in 1980, the McCarthys were 1 of about 160 households in Jackson township, New Jersey, whose wells were contaminated by chemicals from a municipal landfill. From 1972 to 1978, more than 200 million gallons of liquid chemical wastes had been dumped into the landfill. It didn't take long for 38 different chemicals to soak into the underlying water table and migrate to nearby wells. Among the chemicals were benzene and chloroform, both capable of causing cancer and kidney damage.

When local health authorities found out about the contamination, they sent a letter to the residents telling them not to drink the water. "So we stopped using it for drinking and cooking," resident Kathleen Benesch explains. "We were using it for bathing and my children and I were breaking out in rashes—but not like the prickly heat type of rash; it was big, open sores all over the body. So I stopped using the water completely for bathing."[2]

Scattered across the country are a number of such neighborhoods, where the residents suffer from much higher than average rates of cancer, birth defects, and other health problems. The causes of these clusters of illness often remain unexplained. But in some communities, residents suspect contaminated drinking water.

Woburn, Massachusetts, straddles metropolitan Boston's high-technology corridor along Route 128. For years, the stench from local tanneries wafted over the town. Now the tanneries, along with the traditional industries that built the town, have been replaced by light manufacturing plants. But for Woburn's 36,000 residents, one legacy of its industrial past remains: chemical waste.

In 1979, the Massachusetts Department of Environmental Quality Engineering investigated reports of illegal dumping in Woburn. It found a number of barrels of solid polyurethane foam in a lot near two city wells, known as G and H wells. The state tested the wells and found several chemicals, including trichlorethylene (TCE), tetrachlorethylene (PCE), trichloroethane (TCA), dichloroethane, chloroform, and benzene. The wells were closed immediately. Soon after that, ground breaking for a nearby industrial park revealed a 300-acre dump that contained a 130-year accumulation of waste from the manufacture of paper, pesticides, leather, TNT, and glue.

Both sites are now on the EPA's Superfund list, but many residents think the damage has already been done. The city had the dubious distinction of possessing the highest cancer rate of any Massachusetts city of its size during the 1970s. A local citizens' organization called For a Cleaner Environment (FACE) documented at least ten cases of leukemia among Woburn's children over the previous 15 years. Six cases occurred in a six-block area of East Woburn served by G and H wells. Studies by the Massachusetts Department of Public Health subsequently found that the town's rate of childhood leukemia was more than twice the national average, but the department declined to attribute the problem to the contaminated drinking water. Meanwhile, researchers at Harvard University's School of Public Health became interested in Woburn's problems. Their study, based on data gathered from more than 3,200 Woburn households, also found that the 16 cases of childhood leukemia diagnosed in Woburn from 1969 to 1983 were more than twice the national average. But the Harvard study went on to conclude that "exposure to wells G and H is associated with an increase in the incidence of childhood leukemia," accounting for at least 1 and perhaps as many as 5 of the leukemia cases.[3]

The study also found "a consistent pattern of positive associations" between the contaminated water and increased risks of infant deaths; ear and eye birth defects; and urinary, respiratory, neurologic, and skin problems among Woburn's children.[4] The death rate of infants born to mothers who "received at least two-thirds of their water from wells G and H" was ten times higher than would be expected normally.[5] The findings of the Harvard researchers were greeted with a sense of relief among Woburn residents. They felt they were proof that their drinking water was making them sick. But the Harvard study also added fuel to an already raging debate over how harmful the chemical contaminants in our drinking water really are.

More Questions than Answers

About one of every four Americans develops cancer. Some 20 percent of American couples who wish to have children cannot conceive, and a large percentage of pregnancies end in spontaneous abortion or miscarriage.[6] Out of every 100 babies born in the United States, 2 to 3 have serious birth defects.[7] Sometimes, as in Woburn, these problems show up in unusually high numbers in certain communities or neighborhoods. These concentrations of disease are known as clusters. Contaminated drinking water may be one culprit.

• In Tennessee, people drinking water laced with high levels of solvents and pesticide wastes suffered from a wide range of complaints including headaches, nausea, and respi-

(continued on page 136)

Health Effects of Common Drinking Water Contaminants

Although it is extremely difficult to predict the harm of long-term exposures to low levels of toxic chemicals in drinking water, here are some effects that have been observed on humans and animals. Some individuals are more susceptible than others. Children, for example, are often more vulnerable because of their lower body weight, immature and growing body organs, more highly permeable skin, and faster respiratory rate. Genetic factors, general health, and life-style (including smoking and diet) can also affect susceptibility to chemicals.

Inorganic Substances

• *Mercury:* Nervous system and kidney damage. Mercury enters the food chain: fish and other aquatic animals concentrate mercury in their tissues, and humans eating these animals will receive a greater dose.

• *Lead:* Headaches, anemia, nerve problems, mental retardation and learning disabilities in children, birth defects, and possible cancer. The EPA is considering lowering the current 50-ppb limit for lead in drinking water to 25 ppb.

• *Cadmium:* Kidney damage, anemia, pulmonary problems, high blood pressure, possible fetal damage, and cancer.

• *Arsenic:* Liver, kidney, blood system, and nervous system damage and cancer.

• *Chromium:* Suspected cancer from some forms.

• *Asbestos:* Cancer. There is still some controversy over whether asbestos in drinking water causes cancer, but the EPA estimates that drinking water containing 300,000 fibers per liter can result in 1 additional cancer in 100,000 people.

• *Nitrates:* Interference with oxygen metabolism, possibly cancer.

Common Organic Contaminants

• *Trichlorethylene* (TCE): In high concentrations, liver and kidney damage, central nervous system (CNS) depression, skin problems, depression of the contractibility of the heart, and suspected cancer and mutations.

• *Tetrachlorethylene* (PCE): Liver and kidney damage, CNS depression, and suspected cancer.

• *1,1,1 Trichloroethane* (TCA): Liver damage, cardiovascular changes, CNS depression, and possibly cancer and mutations.

• *Carbon tetrachloride:* Liver, kidney, lung, and CNS damage and cancer.

• *1,2 Dichloroethane:* In high concentrations, CNS depression, liver and kidney damage, gastrointestinal problems, pulmonary effects, circulatory disturbances, and suspected cancer and mutations.

• *Vinyl chloride:* Lung, liver, and kidney damage; pulmonary and cardiovascular effects; gastrointestinal problems; cancer; and suspected mutations.

• *Benzene:* Chromosomal damage in both humans and laboratory animals. Benzene affects blood and immune systems to cause anemia, blood disorders, and leukemia.

• *1,1 Dichlorethylene:* At high levels, liver, and kidney damage, CNS depression, suspected cancer, and possible mutations.

• *Dichlorobenzene:* Liver, kidney, and pulmonary damage. There has been no evidence of mutagenicity or carcinogenicity.

• *Polychlorinated biphenyls* (PCBs): Liver damage, skin disorders, gastrointestinal problem, and suspected cancer and mutations.

(continued)

Health Effects of Common Drinking Water Contaminants—Continued

Common Organic Contaminants—continued

• *Chloroform:* Liver and kidney damage, CNS depression, and suspected cancer.

• *Dibromochloropropane* (DBCP): Male sterility and cancer.

• *Ethylene dibromide* (EDB): Male sterility and cancer. EDB is more potent than DBCP.

• *Dioxin:* Skin disorders, cancer, and mutations. Dioxin is extremely toxic.

• *Aldicarb* (Temik): High toxicity to the nervous system. There has been no evidence of mutagenicity, teratogenicity, or carcinogenicity.

Biological Pathogens

• *Viruses and bacteria:* A wide range of ailments ranging from diarrhea, cramps, and nausea to more serious illnesses such as hepatitis and meningitis. Biological organisms are by far the most common cause of *acute* waterborne illness in this country. From 1971 to 1981, more than 82,000 cases of waterborne illness were reported to the federal Centers for Disease Control, a figure that probably greatly understates the actual number of people affected.

Radiation

• *Ionizing radiation:* Even at low levels, alteration of cell structure, which may lead to birth defects, cancer, genetic damage, and sterility.

ratory problems. Exposed individuals also had a high rate of hospitalization and suffered an excessive rate of long-term health damage, including liver enlargement, eye trouble, and neurological changes. A study coauthored by Robert Harris of Princeton University concluded, "The evidence at least strongly suggests that contaminated groundwater . . . was responsible for both reversible and irreversible health damage" and that residents in the vicinity "are at high risk of liver dysfunction and cancer."[8]

• In January 1985, the California State Department of Health Services released a study that found that pregnant women living in neighborhoods south of San Jose, where the drinking water was contaminated, had twice as many miscarriages over a two-year period as women in a similar area with uncontaminated water. The health department also found a high rate of birth defects among children born to women drinking the contaminated water but stopped short of linking the problems to the contamination.[9]

• In 130 counties with heavy concentrations of chemical and petroleum industries, cancer deaths have increased dramatically since the end of World War II, according to the Council on Economic Priorities, a public policy research organization. The increase has particularly affected rural counties, which experienced a 265 percent jump in the cancer death rate from 1950 to 1975. "Cancer mortality trends can be traced, in part, to the chemical, petroleum, and other manufacturing industries generating, treating, and disposing of vast bulks of industrial toxic wastes," the New York–based council suggests.[10]

• In southern Louisiana, a major oil-refining and petrochemical region with extensive water contamination, white males in ten counties have been afflicted with cancer death rates that rank among the top 5 percent in the nation.[11]

It is extremely difficult scientifically to establish a cause-and-effect relationship between chronic health problems and exposure to specific environmental toxins. The easiest problems to detect are acute reactions which occur shortly after exposure to high levels of contaminants. For example, people often develop rashes or headaches soon after bathing or showering in heavily contaminated water. Several years ago, in a rural area of southern

Wisconsin, a train derailment caused a spill of phenol, which contaminated several nearby wells. At least 17 people who drank the highly contaminated water became ill shortly afterward with diarrhea, mouth sores, dark urine, and burning sensations. Six months after the people stopped drinking the water, there were no symptoms of phenol poisoning.[12]

But contaminants usually appear in drinking water at much lower levels, so the greater risk is chronic health problems: cancer; birth defects and reproductive disorders; liver or kidney disease; and damage to the nervous and immune systems. These permanent effects often develop slowly and subtly and may not become obvious for years, or even decades. Often, the victim is no longer exposed to the chemicals that caused the harm. This long latency period means that these diseases are traced to their causes only with great difficulty.

In a recent survey of 881 hazardous waste sites, for example, the EPA identified 444 different chemicals. According to the EPA, "Virtually all of the most commonly encountered of these are known to exhibit chronic toxicity and therefore may cause human health injuries after months or years at extremely low levels of exposure."[13] Among the most commonly detected chemicals were TCE, polychlorinated biphenyls (PCBs), and chloroform, all suspected of causing cancer. Courtney Riordan, EPA assistant administrator for research and development, explained how difficult it is to apply risk assessments to contamination from these waste sites. "Each contains a myriad of hazardous substances that must be identified and quantitated. Not only is our information on health effects limited for many of these substances, but our testing procedures cannot account for multiple risks [and] synergistic [additive] or antagonistic reactions among chemicals."[14]

Our best tools for determining a link between environmental contamination and illness are epidemiological studies, which compare the incidence of disease among people exposed to the toxic substance with the rate among an unexposed (control) group. But medical epidemiology at its best can only suggest—not prove—that chemicals are affecting people's health. Even establishing a *possible* link often proves an awesome task. Epidemiological studies can only detect relatively large excesses in the

incidence of diseases and thus may not even be able to detect an
increased incidence of health problems among people exposed to
toxic substances. "Epidemiological studies are very blunt instruments with which to dissect delicate tragedies," points out Dr.
David Ozonoff of Boston University's department of environmental health.[15] This is particularly true in cases where a relatively
small number of people is exposed. "For example, a neonatal
death—death in the first seven days of birth—happens in 1 out of
200 births," explains Dr. Marvin Zelen, a Harvard public health
professor and a coauthor of the Woburn health study. "If one is
going to interview 50 mothers, unless the rate has changed by a
very large factor, one is not going to see anything."[16] Even if
several hundred people are exposed to an environmental toxin, the
numbers may be too few to confirm that the community is
suffering health problems as a result.

Another difficulty is that a study that doesn't take into
account these long latency periods of diseases may falsely conclude that chemicals have caused no adverse effects. Ozonoff
recently coauthored a study that reported a high rate of respiratory complaints such as coughing, persistent colds, and shortness of
breath but found "no marked increase" in diseases like cancer or
reproductive hazards among people living near a toxic waste site
in Lowell, Massachusetts.[17] Ozonoff compared this finding to "the
man who jumps off the top of the Empire State Building and is
going past the fourteenth floor and says 'so far, so good'—so far, so
good in this particular neighborhood. But we haven't allowed
sufficient time for people to reach the ground yet. And I don't
known what will happen when that occurs. Or whether we'd ever
be able to detect it."[18]

There are other complications. These health studies must
consider age, sex, and life-style and also the length and degree of
exposure.

These variables may make epidemiological studies frustrat-
ingly inconclusive and open to interpretation. Two studies of the
same group of people can reach widely differing conclusions.
While the researchers from the Harvard School of Public Health
linked Woburn's high rate of childhood leukemia to contaminated
drinking water, an earlier study by the Massachusetts Department

of Public Health (MDPH) cautioned that any connection between the leukemia rate and contaminated drinking water supplies was "neither supported nor refuted by study."[19] A second MDPH study the following year reached a similar conclusion: "At the present time there is no evidence to support an environmental toxin in the etiology [origin] of the cases of leukemia in Woburn."[20]

At Love Canal, too, researchers reached contradictory conclusions about the dump's effect on the residents' health. The controversy left a residue of bitterness not only among residents who suspect their health may have been permanently damaged, but among the scientists themselves. Scientists who reported excessive rates of illness and health problems at Love Canal received severe criticism from many of their professional colleagues.

Predictably, industry makes the most of this ambiguity. Says Dr. Robert Neal, president of the Chemical Industry Institute of Toxicology, "Except for acute toxic effects resulting from the contamination of individual wells or, perhaps, small water systems, there is currently no unequivocal evidence that human disease is occurring in the United States as a result of organic chemical contamination of finished drinking water."[21] Many scientists dismiss that argument, however. "There seems to be a widely-believed myth (often asserted 'in the name of science') that when a hazardous chemical is diluted with enough water the health hazards simply disappear," points out Dr. Irwin Bross, director of biostatistics at the Roswell Park Memorial Institute in Buffalo, New York. "It is true that the acute (short-term) effects of some chemicals do disappear in this way. However, the chronic (long-term) effects that are the crux of the public health problems are not diluted out of existence and may be made worse by the wider dissemination involved in dilution."[22]

The absence of conclusive proof linking chemical exposures with disease does not mean that a problem does not exist. As Ozonoff puts it, "We are like people who go into a huge, dark warehouse full of dangerous objects, that is completely dark except for a tiny little miner's light on top of our head. And we look around and say, 'We don't see anything', and walk out again."[23] Thus, even though millions of Americans have drunk water containing harmful chemicals, we may never know the true toll contaminated water has taken on the nation's health. Even if we could make such estimates, it would not tell us what it's like to see a child die of leukemia in Woburn or suffer crippling birth defects in Santa Clara, California. "There are limits to what science can tell us," said former EPA Administrator Douglas Costle. "The more serious limitation is an inability to see the suffering that lies behind the dry projections of injury."[24]

Setting Standards

What little information we possess comes primarily from studies of laboratory animals or groups of people—usually workers—exposed to relatively high levels of chemicals. These studies indicate only that exposure to a chemical carries a *risk* of developing cancer or some other chronic health problem. It is not *certain* that exposure will result in health problems. But many scientists agree that for chemicals that may cause cancer or other chronic diseases, there is no level of exposure so small that there is no danger of developing the disease. The lower the concentration, the lower the risk. This risk is usually expressed as the number of people who will develop the disease at a particular level of exposure over a particular period of time. To arrive at these so-called risk assessments, scientists gather available data from known human exposures and animal tests and apply them to complicated mathematical formulas. The EPA, for example, estimates that if 100,000 people drink water containing 18 parts per billion (ppb) of TCE over their lifetimes, at least 1 person will develop cancer because of the exposure. If the water contains only 1.8 ppb of TCE, only 1 person in a million will get cancer.[25]

Different chemicals have different toxicities. At the same exposure levels, one chemical may produce many more tumors than another. It takes about 100 times more TCE than vinyl chloride in drinking water to produce a similar number of cancers.[26]

The EPA uses these risk assessments to develop national drinking water standards—or maximum contaminant levels (MCLs). Promulgating these standards is a complicated and slow process, however. It can take several years from the time the EPA proposes an MCL to the time the standard goes into effect, and legal challenges along the way may add years more.

This explains in part why the EPA has set only 28 drinking water standards since passage of the Safe Drinking Water Act in 1974. Many of the existing MCLs were simply adopted from old Public Health Service (PHS) maximum allowable concentrations that had been around since the early 1960s. Aside from the PHS guidelines, the EPA has set enforceable MCLs for only certain types of radioactivity, six pesticides, and trihalomethanes.

The EPA has proposed setting standards for nine synthetic volatile organic chemicals because of their toxicity and because they commonly show up in groundwater. They are TCE, vinyl chloride, benzene, TCA, PCE, carbon tetrachloride, 1,1 dichloroethane, 1,2 dichlorethylene, and dichlorobenzene. All but the last chemical are suspected carcinogens. These drinking water standards probably won't go into effect before 1987.

The EPA's maximum contaminant levels are not based solely on predicted health effects. If that were the case, the MCLs for many chemicals, particularly carcinogens, would be zero. The agency also takes into account the available technology for removing contaminants and the costs to water suppliers, industry, and the government. For substances that are not thought to be cancer causing, the EPA sets MCLs at levels supposedly far enough below the lowest concentration known to damage health to provide a margin of safety. This is designed to protect individuals particularly sensitive to chemical exposure—children, the elderly, and the ill.

Although the EPA has set the enforceable national drinking water standards for very few contaminants, it has developed so-called suggested no adverse response levels (SNARLs) for several chemicals that don't have MCLs. SNARLs are not enforceable, but they can give people an idea of what safe levels might be. In the absence of federal action on setting drinking water

National Interim Primary Drinking Water Standards

Constituent	Maximum Contaminant Level (in mg/l° or ppm unless specified)
Inorganic chemicals	0.05
Arsenic	0.05
Barium	1
Cadmium	0.010
Chromium	0.05
Lead	0.05
Mercury	0.002
Nitrate (as N)	10
Selenium	0.01
Silver	0.05
Fluoride	1.4–2.4
Organic chemicals turbidity	1–5 tu°°
Coliform bacteria	1/100 ml (mean)
Endrin	0.0002
Lindane	0.004
Methoxychlor	0.1
Toxaphene	0.005
2,4-D	0.1
2,4,5-TP (Silvex)	0.01
Radionuclides	
Radium 226 & 228 (combined)	5 pCi/l°°°
Gross alpha particle activity	15 pCi/l°°°
Gross beta particle activity	4 mrem/year°°°°
Total trihalomethanes	0.1

°mg/l = milligrams/liter   °°°pCi/l = picocuries/liter
°°tu = turbidity unit   °°°°mrem = millirem

standards, many states have established their own standards for many chemicals not covered by EPA regulations. New York, for example, has set drinking water standards for more than 70 substances.

EPA and state drinking water standards or guidelines shouldn't be accepted as the final word on safety. "Assessments of drinking water safety rely on the assumption that ingestion represents the principal route of exposure," point out researchers from the Massachusetts Department of Environmental Quality Engineering (DEQE) in a recent study. "Such an assumption disregards other routes of exposure such as skin absorption during bathing or swimming, and inhalation of vapors while showering."[27] In one home in Fort Edward, New York, state health officials measured air concentrations of up to 7,000 ppb of TCE, which vaporized after the shower was turned on.

Many chemicals can be absorbed through the skin, and cuts, sunburn, and skin disease can increase absorption. The DEQE study found that skin absorption may account for an average of 64 percent of the total exposure from chemicals in drinking water. "When doses from skin absorption are considered, margins of safety may be significantly narrowed, and currently established guidelines compromised," the DEQE scientists concluded.[28]

Predicting risks becomes even more complex in actual situations. Chemicals may react with each other to increase their toxicities. This is known as a synergistic effect. When the pesticides DDT and dieldrin are mixed together, for example, they greatly increase each other's ability to cause cancer.[29] Acids increase the solubility of heavy metals in water and thereby increase the levels of metals that leach from the pipes and the ground.[30] At the notorious Stringfellow site in southern California, a toxic cocktail of acids and heavy metals such as cadmium and chromium is threatening an underground aquifer that provides drinking water to 500,000 people.

The environment itself may alter toxic substances. Researchers at the drinking water research center at Florida International University found that soil microorganisms in southern Florida transformed TCE and PCE into vinyl chloride and dichloroethane, both more carcinogenic than their parent chemicals. Microorganisms also can convert heavy metals such as mercury into more highly toxic forms.[31]

Warns Dr. Bross of Rosewell Park Memorial Institute, "Compliance with standards based on concentrations of chemicals in drinking water may be better than non-compliance, but compliance does not guarantee that the health and safety of the public has been protected. Water meeting these standards may cause serious health problems."[32]

The Fight over Victims' Compensation

"The guiding principle of the authors of the Superfund was law: those responsible for harm caused by chemical contamination should pay the costs of that harm. That principle was abandoned in 1980 with respect to personal injury." So stated Senator George Mitchell of Maine in testimony before his congressional colleagues.

People who have been harmed by toxic substances cannot expect fair compensation. "Neither logic nor compassion, good government nor common sense compel this result," said Mitchell. "It is simply a failure of will on the part of Congress to deal with what is the most serious part of the problem—injuries to people."[33]

Currently, the only legal recourse for people injured by environmental toxins is to bring a lawsuit against the responsible parties. (These lawsuits are known as toxic torts.) Those injured have a right to a fair hearing in court, but the deck is often stacked against them. As explained by Jeffrey Trauberman, a Washington, D.C., attorney and victims' compensation expert, "A victim will rationally initiate legal action only if he or she calculates that the damage award will probably exceed the time, effort, and actual expenses of bringing suit."[34] And a victim faces many potential stumbling blocks. For one, states may have a statute of limitations which requires a victim to bring suit as soon as a couple of years after exposure, and yet health problems may not become

Bringing a Lawsuit

A lawsuit is not a frivolous undertaking. It requires time, money, and persistence. Additionally, as the Environmental Defense Fund points out, "You may also expose yourself and your family to hostile inquiry by lawyers for the other side regarding your drinking habits."[1]

Citizens can bring two basic types of environmental lawsuits. One aims simply to force a polluter to clean up a site or to comply with environmental laws. The other, which is usually a much more involved undertaking, seeks to collect damages for injuries to health or for economic loss.

For the latter, you need to find a lawyer willing to stick with you for the long haul. The field of environmental law is complex, often uncharted, and therefore risky, so there is little point in spending time and money on inexperienced legal help. Because preparing an environmental lawsuit is extremely expensive, an attorney may be willing to accept a case without taking any money from the client until the suit is settled. If the suit is successful, the attorney will usually take about one-third of the award, plus expenses.

Toxic exposure lawsuits can rest on a number of legal grounds. The most common are trespass, nuisance, and negligence. Trespass, as the name implies, occurs when the contaminants actually enter your property and interfere with your right of possession. Nuisance is somewhat similar to trespass. Chemical contamination can cause a nuisance when it interferes with the right to enjoy property. A public nuisance interferes with the public's use and enjoyment of a community resource, such as a lake or park. A private nuisance affects private property. Negligence occurs when someone does not take the necessary precautions to prevent contamination—for example, does not install the right equipment to contain chemicals at a hazardous waste site. If your health is injured, you may be able to sue for medical damages. If you can prove extreme negligence, you may be able to receive a larger award, known as punitive damages. Punitive damages are designed to punish defendants who act in reckless disregard of health and safety. As Anthony Roisman puts it, "Punitive damages are called smart money. Why? Because it makes defendants a little smarter. It raises the standard."[2]

visible until after this time limit has run out. In 1983, the New York State Supreme Court ruled that the statute of limitations had expired and dismissed 54 cases brought against Hooker Chemical by Love Canal residents. Most trying of all, plaintiffs face the challenge of proving that exposure to a particular toxin actually caused or contributed to an injury.

Toxic exposure cases are extremely complex and expensive to put together. According to Anthony Roisman, an attorney who represents toxic exposure victims, it costs a minimum of $100,000 to $200,000 simply "for gathering the scientific and medical information required to prove a claim."[35] Because of the magnitude of these costs, lawyers typically forgo an hourly rate and take perhaps one-third of the eventual settlement. Many attorneys are simply unwilling to undertake such cases, because of both the risk and expense involved and the well-paid, high-powered corporate legal staffs they may face.

Once plaintiffs sue, the lawsuit usually takes years to wind its way through the legal maze and reach a verdict. "Those who discharge wastes know this," George Mitchell pointed out. "The consequence is legal guerilla warfare in which the objective is to force the other party to settle early." He might have added "and settle for much less money." That strategy has proven successful. "The vast majority of cases, maybe 95 or 99 percent, are settled out of court," says Jeffrey Trauberman. A recent survey of 50 toxic exposure lawsuits found that only 1 resulted in a final judgment; the rest were either settled out of court or are still making their way through the legal system.[36] In 1983, the 1,300 former residents of Love Canal settled more than $15 billion in claims against Hooker Chemical for $20 million. In other toxic exposure case involving contamination from a lead smelter, 206 plaintiffs received an average settlement of little more than $2,800 each.[37]

Settlements such as these may not even cover the medical costs. For James McCarthy of Jackson township, bills for medical care for him and his sick child posed an extreme financial burden. "I am on Social Security disability. When my daughter died, I had basic Blue Cross coverage. The doctor bill for 31 days in the hospital was $31,000. Blue Cross/Blue Shield paid $23,000, and we were responsible for the balance. Luckily, we had some very good doctors who cut their fees, but even as such, we were straddled with a very severe financial problem that took us five years to pay off."[38]

Recognizing the need for a way of fairly redressing the victims of toxic exposure, Congress considered including a victims' compensation provision in the original Superfund legislation. But "enormous pressures from the chemical, hazardous waste, and insurance industries persuaded Congress in 1980 to duck the victims compensation issue in order to enact at least the clean-up provisions of Superfund," said Anthony Roisman, who was chief of the Department of Justice's hazardous waste section at the time.[39] Instead, Congress settled for a study of the issues. In 1982, a panel of 12 legal experts concluded that toxic exposure victims face major obstacles to receiving compensation and endorsed a federal victims' compensation system.

The panel's report spawned several legislative schemes. All would establish a federal compensation system, somewhat akin to current workmen's compensation schemes. The system would supposedly ease some of the more onerous burdens of proving that a disease was caused by a particular exposure. People injured by toxic substances would be able to recover medical expenses and limited loss of income from a special fund financed by a tax on industry. To be eligible for compensation, a person would have to show proof of exposure, proof of disease or injury, and proof that exposure to the chemical in question is capable of producing that disease. People would not be allowed to collect huge punitive damages from this fund, so most of the proposals also permit plaintiffs to sue responsible parties.

Predictably, the chemical industry and the insurance companies which cover them against large legal awards are not happy with the proposed system, calling victims' compensation a solution in search of a problem. "There has not yet been demonstrated that there is a problem that needs to be solved," contends Dr. Bruce Karrh, director of medical safety for Dupont, the nation's largest chemical company. "We have not seen evidence of a significant health problem from hazardous wastes."[40]

The Chemical Manufacturers Association's Dr. Geraldine Cox explains, "It is deceptively easy to look at all the chemicals produced in recent times and to wrongly conclude that there is a major and increasing problem with chemical contamination. This easy, but erroneous, conclusion is reinforced by the horror stories of isolated incidents that then become blown out of proportion by the nation's communications media."[41]

Industry representatives often cite a 1981 study by two of the world's leading epidemiologists, Dr. Richard Doll and Dr. Richard Peto, who estimate that perhaps only 2 to 5 percent of cancer deaths in this country are caused by exposure to toxic substances in our air, water, and food. The rest, they say, is attributable to smoking, diet, viruses, occupation, and life-style. The Reagan administration apparently agrees. In a 1983 memo on victims' compensation, James Tozzi, then of the Office of Management and Budget, remarked, "We can estimate that seven percent of cancer deaths are related to exposure to pollution. Causation is difficult to prove and other factors, such as cigarette smoking and dietary habits, have a much greater effect on cancer mortality. . . . The federal government could make the most efficient use of the nation's resources by focusing new programs on the use of tobacco and encouraging improved dietary habits."[42]

In line with this reasoning, the Reagan administration has been reluctant to fund studies on the effects of exposure to toxic chemicals in the environment. In 1980, Congress mandated the establishment of a federal agency to study the health of people exposed to hazardous wastes; industry, environmentalists, and the scientific community generally went along. But for more than two years, the government failed to establish the new agency. Eventually, the unlikely combination of the Environmental Defense Fund and the Chemical Manufacturers Association filed a lawsuit to force the government to conduct the health studies. Finally, in April 1983, the Department of Health and Human Services established the Agency for Toxic Substances and Disease Registry.

But the battle was not over. Once the agency was set up, the government failed to implement the studies. "The most important activities are only in the preliminary stages, and some of them will be terminated for lack of funds," said Ellen Silbergeld of the Environmental Defense Fund before a congressional committee.

More delays will occur if the Office of Management and Budget has its way. For 1985, it cut the Department of Health and Human Services' funding request for the agency by more than 50 percent. "We know little more than we did in 1979," Silbergeld commented.[43]

A Tidal Wave of Claims?

American Insurance Association representative Sheila Birnbaum raised the possibility of a tidal wave of unwarranted claims if Congress were to pass victims' compensation legislation. "The defendant would be required to pay not only for any cases of cancer caused by the release of the particular carcinogen, but also for all other cases of cancer that may arise from any other cause," Birnbaum claimed. "Thus, 95 percent or more of the damage payments that would be required to be made to those who have cancer and reside near a dumpsite . . . would be for cases *not* caused by any chemical released by the defendant."[44]

The *Washington Post* also warned against opening the floodgates of compensation, asking, "How far . . . is the society prepared to go in requiring compensation for people exposed in the past to toxic substances—especially when the effect of that exposure is far from clear?" The *Post*, echoing the insurance industry's argument, noted that if a chemical dump raised the risk of cancer by 3 percent in a community, "for every 103 people in the community who got the disease, 100 would have gotten it anyway."[45]

Roisman acknowledges, "There will be some people who will recover under the victims compensation scheme here, who aren't entitled." But the former Department of Justice attorney points out that, even accepting Doll and Peto's conclusions, which many researchers don't, there would still be many people injured by toxic exposure. "If all you had were 5 percent . . . dying of cancer in this country who were not being adequately compensated, then the number of people is still quite large . . . not to mention the fact that the toxic chemicals we are dealing with also cause neurological damage, birth defects, genetic problems, mutations, low birth weight, and half a dozen other horrors that have nothing to do with cancer at all."[46]

If the awards given for occupationally caused disease under the workers' compensation system are any indication, there will be little problem with unwarranted claims winning compensation. From 1977 to 1981, there were only six compensation awards for occupationally caused cancer in Colorado. In New York, a much larger industrial state, only three claims for occupationally caused cancer received compensation in 1978.[47] "It is a sad commentary about our view of the morality of the American people that we would deny compensation to admittedly valid claims because we do not want to stimulate other, fraudulent claims," said Senator Mitchell.[48]

Ultimately, victims' compensation is a social, not a medical, dilemma. As Roisman remarked, "The pain and suffering of a man dying of cancer or watching a child die of leukemia is not speculative or hypothetical. It is difficult to predict, and insurance companies and their lawyers have the cheek to suggest that because they can't predict what the cost will be and therefore can't write a policy with exactly the right premium in it to guarantee their rate of return, that you shouldn't allow the system to work that way."[49]

Jeffrey Trauberman suggests that one way to get around the problem of medical uncertainty is to compensate all victims of exposure to the toxic substance in question, but the total award would be based on the number of cases in excess of what would normally be expected. In other words, each victim would receive a share of the total award without having to prove the illness resulted from a toxic chemical exposure. So, in the *Washington Post*'s hypothetical community with a toxic waste site, all 103 cancer victims would receive compensation, but the amount would be based on the fact that there were only 3 cancer cases above the 100 that would normally be expected. Another option would be to award on the basis not of actual injury, but of risk. Under this system, people exposed to toxic substances would be compensated simply because they were theoretically at a higher risk of contracting certain illnesses.

These explanations are obviously simplified. All of the options are fraught with complications that guarantee controversy. "Victims Compensation is an idea whose time has not yet come, though it should have by now," Trauberman says. "It will take some incident to push it through Congress."

In the absence of congressional action, people increasingly have been turning to the courts for redress and compensation for toxic exposures. Billion-dollar lawsuits have been filed over pesticide contamination of groundwater in California and Hawaii. Victims of chemical waste exposure have sued at dozens of sites across the country. And there are signs that courts and juries have become more responsive to the victims' claims. In November 1983, 350 residents of Jackson township, New Jersey, won $15.6 million in damages from the town, which, the jury decided, had negligently operated its landfill, allowing chemicals to contaminate the plaintiffs' wells. The case was hailed as precedent setting because it was one of the first times victims of water contamination won damages in court, not only for the illnesses they already had, but for the increased risk that they would come down with problems at some future date.

The Jackson township verdict may signal a shift that will make it easier for toxic exposure victims to receive compensation from the legal system. But as Jackson township resident Peter Leighton told the *Philadelphia Inquirer*, "My family got $135,000 for the three of us. That's all right as long as I don't get cancer. If I get cancer, what the hell good is it?"[50]

What Can You Do in the Home?

8

Fortunately, you need not wait for America to mend its ways to get a good, clean glass of water. In response to public concern over tainted drinking water, many companies now market a bewildering variety of home-scale purification devices. To decide which is best for your needs (if indeed you need to treat your water at all), you must know the ingredients of the water.

Your tap is delivering more than just water. Even before synthetic chemicals were spread over the earth, there existed no absolutely pure water. That's because any substance will dissolve to some degree in water if given enough time and presented with the right conditions.

Even the clearest untreated tap water contains minerals, salts, trace metals, and organic matter. This is confirmed when water is tested in a laboratory; and simply by allowing a pan of water to evaporate, you'll find a deposit composed of the solids that were once suspended in the water. Fortunately, certain minerals commonly found in water are beneficial to health. Minerals can make the water a better-tasting beverage, as well. What you cannot see, however, are the volatile chemicals and gasses that evaporate along with the water.

Despite the publicity surrounding chemical poisons in our drinking water, bacterial contamination remains the most common water quality problem in individual or small systems. Nationally, 28 percent of rural households drink water that contains more than the federal limit of one coliform bacterium per 100 milliliters.[1] The presence of coliform, which are found mainly in the intestines of warm-blooded animals, does not necessarily mean that drinking water will cause problems. Rather, because the source of most coliform bacteria is animal waste, their presence may indicate the presence of other, harmful bacteria and viruses which cause gastrointestinal problems such as diarrhea.

Public water systems use a variety of additives to treat the water served to the public. The additives include chlorine to kill bacteria and viruses, fluoride to strengthen teeth (see Fluoridation box in chapter 4), and antiflocculents to remove suspended solids. Metals and asbestos can leach into the water from the miles of pipelines carrying it from the raw source to the treatment plant and to your tap.

Sometimes the color, taste, or odor of your water may indicate problems. If your water smells like rotten eggs, it could be that hydrogen sulfide is indicated. Brown stains on fixtures suggest high levels of iron. Green stains indicate elevated levels of copper. A metallic taste may indicate a variety of problems—deteriorating pipes, leachate from new plumbing, or a chemical contaminant.

Usually, if you can detect a taste or smell or can see stains on fixtures, the water contains a high level of a contaminant. Low levels, on the other hand, are often colorless, tasteless, and odorless. Because you aren't able to readily detect the contaminant, you may continue drinking the water for a long time. Of course, ill health is not the ideal indicator of a problem. If you suspect problems, have your water tested by a certified water laboratory. You can do some preliminary legwork to narrow the list of possible contaminants that must be tested for.

Tracking Down Pollutants

Begin your investigation at the point where the water sample was taken. Consider the material from which the pipes in the household water system are made. A worn pump may add lubricating oil or metal from bearings to the water passing through it. Check to see if a garden hose is connected to a faucet that does not have an antisiphoning device; biological contamination may be caused by a hose used to fill a swimming pool and then allowed to sit in the water.

Next, move on to the area surrounding your home. Wells are susceptible to contamination from runoff and seepage; study the path the water takes in getting to your well. Problems are not always as obvious as a landfill operation or a hazardous waste disposal site.

Start with your immediate property. Where is your septic system in relation to your well? Older systems may cause biological contamination if the well is lower than the septic field. Have you disposed of any materials that could be leaching into your water? What sprays or fertilizers do you use to control weeds or pests? Do you bury or burn your trash nearby? Guided by a contour map of your area, available from a county extension agent, look for point sources such as leaking fuel containers, dump sites, and abandoned mines that may have become informal dumps. Consider, too, the path the water takes as it enters the ground after a heavy rain. Although it is difficult to tell the direction in which groundwater moves, assume that it is traveling slowly downhill.

If you live in a rural area, you may want to learn what sprays or fertilizers are used and how much of each chemical is used per acre. Trace the runoff from fields. If a specific agricultural chemical turns up in lab results, ask your neighbors if any spillage has occurred during the past few seasons. Some pesticides and herbicides are residual and could remain in the ground for many years; even those that were banned years ago may be present in your water. Owners of nearby ponds or streams may be using herbicides or pesticides to control unwanted varieties of fish, aquatic weeds, or weeds growing along the banks of the water.

Your region may have water problems peculiar to it. Radon gas, a naturally occurring radioactive substance, is found in groundwater in the New England area. Groundwater in the Southwest often contains uranium. Other areas, especially coastal areas, have high incidences of sulfur and calcium. Some areas of the country have high concentrations of fluoride. Your area could have naturally occurring high levels of any of a number of minerals. Some areas even are susceptible to natural crude oil pollution.

Seasonal factors affect water quality. Because pesticides and fertilizers are applied seasonally, their levels can fluctuate greatly in the same body of water or aquifer over the course of the year. Rainfall or drought, and the amount of water used by your community, can also affect the concentrations of contaminants in your water. Chemicals migrating from a landfill, for example, often appear in high concentrations after heavy rains. The concentrations of fluoride and chlorine added by municipal systems is governed by the source water temperature.

Testing Your Water

Once you have a rough idea of the contaminants that might be in your water, check to see if you are served by a water system covered by the Safe Drinking Water Act (SDWA). If the system has more than 15 individual, year-round hookups, the water supplier is supposed to sample the water periodically for substances regulated under the SDWA—monthly for bacterial contamination and once each year for selected organic and inorganic substances. The specific number of tests required ranges from 1 per month, for systems serving 25 to 1,000 persons, to 500 per month, for systems serving more than 4.7 million persons. Systems using surface water sources are required to monitor the water daily for turbidity, an indicator of coliform bacteria contamination.

You should be able to obtain the test results—if in fact your water supplier conducts the required testing. A recent survey by the congressional General Accounting Office (GAO) found that 93 of 140 community water systems failed to comply with federal testing requirements. "Noncompliances ranged from missing a single monthly coliform bacteria sample to not testing an entire system for any contaminants during the 12-month period," the GAO found.[2] Still, whatever information you can obtain from a supplier can help to narrow the list of pollutants you must test for. If you suspect your water system is not conducting all the required testing, you may consider contacting the state regulatory agency.

But even if your water supplier is conducting all the required testing, you are still not necessarily guaranteed safe drinking water. The SDWA requires water suppliers to check only those substances for which the EPA has set maximum contaminant levels, or MCLs. These regulated substances include ten metals, six pesticides, and total trihalomethanes (a group of organic chemicals formed when chlorine reacts with humic acid from decaying vegetation particles).

Suppliers are not required to test for the vast majority of organic chemicals that have shown up in drinking water, although the EPA is considering adding more than 30 pesticides and herbicides to its revised primary drinking water regulations list. Recommended and maximum contaminant levels would then be set. The list, if approved, would include many commercially available and registered pesticides, such as aldicarb, chlordane, carbofuran, simazine, atrazine, and dinoseb. If your water system is currently contaminated with organic chemicals that are not on the list, the supplier may not know that they are present.

A few states, particularly those with widespread chemical pollution of their water supplies, have voluntarily established much more stringent testing requirements than the EPA's. New Jersey drinking water quality standards now include 25 organic chemicals not on the SDWA list. Florida requires water suppliers to test for the organic chemicals most likely to turn up in their water.

If you get your water from a private well or a system serving fewer than 15 hookups, you're not protected by the SDWA. There is no requirement for any government agency to check your water quality. You'll have to take the responsibility for testing. Luckily, it is relatively inexpensive to check your water for coliform bacteria. The tests usually cost less than $25, although prices vary widely from county to county and state to state. County health departments may do routine bacteriological tests free of charge. In California, the Fresno County Health Department will check for bacteria if a physician requests it on behalf of a patient. Otherwise, it costs $23.[3] The Ohio Department of Health laboratory will do a bacteria test for $5.[4]

Beyond checking for bacteria, local health departments will rarely conduct routine tests of well water quality unless a specific problem is suspected or a physician recommends it. If you do request testing from a local health department, be sure to explain why you think there may be a problem, and describe any symptoms you and your family have. There is no guarantee you will be successful. Many local health departments don't have the equipment or staff to test for more than a few conventional contaminants.

Your local health department may refer you to a state-run laboratory or to a state-approved private lab. Water quality tests at these labs are often more expensive, and the prices can vary widely, so "it definitely pays for the consumer to shop around," advises William Hurst of the New Jersey Office of Water Quality Assurance. Test samples can be mailed from anywhere in the country to WaterTest Corporation, Box 186, New London, NH 03257 (1-800-426-8378).

If you suspect that your water contains organic chemicals, be prepared to spend a good deal more money—hundreds and even thousands of dollars. Some labs will "screen" the water for a wide variety of contaminants, and will narrow your search without giving very specific results, for a more modest fee.

Usually, this screening involves a TOC test to determine the total amount of organic carbon. A TOC test is of little practical value, however, since *most* substances contain organic carbon and this test does not differentiate between those that are harmful and those that aren't. Also included in many screenings is a TOX test for halogenated organic chemicals, also known as organic halides. These include a family of the most toxic chemicals most commonly found in drinking water. Vinyl chloride, trichlorethylene (TCE), ethylene dibromide (EDB), and dibromochloropropane (DBCP) are all organic halides.

You should be aware that a negative result on a TOX test—one that shows no detectable level of organic halides—does not guarantee that your water is free of chemical pollutants. A number of toxic contaminants are not organic halides. Among the most serious and common of these are gasoline, benzene, toluene, and organophosphate pesticides such as aldicarb. If you do not feel secure about the safety of your water after a TOX test, you may consider a screen test for hydrocarbons or for organophosphate pesticides.

You can compare your test data with the recommended maximum contaminant levels (RMCLs) and the maximum contaminant levels (MCLs) set by the EPA. These figures are available free of charge by writing to the Office of Drinking Water Criteria and Standards, Environmental Protection Agency, 401 M Street, SW, Washington, DC 20460; or call the EPA offices at (202) 382-7575. You will also receive background information on these contaminants. By checking the EPA lists, you can see just how good or how bad your water is. You may wish to retest the water, perhaps with another lab, to double-check the results.

Quality control at laboratories—both government and private—is sometimes poor, and the results you get back may not be accurate. Stephen Lester, a science advisor with the Citizens Clearinghouse for Hazardous Wastes, recommends "splitting a sample" by sending one sample to a state-run laboratory and a second (taken from the same source at the same time) to a private or university lab. If the results show the same levels of contaminants, then you can be sure of what is in the water. If the second round of results confirms high levels, you have a problem that requires immediate attention. Call local authorities, including the water treatment facility if you are supplied with municipal water, and start asking questions. Share the lab results with your neighbors so that they can take action also.

You may want to have your water tested periodically. A single test tells you only what your water contains at any particular moment, but water quality is constantly changing. Contaminants not present in one set of samples may show up in another set taken a few weeks or months later.

If you are buying a house with an individual well, you may want to request the seller to have the water tested at least for the contaminants covered by the SDWA.

People served by larger municipal systems should not have to run as many tests, because municipal water quality usually remains relatively constant, at least for the contaminants covered by the SDWA.

The sad fact is that it is usually up to the public to prove that their water is contaminated and to find the source of the contamination. Don't expect health officials to agree to requests to have your water tested for chemical contaminants. The tests require manpower and facilities often unavailable to smaller communities; also the costs of the tests may not be in the municipal budget. Many health officials are trained to deal with only traditional water quality problems, such as bacteriological contamination. Although the situation is changing as more and more communities are confronted with chemically contaminated water, health officials may feel threatened by citizens' questions about chemical contamination.

When taking water samples, be sure to follow the laboratory's instructions carefully. If you are testing for heavy metals leaching from plumbing, take the samples when you first run the tap in the morning: concentrations will have built up in the water sitting in pipes overnight, and the test will give you a better idea of the maximum doses you are getting. You don't need to do this if you are testing for organic chemicals. Samples are usually drawn into sterilized, airtight containers. Volatile organic chemicals may escape into the air if the vessel is open to the air.

Armed with the information you have gathered, present your case to local water officials, county agents, or even to the responsible party. In the meantime, you will need another source of water, or a way to rid your water of the contamination. The following section provides some answers to this immediate problem.

Bottled Water

If you find your water either is contaminated or has such an unpleasant taste or odor that you don't want to drink it, you have two basic options. You can buy bottled water or use in-home water purification devices. (Sinking a new well is a third option, but there is no guarantee that it will provide you with a clean source of water because of the difficulty in predicting how contaminants move through groundwater.) Either choice will cost money.

Until a few years ago, few Americans used bottled water. But now bottled water is the nation's fastest-growing beverage market. In the five-year period ending in 1983, bottled water sales climbed 93 percent (wine sales came in a distant second with a 28 percent increase).[5] In 1982, Americans shelled out nearly $850 million for more than 700 million gallons of bottled water.[6] The International Bottled Water Association estimates that 1 of every 18 Americans now relies on bottled water as a primary source of drinking water. In southern California, one of three households buys bottled water.[7]

Why would millions of Americans pay a dollar or more a gallon for what they can get from the tap for a fraction of a cent? For many people, the reason is taste and appearance. But more compelling is concern over the effects of chemical contamination on health. After TCE was discovered in drinking water serving 4.5 million metropolitan Los Angeles residents, bulk water companies signed up customers at five times the normal rate. In Duluth, Minnesota, bottled water sales shot up after asbestos was discovered in the city's water. In New Orleans, many people turned to bottled water after scientific reports linked the city's unusually high rates of certain cancers to chemical contamination of the city's drinking water. In many instances of contamination, responsible parties or government agencies are providing bottled water free of charge to affected households.

The International Bottled Water Association sees no slowing of the sales boom in the next few years. They project the bottled water market in this country will reach almost $2 billion annually by 1990, more than twice the 1983 figure.[8]

What are their customers getting for all this money? The nonsparkling waters, which account for the vast majority of the bottled water sold in this country, are of several types:

> • *Still or drinking water* is often ordinary municipal drinking water from which chemicals and minerals have been removed by filtration or distillation. Minerals may be added back to achieve the desired taste.

Quick Fixes

Here are a few short-term measures for reducing the concentrations of pollutants in your water. They are simple, but limited in the protection they provide.

• Let your water run at full force for two or three minutes first thing in the morning. This will clear out relatively high levels of lead, cadmium, and copper that may have built up in the water sitting overnight in the pipes.

• You can eliminate bacteria and some organic chemicals from your water by boiling it at least 20 minutes. Experiments conducted by the EPA have shown that boiling removes only *volatile* organic chemicals—or those that evaporate easily.[1] The chemicals escape into the air, so try not to breathe the air directly over the boiling water. Boiling is time-consuming and energy intensive and may concentrate the nonvolatile organics, heavy metals, and nitrates left behind in the water.

• Whipping your water in an electric blender can remove some volatile chemicals. You should blend the water for about 15 minutes, with the top off.[2]

• *Spring or natural water* is obtained from a well or spring. The term "natural" implies the water has not been processed before bottling, although it may be disinfected, usually with ozone.

• *Fluoridated water* contains fluoride, which may come from a natural source or may have been added by the bottler.

• *Mineral-free or purified water* contains less than 10 parts per million (ppm) of minerals. The minerals are often removed by reverse osmosis, a process that forces the water through a membrane.

• *Mineral water* may be any water that contains minerals, because the federal government has declined to define the term. A product calling itself a mineral water may actually contain fewer minerals than tap water. The state of California requires a product sold as mineral water to contain either more than 500 ppm of total dissolved solids or at least one mineral in excess of federal drinking water standards; if the product is labeled "natural" mineral water, the manufacturer is not supposed to alter the mineral content of the original water.

Sparkling bottled water contains carbon dioxide gas. There are three basic kinds of sparkling water:

• *Seltzer* is generally tap water that has been filtered and carbonated with manufactured carbon dioxide.

• *Club soda* is usually filtered and carbonated public drinking water, but minerals and mineral salts are added for flavoring.

• *Naturally sparkling water* contains enough naturally occurring carbon dioxide to make it bubbly. Because a lot of the gas is lost when the water is taken out of the ground, the carbon dioxide is usually drawn off and reinjected during the bottling process.

Most bottled water is disinfected with ozone, a form of oxygen gas, before bottling. Unlike chlorine, ozone does not leave a residual taste or odor and it forms no chemical by-products. Bottled water from public systems is also generally filtered to remove organic chemicals.

The U.S. Food and Drug Administration (FDA) regulates bottled water as a food product. Under the SDWA, the FDA must adopt standards for bottled water comparable to the EPA's national drinking water criteria. Congress included bottled water in federal standards after EPA and FDA surveys in the early 1970s found "lapses in quality control and sanitation of plants, facilities, employee practices, containers, and closures which rendered some of the products, if not unfit for consumption, certainly below federal standards," according to an FDA publication.[9] Interestingly, the FDA doesn't regulate mineral or sparkling waters as bottled water. Manufacturers of these products are not allowed to add artificial sweeteners, vitamins, minerals, or proteins for nutritional purposes to sparkling water, but they may add any other "safe and suitable optional ingredient," provided each is listed on the label. Bottlers are not allowed to make any health or medicinal claims for bottled water of any type.[10]

But federal regulations do not require bottlers to list the source of their water on the label, and many don't. According to The International Bottled Water Association's Executive Vice-President William Deal, 75 percent of bottled water comes from underground sources.[11] Although the association conducts yearly inspections to ensure good quality, no federal monitoring program for bottled water has taken place for anything other than aesthetic qualities, says Deal.

But is bottled water safe? In 1980, *Consumer Reports* magazine tested more than 40 brands of still and sparkling water for sodium, fluoride, chloride, nitrates, four heavy metals (arsenic, cadmium, lead, and iron), trihalomethanes (THMs), and a few pesticides. For most substances surveyed, no safety problems were found. There were no detectable levels of THMs or pesticides in any of the waters, and the levels of chloride, nitrate, cadmium, lead, and iron were all within federal standards. Nor did the magazine find serious bacterial contamination. The main water quality concerns were arsenic, which appeared in four brands of mineral water at levels close to or a little above the federal standard, and sodium, which is linked to hypertension and a greater risk of heart disease.[12]

But bottled water has not escaped the taint of chemical contamination. Tests conducted in 1982 by the Suffolk County Health Department on Long Island found chloroform, a suspected carcinogen, in several brands of bottled water. The source of the contamination is unknown, but Paul Pontura, a senior public health engineer with the Suffolk County Health Department, says the chloroform may have formed while the chlorinated water sat on the shelves.[13] Suffolk County also found benzene when it tested Poland Spring mineral water. Because other samples of Poland Spring did not contain benzene, Pontura speculates that the contamination may have resulted from the packaging.[14]

There has generally been little testing of bottled water for chemical contamination, and the federal government does not require any. The bottom line, Pontura says, is that "these substitutes to the public water supply are sometimes not as well regulated as the public supply."[15]

Even though bottled drinking water generally appears to be of good quality, you may want to ask the bottler for all available information on its mineral, bacteriological, and chemical content. (If you are concerned about the levels of either sodium or arsenic, ask the bottler to provide you with information specifically about the mineral content of its product.) You may also contact your state health department to find out if it has any data on the purity of a particular brand. To be absolutely certain that the water is of good quality, you will probably have to have it tested at a private laboratory.

With the cost of plain bottled water pushing $1 a gallon, a year's supply may run around $200 for each household member. Given this expense, many people are turning to another option—home water treatment units designed to remove contaminants.

Home Treatment

Like bottled water, the market for home treatment units has taken off in the last decade. The reason is the same: reports of poor water quality across the country. The EPA estimates that Americans bought 2 million residential drinking water treatment units in 1979.[16] The Water Quality Association, the water treatment trade association, predicts sales could increase as much as 20 percent annually in the coming year.[17]

A filter will remove only certain contaminants. Given this, and the fact that filters may require a fair amount of maintenance, consider whether you really need one. Do the impurities in your water make a filter necessary? Some of them may actually be beneficial. Water is often a significant source of iron, which can prevent anemia, a deficiency of iron in the blood. The calcium in hard water may cause the body to absorb less cadmium and lead, both toxic heavy metals. Iron and zinc also counteract the absorption of cadmium. There is evidence that calcium and magnesium may help prevent heart attacks. Numerous studies have shown lower rates of heart disease in areas with hard water compared to areas with water low in calcium and magnesium.[18]

In shopping for a unit, you are faced with a wide range of devices. Some of these are complicated to install and operate, while others are quite simple. Many are quite specialized in their functions and will remove only certain contaminants. These devices fall into five main categories: activated carbon filters, sediment filters, distillers, reverse osmosis systems, and ultraviolet systems. There are many variations and combinations of systems, and prices are apt to range widely.

Domestic devices that remove bacteria and viruses are technically known as purifiers. Any filter system that does not perform this function cannot legally be called a purifier. Water purifiers commonly employ a chemical "feeder" that injects small amounts of chlorine either into the well or into the water. Iodine is also an efficient disinfectant, but it is not considered safe for long-term use or by pregnant women (it can adversely affect fetuses). Ultraviolet (UV) radiation also effectively kills bacteria. In UV home treatment units, microorganisms are exposed to UV radiation from a lamp that shines on the water as it flows by. Although UV units do not add any chemical to the water, they cost at least several hundred dollars and require a lot of maintenance. Their effectiveness is reduced in water with high turbidity or high iron levels.

You will note that this list does not include water softeners. These appliances are not filters, in the strict sense of the word, but operate by changing the chemical makeup of the water. They remove the calcium and magnesium ions responsible for hard water, but the water produced by these appliances contains elevated levels of salt, which is linked with hypertension and heart diseases. Consequently, many people install bypass lines so that the softener is providing water only to the hot water lines and those cold water lines that are not used for drinking water.

Reverse Osmosis

Reverse osmosis (RO) systems are fast becoming the standard in home water treatment devices. The process involves three filters arranged in series. Water from a cold water line first enters a sediment filter, which removes large particulate matter. Without this component, the system would soon be fouled with sediment. The pore size of the membrane in the sediment filter is from one to five microns, or about the diameter of human hair. The filter consists of a paper cartridge inside a plastic cannister. Some manufacturers use clear plastic containers so the home owner can see the amount of sediment that has been strained from the water. The brown, green, or orange deposits may be quite shocking, especially if the filter paper is discolored after only a few hours of operating time.

The water then enters a second cannister containing the reverse osmosis membranes. These membranes resemble cellophane. The pore size is carefully controlled in the manufacturing process; ideally only a single water molecule can pass through at a time. The surface area of the membranes ranges from 5 to 15 square feet. Water is forced against the outer layer of the membrane. Here, the initial separation of contaminants from the water molecules occurs. The larger contaminant molecules are flushed from the membrane surface with waste water, and the smaller water molecules are squeezed through the ultrafine membrane pores. Each successive layer of membrane further refines the water so that clean water finally reaches a tube in the center, which is connected to the last filter cannister.

The third cannister contains an activated carbon filter cartridge, which removes contaminants—especially lighter-weight organic contaminants and dissolved gasses—that may have passed through the RO membrane.

Reverse osmosis systems are quiet and effective. It takes only a few minutes to replace filters. The units are permanently installed under the kitchen sink, and are connected to the feed and drain lines of the home's plumbing. The water is delivered through a third faucet installed on the sink. In this way, untreated water can be used for washing and other needs. The average price for such a system is $500 at this writing.

RO systems are not without their drawbacks. Most people rely on dealer technicians to install them, although someone accustomed to working on home plumbing systems could install one without much difficulty. Another consideration is the cost and bother of replacing membrane cartridges after one to three years, carbon filters more often, and sediment filters as necessary. Exact life spans for these elements can't be calculated, because the quality of the incoming water determines how often each element must be replaced. This uncertainty places more responsibility on the owner of an RO unit.

These units are dependent on water pressure for proper operation. They won't perform if the pressure is below 35 pounds per square inch (psi). Very high pressures, over 200 psi, will compress the membranes and reduce efficiency or cause complete failure. Low pressures can be remedied by adding a small pump to the system; high pressures are relieved with a regulator valve.

Ultraviolet

Ultraviolet (UV) light water treatment systems for the home are still in the development stage, but they offer promise and should be included here. Some municipal water systems use UV systems to kill bacteria and to reduce organic chemicals. Water passes through clear glass tubes and is subjected to ultraviolet rays from light bulbs. Bacteria and viruses are killed by ultraviolet light, and certain organic chemicals are altered in such a way that they are not harmful.

UV systems are rendered ineffective if the water is turbid or even slightly cloudy. Bacteria actually cling to particulates in the water and are protected from the UV light. Also, UV light has difficulty penetrating cloudy water. Operating costs are high when compared with traditional treatments. Usual maintenance includes clearing the glass tubes of scale and debris and replacing burned-out light bulbs. As designs are refined, UV systems could become more popular.

Activated Carbon Filters

Most people are familiar with activated carbon (AC) water filters. These are sold through retail stores and can be found in a variety of designs. The popularity of these devices was set back recently when it was found that bacteria breeded in some brands. The problem was usually traced to poor maintenance of the filters, however, and not to poor design or construction.

Not all AC filters are equal. The smaller units contain too little activated carbon to be effective. You will get more for your money by purchasing a larger filter; it will have a longer service life and will present less risk of bacterial contamination.

Activated carbon is highly porous. It is estimated that one pound of AC has a surface area of an acre. Molecules passing over the surface area are captured by the carbon. AC is available in three forms. Avoid powered AC; it is apt to release particles of carbon into the finished water, and if the particles are charged with contaminants, you will consume concentrated doses of the very chemicals you intend to remove.

Granulated AC is found in the majority of filters. The particles are larger. Water may pass through the filter in channels between granules. Because this reduces the amount of carbon available to filtration, these filters should be equipped with a back-flush valve to rearrange and clean the carbon.

Solid-block AC filters are considered superior. Channeling can't occur, and the solid-block filters usually last longer, compensating for their greater cost.

Several configurations of AC filters are available. Sink-mounted models are placed on the end of the faucet. Most have a bypass valve so that you have the option of drawing unfiltered water for washing. This feature greatly increases the filter life.

Under-the-sink models are usually larger and use a cannister or cartridge connected with the cold water line. Most offer the option of allowing unfiltered water to be tapped separately.

Pour-through and appliance units operate independently of the plumbing system. Much like a pour-through coffee maker, water is poured through a filter cannister and into a vessel. Some units employ a small electric pump to force the water through the carbon; the water can be circulated through the unit continuously to remove more contaminants with each passage through the carbon.

Spurred by the growing consumer demand for water treatment devices, the EPA and two magazines have tested a number of units. The effectiveness of the filters varied greatly in each test.

Beginning in 1979, Gulf South Research Institute in Louisiana, under contract to the EPA, tested 31 filters on their ability to remove THMs and nonvolatile carbon. Generally, under-the-sink line-bypass models proved especially effective in removing both THMs and organic carbon. The 14 line-bypass units tested removed 23 to 99 percent of THMs and 0 to 87 percent of organic carbon, compared with only 6 to 69 percent of the THMs and 6 to 31 percent of organic carbon for end-of-faucet bypass models, the next most effective type of filter.[19]

In February 1983, *Consumer Reports* magazine (CR) published the results of its tests on 17 activated carbon filters. CR chose to test the effectiveness of the filters in removing chloroform, because this carcinogen is commonly found in tap water and "because activated-carbon filters don't retain chloroform as well as they do larger organic molecules such as pesticides." According to the magazine, this meant theirs was "a tough test of a filter's ability to remove organic chemicals."[20]

Again, the CR results showed that under-the-sink models were more effective than smaller, end-of-faucet models in removing chloroform from tap water. CR discovered, however, a disturbing feature in three under-the-sink models they tested. Each effectively removed chloroform from the first 150 gallons of water, but after 300 gallons the filters began releasing chloroform into the filtered water. CR concluded that the filters were unloading the chloroform that had been absorbed from the raw water;[21] they apparently did so because they used powdered activated carbon, and particles of it were passing through to the filtered water. Models with granulated activated carbon or solid-block carbon, on the other hand, showed no unloading. Today, few manufacturers use activated powdered carbon in their filters.

End-of-faucet units are generally easier and less expensive to install than under-the-sink models, but in CR's tests they were less effective in removing chloroform; two units removed less than half the chemical.

Rodale's *New Shelter* magazine tested ten water filters for their ability to remove organic halogens from Philadelphia tap water. The models removed from 0 to 73 percent of these chemicals; on one unit, more organic halogens flowed out than flowed in (this was traced to a defect in the filter cannister, and the problem was subsequently corrected by the manufacturer).[22]

The *New Shelter* study found that the effectiveness of most filters declined markedly after 75 percent of the manufacturers' suggested lifetimes. Therefore, you would be wise to replace filter cartridges earlier than the manufacturer's recommendation if your water has significant levels of organic chemicals. A unit that has a life expectancy of 250 gallons, for example, should ideally be replaced after about 190 gallons have been filtered (250 gallons × 0.75 = 187.50 gallons).

Carbon filters have some clear limitations. Although they will remove rust particles, they are not very effective in removing dissolved inorganics such as heavy metals. They are also ineffective against bacteria. In fact, because wet carbon provides an excellent breeding ground for bacteria, you should be sure that the water going into a filter is free of harmful bacteria. Chlorinated municipal systems are usually safe, but private wells should be tested annually, at least, for bacterial contamination. The Canadian Health Protection Branch has identified nearly a dozen types of potentially harmful bacteria that can grow on carbon filters.[23]

Several filters contain silver to kill bacteria, but both the EPA and the Health Protection Branch have expressed doubts as to the effectiveness of this method.[24] The best way to control bacterial growth is to conscientiously replace filters. Neglected filters may also be clogged by sediment. If you are not inclined to tend to such details, you may consider buying a service contract from the dealer.

Distillers

The process used in distillers is much like the solar-powered hydrological cycle in nature. When the sun's heat vaporizes water, impurities are left behind. The vapor condenses back into water particles as it is drawn into the atmosphere. These water particles appear as naturally distilled dew, rain, and snow.

In a distiller, water is either poured or fed automatically into a vaporizing chamber, where it is boiled by an electrical resistance heating element. As the steam rises, most chemicals, minerals, bacteria, viruses, and other pollutants are removed. The steam travels by convection to a condensing chamber, where it is cooled by a fan or cooling coils, to condense into distilled water.

Some maintenance is necessary. Distillers should be cleaned periodically to remove sediment and scale that build up over time. Most models give off some heat, and they may gurgle or whir as they operate; for these reasons some owners install distillers away from the busiest part of the home, such as in the laundry room. If properly maintained, distillers provide a constant supply of high-quality water. Filters and reverse osmosis units, on the other hand, are at their best when first installed, and efficiency inevitably declines with use.

Where Do We Go from Here?

9

Joel Hirschhorn, at the congressional Office of Technology Assessment, is Capitol Hill's resident expert on hazardous waste. Working out of a cluttered office crammed from floor to ceiling with papers, files, and reports, Hirschhorn has produced a steady stream of reports on the subject, testified before congressional committees more times than he can count, and spoken endlessly before industry and government conferences.

Lois Gibbs also spends much of her time giving presentations on hazardous waste. Unlike Hirschhorn, Gibbs doesn't have any engineering degrees, and she speaks instead to citizens whose communities are contaminated by toxic chemicals. As a former resident of Love Canal, she runs the Citizens Clearinghouse for Hazardous Wastes, which coordinates groups protesting toxic contamination in their communities.

Despite their different approaches, both Gibbs and Hirschhorn have arrived at a similar conclusion: contamination has to be prevented before it happens. That means reducing the amount of toxic material produced. "It is necessary to squarely face the fact that billions of tons of hazardous waste are already in our land, and that it makes little sense to unnecessarily add more to that threat," Hirschhorn says. Gibbs says more pointedly: "Don't come to me with your garbage can and say we're going to put it here, because if we don't stop at this level, [the contamination] will just continue."

Reducing the Threat

No single technology offers a panacea, nor will we ever be able to eliminate completely the threat of contamination, but we *can* substantially reduce our output of waste. A 1981 report by the California Office of Appropriate Technology found that it is technologically feasible to recycle, treat, or destroy 75 percent of the hazardous waste that now goes into the state's land disposal facilities.[1] A 1983 report by the National Academy of Sciences concluded, "There exists some technology or combination of technologies capable of dealing with every hazardous waste so as to eliminate concern for future hazards."[2] Most of these technologies "are in common practice or are commercially available in the United States today," says William Sanjour, waste policy analyst for the EPA.[3]

First, water systems can ozonate drinking water rather than rely heavily on chlorine, which may be converted into cancer-causing trihalomethanes (THMs). Rip Rice, a technical consultant to the International Ozone Association, points out that water from a pilot ozone treatment plant in Belle Glade, Florida, tested as low as 25 parts per billion (ppb) of THMs, while the city's conventional chlorine treatment resulted in THM levels of 600 to 900 ppb. That's significantly higher than the EPA's standard of 100 ppb. As recently as 1977, only 2 municipal ozone treatment plants were operating in the United States, but Rice says that by 1984 there were 17 ozone treatment plants operating and another 5 under construction.[4]

Another way to reduce the hazardous chemicals in drinking water is simply to produce fewer toxic products to begin with. We already have phased out most lead-based interior paints, for example, which means that less lead-contaminated waste is generated. Zinc can be use in electroplating processes in place of cadmium, a much more toxic metal. To reduce the use of toxic pesticides, scientists are exploring biological controls such as natural predators, pest sterilization, and resistant plant varieties. The National Park Service managed to cut its use of pesticides in the Washington, D.C., area by more than half, from 15,000 pounds of active ingredients in 1979 to 7,000 pounds in 1983, by planting disease-resistant plant varieties, using biological pest controls, and modifying cultivation techniques.[5]

Often the amount of waste produced can be substantially reduced through simple housekeeping measures. Union Carbide, for example, reported that when it plugged leaks in production pipelines, it conserved a total of 20,000 pounds of solvents and saved $2,000 a day.[6]

Many firms have found that they can reuse by-products they formerly discarded. Allied Chemical is annually converting 25,000 tons of highly alkaline sludge into an ingredient used in the manufacture of another product.[7] An ICI American plant at Bayonne, New Jersey, has earned $700,000 over the past five years from the sale of solvents and other materials recovered from its waste.[8] The 3M Corporation claims its "pollution prevention pays" program spares nearly 250,000 tons of waste each year by recovering chemicals for reuse.[9]

Smaller companies often do not have the money or expertise to process their wastes. Take the case of the small firms which make up the metal-finishing industry; they produce a large amount of waste containing toxic heavy metals and cyanide, but many cannot afford the technology to recover the metals and neutralize the cyanide. To fill this need, one southern California company, ENV, Incorporated, uses mobile treatment vans, each with the capacity to treat 5,000 gallons of these wastes per day.[10]

Through an innovative waste exchange, waste generators can locate potential users for their by-products. The first such exchange in the United States was started in 1975; 34 were operating by 1981. Several companies have taken the concept further. Functioning as waste brokers, they pick up waste and then actively find buyers for it.

Still, we will always be burdened with some hazardous waste that can't be recovered, recycled, or reused. This must be destroyed or treated to render it less harmful to the environment. Dow Chemical now burns more than 90 percent of the organic waste it generates, and this annually yields the company the equivalent of 9.2 million gallons of gasoline in heat—energy that otherwise would simply go up in smoke.[11] Incineration is currently the most popular method of destroying unwanted waste. There are currently about 50 chemical incinerators operating around the world and another 14 under construction, according to the National Solid Waste Management Association.[12]

Incineration is not without its problems. The process does emit some pollutants, although a relatively small amount is allowed by EPA specifications. Incinerators also produce a residue of ash that must be land disposed. For example, for every 100 tons of hazardous waste Dow burns at its incinerator in Plaquemine, Louisiana, 15 tons of ash and other residue must be disposed of in a landfill on the plant site.[13]

Waste that cannot be destroyed or reused can often be treated to render it harmless or inert. Acids, for example, can be neutralized. Cyanide can be chemically altered to make it harmless. Fly ash can be fixed in cement.

We will not do away with landfilling completely. "You can't say, 'We will landfill nothing'—you can only minimize so far," says David Carroll, director of environmental programs for the Chemical Manufacturers Association. But by the year 2000, we could reduce the amount of waste we generate by 30 percent, without the use of incineration, according to Robert Pojasek, a member of the National Academy of Sciences hazardous waste committee. "What is needed is not so much a 'technical fix' to be hatched from the laboratory," Hirschhorn points out, "but rather bold institutional programs encouraged by the public, supported by policymakers, and implemented effectively by bureaucrats."[14] For several reasons, these bold programs do not appear about to happen.

What Did We Learn from Love Canal?

"The biggest mistake we probably made was not taking an alternate method maybe within six months after Love Canal," points out M. R. Speach of ENV, a California waste treatment firm.[15] One reason we did not is put forth by Dr. Donald Huisingh, an environmental science professor at North Carolina State: most engineers are not oriented toward waste reduction but, rather, focus on how to dispose of waste once it is produced. Huisingh, a leading waste management expert, adds, "99.9 percent" of engineers have what he calls the " 'anal point of view.' That's how we've taught them."

Another disincentive to alternatives is cost: land disposal remains the cheapest waste management option. Couple this with the EPA's lack of enthusiasm for alternatives, and it isn't surprising that 80 percent of our waste continues to be buried. "It's a basic fact of life that doing something costs more than doing nothing," says Richard Fortuna, executive director of the Hazardous Waste Treatment Council, which is composed of more than two dozen high-technology waste management firms. "And, if doing something is not required—doing treatment or something more protective–people just aren't going to do it." Fortuna blames "a lack of regulatory restructuring of the marketplace to protect public health." EPA regulations have always favored land disposal. Hirschhorn explains why: "You wouldn't expect a regulatory agency to be pushing economic incentives to put themselves out of business, essentially. It's not the way regulators think."

Under Anne Burford, the EPA "couldn't find a land disposal facility they didn't like," according to Fortuna. Although the agency was automatically permitting many existing land disposal facilities, it was slow to permit those that employed alternative waste management technologies. "There is this unwillingness to use untested, unproven technologies," says Hirschhorn, "even though land disposal is proven not to work." The EPA also has done little to support research on waste reduction. The agency's efforts have been "underfunded and undermanned from the beginning," says Penny Hansen of the EPA's hazardous waste treatment branch.

Congress and the States React

Because of the EPA's inaction, it was left to Congress in 1984 to amend the Resource Conservation and Recovery Act so that it sharply limited the disposal of waste in landfills. "The law is a reflection on Burford and Lavelle," says Mark Anthony Reisch, a waste expert with the Congressional Research Service. "If the agency had done its job right, this law would never have happened."

Fortuna calls the bill "the beginning of the end for unrestricted land disposal." Hirschhorn agrees that it "will enhance the trend to move away from land disposal."

The hazardous waste bill is, in fact, the only major piece of environmental legislation to pass Congress in the first half of the 1980s. For several years Congress has failed in its efforts to amend the major environmental laws governing drinking water quality, including the Safe Drinking Water Act, the Clean Water Act, and Superfund. Lois Gibbs thinks Congress has failed to act on environmental legislation because "now the magnitude of the problem is much greater than when those laws were first passed and so the impact of the legislation is much greater on both corporations and government. Five or six years ago, you weren't talking about 29 percent of Americans' groundwater supply being contaminated."

With the Reagan administration in power until 1989, and an ongoing federal budget crisis, we can expect still greater pressure to reduce the agency's meager resources. This will mean more delays, more missed deadlines, and continued lax enforcement. Paralysis at the federal level has placed more responsibility on state and local resources. Florida's "amnesty days" program is a model of the innovative steps that can be taken regionally. Prior to the program, waste management firms had no incentive to bother collecting waste from small businesses and home owners. As a result, toxic products sat around in garages and basements or were taken to town dumps. But by setting up mobile waste collection centers, the state made it feasible to pick up waste from thousands of different sources. Now the wastes are taken to be recycled, treated, or, at the very least, disposed of in an EPA-permitted landfill.

In New York, the state-run Environmental Facilities Corporation gives advice on waste reduction, primarily to small and medium-sized firms, and operates a waste exchange. In North Carolina, the state Waste Management Board has set up a clearinghouse of toxic waste and hazardous substances to help companies recycle and reuse waste. A key advantage of such programs is that they do not require the establishment of yet another huge government bureaucracy. "You don't need a regulatory agency," Hirschhorn points out. "What you need is technology transfer, information transfer, capital assistance."

These programs are increasingly attractive to state and local governments because they are a cheaper alternative to expensive regulatory programs. According to Frank Walper, administrator of Florida's amnesty days program, at least 25 other states have called his office asking for information on how to set up similar programs.

The Citizen's Role— Creating the Environment

But these innovative programs and technologies are successful only when the right motivation exists. It boils down to economics. Companies reduce the risk only if it pays them to do so—and that happens only through economic incentives such as tax credits for reducing waste. Increasingly, waste generators are forced to take into account the long-term costs of unsafe practices, because of both legal action under Superfund and lawsuits by citizens. Federal and state regulations promise to make it still more expensive for polluters to continue their ways.

These laws did not come out of a vacuum but were enacted largely because the public demanded that the government do something about pollution. As Lois Gibbs points out, "There's very stringent laws being passed state by state. And that depends on how strongly organized or how many groups there are at a grassroots level." Once laws are on the books, it again is up to citizens to make sure that the government enforces them. When that has failed, citizens and environmental groups have gone to court to force compliance.

Hirschhorn says that states would attempt innovative programs if there were enough public pressure. This is beginning to happen. Around the country, people have successfully closed or stopped waste facilities that threatened their communities. With waste piling up and disposal capacity dwindling, government officials and industry are now forced to look at possible alternatives. "Basically what citizens are saying is, 'Show me what's left after you've used everything available, and then we'll sit down and talk about what to do with it,' " Gibbs says.

People such as the Arlingtons of Fort Edward, the Woodmans of Jacksonville, and Sharilyn Dienst of Benton, have shown that citizens can make a difference. At Love Canal, when Lois Gibbs first suspected that her children's illnesses might be caused by toxic chemicals, she didn't know where to turn. But over the past several years, she has found that the situation is changing dramatically. "I think the difference between then and now is that there has been a groundswell of grassroots people across the country who are faced with these problems, who have seen what was done at Love Canal, who have seen what was done at Times Beach, and as a result are taking situations into their own hands."

For Gibbs, this involvement will make all the difference in the fight to protect this precious resource. "I'm really very optimistic. I see people moving, and I see things happening."

Appendix: State Groundwater Contacts

ALABAMA
Water Improvement Commission
Alabama Dept. of Environmental Management
1751 Federal Dr.
Montgomery, AL 36130
(205) 271-7700

ALASKA
Division of Land and Water
Dept. of Natural Resources
Pouch #7-005
Anchorage, AK 99510
(907) 276-2653

Water Quality Management
Dept. of Environmental Quality Management
Pouch 0
Juneau, AK 99811
(907) 465-2653

ARIZONA
Dept. of Water Resources
99 E. Virginia Ave.
Phoenix, AZ 85004
(602) 255-1554

ARKANSAS
State Soil and Water Conservation Commission
Dept. of Commerce
1 Capital Mall, Suite 2D
Little Rock, AR 72201
(501) 371-1611

CALIFORNIA
Dept. of Water Resources
P.O. Box 388
Sacramento, CA 95802
(916) 445-9248

COLORADO
Water Quality Control
Dept. of Health
4210 E. 11th Ave.
Denver, CO 80220
(303) 320–8333

Water Resources Division
Dept. of Natural Resources
1313 Sherman St., Room 818
Denver, CO 80203
(303) 866–3587

CONNECTICUT
Dept. of Environmental Pro-
    tection
Natural Resources Center
165 Capital Ave., Room 553
Hartford, CT 06106
(203) 566–3540

DELAWARE
Dept. of Natural Resources and
    Environmental Control
Water Supply Branch
Richardson Robins Bldg.
P.O. Box 1401
Dover, DE 19903
(302) 736–4793

FLORIDA
Dept. of Environmental Regu-
    lation
Division of Environmental
    Programs
Groundwater Section
2600 Blair Stone Rd.
Tallahassee, FL 32301
(904) 488–0300

GEORGIA
Geological Survey
Environmental Protection Di-
    vision
Dept. of Natural Resources,
    Room 14
19 Martin Luther King, Jr. Dr.,
    SW
Atlanta, GA 30334
(404) 656–3214

HAWAII
Division of Water and Land
    Development
Dept. of Land and Natural Re-
    sources
P.O. Box 373
Honolulu, HI 96809
(808) 548–7619

IDAHO
Dept. of Water Resources
State House
Boise, ID 83720
(208) 334–2190

ILLINOIS
State Water Survey
605 E. Springfield Ave.
P.O. Box 5050, Sta. A
Champaign, IL 61820
(217) 333–2210

Water Pollution Control Divi-
    sion
Illinois Environmental Protec-
    tion Agency
2200 Churchill Rd.
Springfield, IL 62706
(217) 782–1654

INDIANA
Division of Pollution
Indiana State Board of Health
5500 W. Bradbury Ave.
Indianapolis, IN 46241
(317) 243-9100

Division of Water
Indiana Dept. of Natural Resources
2475 Directors Row
Indianapolis, IN 46241
(317) 232-4160

IOWA
Water, Air and Waste Management
Field Services Division
Henry A. Wallace Bldg.
900 East Grand Ave.
Des Moines, IA 50319
(515) 281-8690

KANSAS
Oil Field and Environmental Geology
Dept. of Health and Environment
Bldg. 740
Forbes Field
Topeka, KS 66620
(913) 862-9360

KENTUCKY
Division of Water
Dept. for Natural Resources and Environmental Protection
18 Reilly Rd.
Frankfort, KY 40601
(502) 564-3410

Water Patrol Division
Dept. for Natural Resources and Environmental Protection
107 Mero St.
Frankfort, KY 40601
(502) 564-3074

LOUISIANA
Office of Water Resources
Dept. of Environmental Quality
P.O. Box 44066
Baton Rouge, LA 70804
(504) 342-6363

MAINE
Office of Legislative Assistance
State House, Sta. 13
Augusta, ME 04333
(207) 289-1670

MARYLAND
Division of Water Supply
Dept. of Health and Mental Hygiene
O'Conor Bldg.
201 W. Preston St.
Baltimore, MD 21201
(301) 383-4249

Water Resources Administration
Dept. of Natural Resources
Tawes State Office Bldg.
580 Taylor Ave.
Annapolis, MD 21401
(301) 269-3846

MASSACHUSETTS
Dept. of Environmental Management
Water Resources Division
100 Cambridge St.
Boston, MA 02202
(617) 727-3267

MICHIGAN
Dept. of Public Health
Water Supply Division
3500 N. Logan
P.O. Box 30035
Lansing, MI 48909
(517) 373-1376

Groundwater Quality Division
Dept. of Natural Resources
P.O. Box 30028
Lansing, MI 48909
(517) 373-1947

Surface Water Quality Division
Dept. of Natural Resources
P.O. Box 30028
Lansing, MI 48909
(517) 373-1949

MINNESOTA
Dept. of Health
717 Delaware St., SE
Minneapolis, MN 55440
(612) 623-5000

Dept. of Natural Resources
Division of Water
500 Lafayette Rd., Box 32
St. Paul, MN 55146
(612) 296-4800

Pollution Control Agency
1935 W. County Rd., B-2
Roseville, MN 55113
(612) 296-7373

MISSISSIPPI
Board of Health
Bureau of Environmental Health
Water Supply Division
Jackson, MS 39209

Bureau of Land and Water Resources
Dept. of Natural Resources
P.O. Box 10631
Jackson, MS 39209
(601) 961-5202

MISSOURI
Missouri Dept. of Natural Resources
Division of Environmental Quality
Public Drinking Water Program
P.O. Box 1368
Jefferson City, MO 65102

Missouri Dept. of Natural Resources
Division of Environmental Quality
Water Supply Program
P.O. Box 176
Jefferson City, MO 65102
(314) 364-1752

State Geological Survey
P.O. Box 250
Rolla, MO 65401

MONTANA
Water Quality Bureau
Dept. of Health and Environ-
mental Science
Helena, MT 59601

Water Rights Bureau
32 S. Ewing
Helena, MT 59620
(406) 444-6610

NEBRASKA
Dept. of Environmental Control
301 Centennial Mall South
P.O. Box 94877
Lincoln, NE 68509
(402) 471-2186

Dept. of Water Resources
301 Centennial Mall South
P.O. Box 94676
Lincoln, NE 68509

NEVADA
State Engineer
Dept. of Conservation and
Natural Resources
201 S. Fall St.
Carson City, NV 87710
(702) 885-4360

NEW HAMPSHIRE
Office of State Planning
Division of Water Supply
2½ Beacon St.
Concord, NH 03301
(603) 271-1110

NEW JERSEY
Dept. of Environmental Pro-
tection
Division of Water Resources
P.O. Box CN-029
Trenton, NJ 08625
(609) 292-2203

NEW MEXICO
New Mexico Interstate Stream
Commission
Bataan Memorial Bldg.
Santa Fe, NM 87503

Water Pollution Control Bu-
reau
Environmental Improvement
Division
P.O. Box 968
Santa Fe, NM 87503
(505) 988-6307

Water Resources Division
Natural Resources Dept.
Bataan Memorial Bldg.
Santa Fe, NM 87503

NEW YORK
Dept. of Environmental Conservation
Division of Pure Waters
50 Wolf Rd.
Albany, NY 12233
(518) 474-2121

NORTH CAROLINA
Division of Environmental
Management
Dept. of Natural Resources
Raleigh, NC 27611
(919) 851-0276

NORTH DAKOTA
Division of Water Supply and
    Pollution Control
Dept. of Health
1200 Missouri Ave.
Bismarck, ND 58505

State Water Commission
900 East Blvd.
Bismarck, ND 58506

OHIO
Dept. of Natural Resources
Division of Water
Groundwater Section
Fountain Square, Bldg. E3
Columbus, OH 43224
(614) 265–6717

OKLAHOMA
Chief, Planning and Develop-
    ment Division
Water Resources Board
P.O. Box 53585
N.E. 10th and Stonewall St.
Oklahoma City, OK 78152
(405) 271–2573

OREGON
Groundwater Section
Water Resources Dept.
555 13th St., NE
Salem, OR 97310
(503) 378–3739

Water Quality Control Divi-
    sion
522 S.W. 5th St.
Portland, OR 97204

PENNSYLVANIA
Dept. of Environmental Re-
    sources
Bureau of Water Quality Man-
    agement
Box 1467
Harrisburg, PA 17120
(717) 787–2666

RHODE ISLAND
Water Resources Board
265 Melrose St.
Providence, RI 02907
(401) 277–2217

SOUTH CAROLINA
Water Resources Commission
Division of Hydrology
3830 Forest Dr.
P.O. Box 4440
Columbia, SC 29240
(803) 758–2514

SOUTH DAKOTA
Water and Natural Resources
Joe Foss Bldg.
Pierre, SD 57501
(605) 773–3151

TENNESSEE
Dept. of Public Health
Division of Water Quality
    Control
Terra Bldg.
150 9th Ave., N
Nashville, TN 37219–5404
(615) 741–3111

Health and Environmental
  Dept.
Terra Bldg.
150 9th Ave., N
Nashville, TN 37219–5404
(615) 741–2275

TEXAS
Dept. of Water Resources
Box 13087, Capital Sta.
Austin, TX 78711–3087
(512) 475–7036

UTAH
State Engineer
Dept. of Natural Resources
1636 W. North Temple
Salt Lake City, UT 84116
(801) 533–6071

VERMONT
Agency of Environmental Conservation

State Office Bldg.
Montpelier, VT 05602
(802) 828–2761

VIRGINIA
Bureau of Water Supply Engineering
State Health Dept.
109 Governor St.
Richmond, VA 23219
(804) 786–6277

State Water Control Board
P.O. Box 11143
2111 Hamilton St.
Richmond, VA 23230
(804) 257–0056

WASHINGTON
Dept. of Ecology
Office of Water Programs
Water Resources Management
Olympia, WA 98504

Notes

Introduction

1. *Hazardous Waste Control and Enforcement Act of 1983*, hearings before the Subcommittee on Commerce, Transportation, and Tourism, House Committee on Energy and Commerce, No. 98–32, March 22 and 24, 1983, testimony of Neal Potter, p. 561.

2. Joel S. Hirschhorn, statement before the Senate Full Committee on Environment and Public Works, September 10, 1984, p. 4.

3. Citizens for a Better Environment and Natural Resources Defense Council, *Hazardous Waste Surface Impoundments: The Nation's Most Serious and Neglected Threat to Groundwater*, September 15, 1983, p. 3.

4. EPA Office of Solid Waste and Emergency Response, *Extent of the Hazardous Release Problem and Future Funding Needs*, December 1984, pp. 5–9.

5. Ibid.

6. *Hazardous Waste Control and Enforcement Act of 1983*, statement of Jane Bloom, p. 503.

7. *Safe Drinking Water Act Amendments of 1983*, hearings before the Subcommittee on Health and the Environment, House Committee on Energy and Commerce, No. 98–49, June 15, 21, and 22; July 27 and 28, 1983, statement of Bruce Brower, p. 74.

8. Erlinda Villamor, "The Idea Is to Keep New Jersey's Water Drinkable," *Asbury Park Press*, May 6, 1984.

9. Representative Mike Synar, remarks at the Second National Water Conference, Philadelphia, Pa., January 24, 1984.

10. Ibid.

11. *Ground Water Contamination*, hearings before the Subcommittee on Toxic Substances and Environmental Oversight and the Senate Full Committee on Environment and Public Works, No. 98–721, November 21 and 29, 1983; January 18; March 1 and 9, 1984, statement of Jack E. Ravan, EPA Assistant Administrator for Water, p. 73.

12. *Toxic Waste Contamination of Ground Water: EPA Oversight*, hearings before a subcommittee of the House Committee on Government Operations, July 24 and 25; September 18, 1980, statement of Representative Toby Moffett, p. 3.

13. Ibid., statement of Robert Harris, p. 9.

14. *Federal Register*, June 12, 1984, p. 24335.

15. Council on Environmental Quality, *Contamination of Ground Water by Toxic Organic Chemicals*, January 1981, p. 36.

16. Environmental Policy Institute, *Toxics and Groundwater Crisis: Toward a National Strategy*, May 24, 1984, p. 1.

17. *Toxic Waste Contamination of Ground Water: EPA Oversight*, statement of Eckhardt C. Beck, p. 81.

18. Ralph Nader, "Not All of Our Drinking Water Meets Healthful Standards," *Today's Health*, December 1975, pp. 10–11, 51–55.

19. William D. Ruckelshaus, "Putting the Hazardous Waste Issue in Perspective," *EPA Journal*, October 1984, pp. 2–3.

20. *Safe Drinking Water Act Amendments of 1983*, statement of Representative Dennis E. Eckart, p. 9.

21. Joel S. Hirschhorn, interview with the authors.

22. From statistics compiled by the International Bottled Water Association and the Water Quality Association.

23. Office of Technology Assessment, *Technologies and Management Strategies for Hazardous Waste Control*, March 1983, p. 6.

24. Ibid.

25. Penny Hansen, Branch Chief, EPA Hazardous Waste Treatment Branch, Analysis and Assessment Program, Office of Solid Waste, interview with the authors.

26. *Health Effects of Hazardous Waste Disposal Practices, 1980*, joint hearings before the Subcommittee on Health and Scientific Research, Senate Committee on Labor and Human Resources, and the Senate Committee on the Judiciary, June 6, 1980, testimony of Kathleen Benesch, p. 15.

27. Sharilyn Dienst, statement before the Subcommittee on Natural Resources, Agriculture Research, and Environment, House Committee on Science and Technology, July 30, 1983.

1: Toxic Waste

1. *Federal Register*, June 12, 1984, p. 24340.

2. State of New York Department of Environmental Conservation, "In the Matter of the Summary Abatement Order Issued to the General Electric Company." July 7, 1983.

3. Dominic Tom, "Fort Edward Homeowners Reject GE Pact," *Glens Falls Post-Star*, January 21, 1983.

4. Samuel Epstein, Lester Brown, and Carl Pope, *Hazardous Waste in America* (San Francisco: Sierra Club Books, 1982), p. 7.

5. U.S. General Accounting Office, "EPA's Efforts to Identify and Control Harmful Chemicals in Use," RCED–84–100, June 13, 1984, pp. 1–2.

6. *Toxic Waste Contamination of Ground Water: EPA Oversight,* hearings before a subcommittee of the House Committee on Government Operations, July 24 and 25; September 18, 1980, statement of Representative Toby Moffett, p. 3.

7. Robert H. Harris et al., "Adverse Health Effects at a Tennessee Hazardous Waste Disposal Site," unpublished paper.

8. *Toxic Waste Contamination of Ground Water: EPA Oversight,* statement of Robert Harris, p. 13.

9. Ibid., statement of Eckhardt C. Beck, p. 86.

10. Ibid., statement of Robert Harris, p. 11.

11. Michigan Department of Natural Resources, "Groundwater Management Strategy for Michigan," p. i.

12. Council on Environmental Quality, *Contamination of Ground Water by Toxic Organic Chemicals,* January 1981, p. 32.

13. Cited in Epstein, Brown, and Pope, *Hazardous Waste in America,* pp. 28–29.

14. William Drayton, *America's Toxic Protection Gap: The Collapse of Compliance with the Nation's Toxics Laws,* July 1984, p. 7.

15. Office of Technology Assessment, *Technologies and Management Strategies for Hazardous Waste Control,* March 1983, p. 8.

16. Citizens for a Better Environment and Natural Resources Defense Council, *Hazardous Waste Surface Impoundments: The Nation's Most Serious and Neglected Threat to Groundwater,* September 15, 1983, p. 1.

17. EPA, *Environmental Progress and Challenges: An EPA Perspective,* June 1984, p. 82.

18. Ibid., p. 72.

19. James P. Lester, "The Process of Hazardous Waste Regulation: Severity, Complexity, and Uncertainty," in James P. Lester and Ann O'M. Bowman, eds., *The Politics of Hazardous Waste Management* (Durham, N.C.: Duke University Press, 1983), p. 8.

20. Office of Technology Assessment, *Technologies and Management Strategies for Hazardous Waste Control,* p. 131.

21. Quoted in Lester, "The Process of Hazardous Waste Regulation," in Lester and Bowman, *The Politics of Hazardous Waste Management,* p. 1.

22. Richard Riley, "Toxic Substances, Hazardous Wastes, and Public Policy: Problems in Implementation," in Lester and Bowman, *The Politics of Hazardous Waste Management,* p. 37.

23. EPA Region 10, *Environmental Management Report,* March 1983, p. 15.

24. Erlinda Villamor, "The Idea Is to Keep New Jersey's Water Drinkable," *Asbury Park Press,* May 6, 1984.

25. *Amending and Extending the Comprehensive Environmental Response, Compensation, and Liability Act of 1980 (Superfund),* hearings before the Senate Full Committee on Environment and Public Works, April 11 and 25; May 16, 23, and 24; June 4 and 25; July 31, 1984, testimony of John Gaston, p. 1177.

26. Villamor, "The Idea Is to Keep New Jersey's Water Drinkable."

27. EPA Region 10, *Environmental Management Report,* May 1983, p. 40.

28. EPA, "Drinking Water Supplies Contaminated by Organic Chemicals in New England," cited in Congressional Research Service, *Groundwater Contamination by Toxic Substances: A Digest of Reports,* November 1983, p. 3.

29. EPA Region 5, *Environmental Management Report: Attachment A,* May 1983, p. 258.

30. Alvin L. Morris, "Superfund Task Force Preliminary Assessment," EPA memorandum to Alvin L. Alm, Deputy Administrator, and Lee M. Thomas, Assistant Administrator for Solid Waste and Emergency Response, December 8, 1983.

31. James J. Westrick, J. Wayne Mello, and Robert F. Thomas, "The Ground Water Supply Survey: Summary of Volatile Organic Contaminant Occurrence Data, " EPA Office of Drinking Water, January 1983, p. i.

32. *Review of Ground Water Protection Strategy Recently Proposed by the Environmental Protection Agency*, hearings before a subcommittee of the House Committee on Government Operations, April 11 and 12, 1984, statement of Representative Mike Synar, p. 2.

33. Congressional Research Service, *Groundwater Contamination by Toxic Substances: A Digest of Reports*, November 1983, p. xi.

34. Office of Technology Assessment, *Technologies and Management Strategies for Hazardous Waste Control*, p. 5.

35. *Federal Register*, February 5, 1981, p. 11128.

36. Citizens for a Better Environment and Natural Resources Defense Council, *Hazardous Waste Surface Impoundments: The Nation's Most Serious and Neglected Threat to Groundwater*, p. 1.

37. Ibid., p. i.

38. Ibid.

39. Ibid.

40. Ibid., p. 3.

41. EPA, "Waste Disposal Practices and Their Effects on Ground Water—The Report to Congress," January 1977.

42. Citizens for a Better Environment and Natural Resources Defense Council, *Hazardous Waste Surface Impoundments: The Nation's Most Serious and Neglected Threat to Groundwater*, p. ii.

43. California Assembly Office of Research, "Is Our Water Safe to Drink?" April 1983, pp. 79–82.

44. Lyle R. Silka and Francoise M. Brasier, "National Assessment of the Ground-Water Contamination Potential of Waste Impoundments," EPA, presented at the Symposium on Surface-Water Impoundments, Minneapolis, Minn., June 2–5, 1980, p. 4.

45. Veronica I. Pye, Ruth Patrick, and John Quarles, *Groundwater Contamination in the United States* (Philadelphia: University of Pennsylvania Press, 1983), p. 64.

46. *Safe Drinking Water Act Amendments of 1983*, hearings before the Subcommittee on Health and the Environment, House Committee on Energy and Commerce, No. 98–49, June 15, 21, and 22; July 27 and 28, 1983, testimony of Michael Dalton and James Irwin, pp. 529–46.

47. Chris Shuey, *The Workbook*, Southwest Research and Information Service, October/December 1984, p. 144.

48. Ibid.

49. Thomas Petzinger, Jr., and George Getschow, "In Louisiana, Pollution and Cancer Are Rife in the Petroleum Area," *Wall Street Journal*, October 23, 1984.

50. Donald V. Feliciano, "Underground Injection of Wastes," Congressional Research Service, October 20, 1983, p. 2.

51. Citizens for a Better Environment and Natural Resource Defense Council, *Hazardous Waste Surface Impoundments: The Nation's Most Serious and Neglected Threat to Groundwater*, p. 1.

52. Suellen Pirages, statement before the Subcommittee on Toxic Substances and Environmental Oversight, Senate Full Committee on Environment and Public Works, June 26, 1984.

53. *Safe Drinking Water Act Amendments of 1983*, testimony of Phillip Palmer, p. 713.

54. R. Allan Freeze and John A. Cherry, *Groundwater* (Englewood Cliffs, N.J.: Prentice Hall, 1979), p. 456.

55. Office of Technology Assessment, "Use of Injection Wells for Hazardous Waste Disposal," staff memorandum prepared by the Industry, Technology, and Employment Program, July 13, 1983, pp. 8–9.

56. Feliciano, "Underground Injection of Wastes," p. 4.

57. Bob Drogin, "Gasoline Pollution Plagues Residents of Maine Town," *Los Angeles Times*, December 11, 1983.

58. Ibid.

59. EPA Office of Solid Waste and Emergency Response, *Extent of the Hazardous Release Problem and Future Funding Needs*, December 1984, pp. 5–9.

60. Ibid.

61. Michael Harder, remarks to the Conference on Underground Fuel Tanks: Regulatory and Remedial Outlook, Arlington, Va., July 9, 1984.

62. Patrick Fitzgerald, "Gasoline in Wells Fouls State Water," *Lansing State Journal*, January 2, 1984.

63. *USA Today*, September 2, 1983.

64. *Ground Water Contamination*, hearings before Subcommittee on Toxic Substances and Environmental Oversight and the Senate Full Committee on Environment and Public Works, No. 98–721, November 21 and 29, 1983; January 18; March 1 and 9, 1984; testimony of Dr. Vernon Houk, p. 82.

65. Marcel Moreau, "Leaking Underground Storage Tanks: Status Report," Maine Department of Environmental Protection, p. 1.

66. Donald V. Feliciano, "Leaking Underground Storage Tanks: A Potential Environmental Problem," Congressional Research Service, January 11, 1984, p. 5.

67. Marcel Moreau, "A Little Gasoline: A Lot of Problems," *Maine Audubon Magazine*, reprinted in proceedings of the Conference on Un-

derground Fuel Tanks: Regulatory and Remedial Outlook, Arlington, Va., July 9–10, 1984.

68. Feliciano, "Leaking Underground Storage Tanks: A Potential Environmental Problem," p. 4.

69. Office of Technology Assessment, *Technologies and Management Strategies for Hazardous Waste Control*, p. 9.

70. EPA Office of Solid Waste and Emergency Response, *Extent of the Hazardous Release Problem and Future Funding Needs*, pp. 5–6.

71. *Hazardous Waste Control and Enforcement Act of 1983*, hearings before the Subcommittee on Commerce, Transportation, and Tourism, House Committee on Energy and Commerce, No. 98–32, March 22 and 24, 1983, testimony of Neal Potter, p. 561.

72. New York State Comptroller, press release, December 4, 1984.

73. John England, interview with the authors.

74. EPA Office of Solid Waste and Emergency Response, *Extent of the Hazardous Release Problem and Future Funding Needs*, p. i.

75. Ibid., pp. 5–7.

76. EPA, *Nonpoint Source Pollution in the U.S.*, report to Congress, January 1984, pp. 2–23.

77. Terry Murphy, "GE: We'll Pay for Water," *Tri-County Saratogean*, January 7, 1983.

78. Terri Axton, "GE: State 'Forcing' Us into Court," *Tri-County Saratogean*, April 26, 1983.

79. Ibid.

80. *Safe Drinking Water Act Amendments of 1983*, testimony of Richard Arlington, p. 698.

81. Brian Fear, New York state health officer, interview with the authors.

High-Tech Contamination box

1. Andy Pasztor, "Underground Pollution in Silicon Valley Is Widespread, Federal Officials Report," *Wall Street Journal*, November 11, 1984.

2. EPA Office of Solid Waste and Emergency Response, *Extent of the Hazardous Release Problem and Future Funding Needs*, December 1984, pp. 5–9.

3. Ibid., pp. 3–6.

2: Military Contamination

1. John Burr, "Navy Northeast Florida's Top Toxic Waste Producer," *Florida Times-Union*, August 7, 1983.

2. Navy Environmental Support Office, *Navy Hazardous Materials Management Guide*, OPNAVNOTE 6240.

3. *Department of Energy Authorization Legislation (National Security Programs) for Fiscal Year 1983*, hearing before the Subcommittee on Procurement and Military Nuclear Systems, House Committee on Armed Services, No. 97–41, April 26, 27, and 28, 1982, statement of Gen. William W. Hoover, p. 73.

4. Representative Mike Synar, statement before the Subcommittee on Environment, Energy, and Natural Resources, House Committee on Government Operations, August 15, 1983.

5. U.S. General Accounting Office, "Status of the Air Force Efforts to Deal with Groundwater Contamination Problems at McClellan Air Force Base," NSIAD–84–37, November 28, 1983.

6. Lt. Col. William Shimkus, Director of Public Affairs at McClellan Air Force Base, interview with the authors, January 28, 1985.

7. Jane Kay, "Ground-Water Cleanup Could Cost $79 Million," *Arizona Daily Star*, September 21, 1984.

8. Representative Mike Synar, memorandum to the Subcommittee on Environment, Energy, and Natural Resources, House Committee on Government Operations, August 8, 1983.

9. Statement of Kenneth Kamlet before the Subcommittee on Commerce, Transportation, and Tourism, House Committee on Energy and Commerce, March 1, 1984.

10. Cited in Representative Mike Synar's memorandum to the Subcommittee on Environment, Energy, and Natural Resources, August 8, 1983.

11. U.S. Assistant Attorney General Robert A. McConnell, Department of Justice, Office of Legislative Affairs, letter to Representative John Dingell, October 11, 1983.

12. U.S. General Accounting Office, "DOD Efforts to Clean Up Inactive Hazardous Waste Sites" (draft), October 31, 1984, p. ii.

13. Representative Mike Synar, statement before the Subcommittee on Environment, Energy, and Natural Resources, August 15, 1983.

14. Carl J. Johnson, "Contamination of Municipal Water Supplies in the Denver Metropolitan Area by the Rocky Flats Plutonium Plant," paper presented at the annual meeting of the American Association for the Advancement of Science, San Francisco, Calif., January 3–8, 1980.

15. "The Case for Monitoring Radioactive Wastes at the Idaho National Engineering Laboratory (INEL)," paper presented by the Snake River Alliance, 1981.

16. Barney Lewis, Acting Project Chief for U.S. Geological Survey office, Idaho Falls, Idaho, interview with the authors.

17. *The Impact of Mercury Releases at the Oak Ridge Complex*, hearing before the Subcommittee on Investigations and Oversight and the Subcommittee on Energy Research and Production, House Committee on Science and Technology, No. 44, July 11, 1983, testimony of Stephen Gough, pp. 388–89.

18. "Mercury Inventory at Y-12 Plant 1950–1977," Union Carbide Corporation, June 9, 1977.

19. *The Impact of Mercury Releases at the Oak Ridge Complex,* statement of Michael Bruner, pp. 186–87.

20. Ibid., statement of David Freeman, p. 199.

21. Ibid., statement of Frank D'Itri, p. 313.

22. Ibid., statement of Michael Bruner, p. 188.

23. J. A. Stone and E. J. Christensen, eds., *Technical Summary of Groundwater Quality Protection Program at Savannah River Plant: Volume II—Radioactive Waste,* DPST–83–829, E.I. Dupont de Nemours & Co., December 1983, pp. 2–15.

24. Colleen Walsh, "Nuclear Plant Continues Groundwater Cleanup," *Augusta Chronicle,* May 19, 1983.

25. Chris Shuey, Southwest Research and Information Center, interview with the authors.

26. Chris Shuey, "Uranium Mill Tailings as Hazardous Waste: A Brief Overview," Southwest Research and Information Center Fact Sheet, March 1984.

27. Ibid., and Chris Shuey, interview.

28. Chris Shuey, interview.

29. Terry Williams and Randell Beck, "OR Plants 'Above Law,' " *Knoxville Journal,* December 1, 1983.

30. *The Impact of Mercury Releases at the Oak Ridge Complex,* testimony of Howard Zeller, p. 183.

31. Gabriel J. Marciante, "Report on Meeting with U.S. EPA and Tennessee State Health Department Representatives," April 8, 1983, memorandum to the files, April 26, 1983.

32. *Implementation of the Comprehensive Environmental Response, Compensation, and Liability Act of 1981,* hearings before the Subcommittee on Environmental Pollution, Senate Full Committee on Environ-

ment and Public Works, No. 97–H31, July 8 and 20, 1981, testimony of George Marienthal, p. 99.

33. U.S. General Accounting Office, "DOD Efforts to Clean Up Inactive Hazardous Waste Sites," p. 1.

34. Kay, "Ground-Water Cleanup Could Cost $79 Million."

35. U.S. General Accounting Office, "DOD Efforts to Clean Up Inactive Hazardous Waste Sites," p. 30.

36. Statement of Representative Vic Fazio, November 1, 1984.

37. Grover A. Smithwick, "Environmental Program Briefing," presented to Bob Bayer, Legislative Assistant for Military Affairs for Senator Sam Nunn, March 15, 1984.

38. Cass Peterson, "Oak Ridge Told to Obey Waste and Water Laws," *Washington Post*, April 14, 1984.

3: The Pesticide Trickle-Down

1. Lawrence Gladieux, testimony before the Florida State Assembly Committee on Community Affairs, November 1, 1983, and interview with the authors.

2. Thomas Atkinson, Florida Department of Environmental Regulation, interview with the authors.

3. EPA Office of Solid Waste and Emergency Response, *Extent of the Hazardous Release Problem and Future Funding Needs*, December 1984, pp. 5–10.

4. EPA Scientific Advisory Panel meeting, Arlington, Va., June 13–14, 1984.

5. David Cohen, Program Manager, Toxic Substances Control Program of the California State Water Resources Control Board, interview with the authors.

6. Ramlit Associates, *Groundwater Contamination by Pesticides: A California Assessment*, report to California State Water Resources Control Board, June 1983, p. ix.

7. Greg Becker, Wisconsin Department of Natural Resources, interview with the authors, and Wisconsin Department of Natural Resources, "Groundwater Pesticide Sampling Program Summary."

8. Dennis Moran, Suffolk, N.Y., County Health Department, interview with the authors.

9. Office of Technology Assessment, *Impacts of Technology on U.S. Cropland and Rangeland Productivity*, August 1982, p. 52.

10. William J. Storck, "Pesticides Head For Recovery," *Chemical and Engineering News*, April 9, 1984, pp. 35–57.

11. Philip M. Boffey, "20 Years after 'Silent Spring': Still a Troubled Landscape," *New York Times*, May 25, 1982.

12. Stanford Research Institute, *Environmental Indicators for Pesticides, 1972*, quoted in California Department of Food and Agriculture, *Pesticide Movement to Ground Water* (draft of final report), pp. 1–2.

13. Mike Brusko, "The Trouble with Temik: Your Well Is Poisoned," *New Farm*, September/October 1983, pp. 27–32.

14. Lewis Regenstein, *America the Poisoned* (Washington, D.C.: Acropolis Books, 1982), p. 317.

15. Ramlit Associates, *Groundwater Contamination by Pesticides: A California Assessment*, p. 39.

16. Ehud Yonay, "The Nematode Chronicles," *New West*, May 1981, pp. 66–74, 144–53.

17. Deborah Blum, "Day and Night with the Invisible Foe," *Fresno Bee*, November 28, 1982.

18. Richard Jackson et al., *An Epidemiological Comparison of Patterns of DBCP Drinking Water Contamination with Mortality Rates from*

Selected Cancers in Fresno County, California, 1970–1979, California Department of Health Services, June 1, 1982.

19. House Committee on Government Operations, *Problems Plague the Environmental Protection Agency's Pesticide Registration Activities,* HR 98–1147, October 5, 1984, p. 9.

20. Myron Struck, "Medfly Fumigant Risky, EPA Scientist Says," *Washington Post,* October 8, 1981.

21. Philip Shabecoff, "U.S. Officials' Talks on Pesticide Faulted by Environmentalist," *New York Times,* January 31, 1984.

22. Representative Andy Ireland, letter to Dr. John Todhunter, EPA Assistant Administrator for Pesticides and Toxic Substances, July 15, 1982.

23. Shabecoff, "U.S. Officials' Talks."

24. Representative Mike Synar, *EPA's Pesticide Registration Activities* (Part 1), hearing before a subcommittee of the House Committee on Government Operations, September 26, 1983, p. 2.

25. John A. Moore, EPA Assistant Administrator for Pesticides and Toxic Substances, letter to Doyle Conner, Commissioner, Florida Department of Agriculture and Community Services, December 12, 1983.

26. Kim Kleman, "Conner Says Floridians Well Protected from Pesticides," *Tampa Tribune,* October 12, 1983.

27. Quoted in Regenstein, *America the Poisoned,* p. 115.

28. House Committee on Government Operations, *Problems Plague the Environmental Protection Agency's Pesticide Registration Activities,* p. 18.

29. Ibid., pp. 5–6.

30. Ibid., p. 6.

31. Cass Peterson, "Overseer of Pesticides, Toxic Safety Freely Admits Agency's Pace Is Slow," *Washington Post,* April 20, 1984.

32. *EPA's Pesticide Registration Activities* (Part 1), testimony of Jacqueline Warren, p. 154.

33. Ronald Taylor, "Discovery of DBCP in Oahu Well Catches EPA by Surprise," *Los Angeles Times*, May 5, 1980.

34. John G. Mink, testimony before the EPA on the proposed withdrawal of notice of intent to cancel DBCP registration for use on pineapples in Hawaii.

35. Stuart Z. Cohen, chemist, EPA Hazard Evaluation Division, memorandum, "Findings on DBCP Contamination of Groundwater in Hawaii," March 5, 1981, p. 1.

36. Legal Aid Society of Hawaii, "Memorandum in Opposition to the Proposed Withdrawal of Notice of Intent to Cancel DBCP Registration for Use on Pineapples in Hawaii," hearings before the EPA, 1981, p. 4.

37. House Committee on Government Operations, *Problems Plague the Environmental Protection Agency's Pesticide Registration Activities*, p. 21.

38. Scott Johnson, "Clemson, Peach Growers Continue Fight to Use DBCP," *Columbia Record*, September 8, 1982.

39. *Reauthorization of the Federal Insecticide, Fungicide, and Rodenticide Act*, hearing before the Subcommittee on Agricultural Research and General Legislation, Senate Committee on Agriculture, Nutrition, and Forestry, May 24, 1983, written responses of Jay Feldman, p. 44.

40. Ibid.

41. *EPA's Pesticide Registration Activities* (Part 2), hearing before a subcommittee of the House Committee on Government Operations, June 7, 1984, submission for the record, p. 85.

42. Stephen Barlas, "EPA under Increasing Pressure to Grant Pesticide Exemptions," *Washington Post*, August 14, 1982.

43. Ward Sinclair, " 'Streamlining' at EPA Raises Questions about Safeguards," *Washington Post*, January 31, 1984.

44. Stuart Z. Cohen et al., "Potential for Pesticide Contamination of Ground Water Resulting from Agricultural Uses," unpublished paper.

45. David A. Wagoner, Director of Air and Waste Management Division, EPA Region 7, memorandum to Edwin L. Johnson, Director of EPA Office of Pesticide Programs, undated.

46. C. E. Poindexter, EPA Community Safety Officer, "Trip Report," February 16, 1984.

47. Office of Technology Assessment, *Impacts of Technology on U.S. Cropland and Rangeland Productivity* (chart), p. 6.

48. Fred Zahradnik, "Nitrates—A Needless Danger," *New Farm*, November/December 1983, pp. 10–13.

49. EPA Office of Drinking Water, *Nitrate Removal for Small Public Water Systems*, Report No. 570/9–83–009, June 1983, p. ii–3.

50. EPA, "National Statistical Assessment of Rural Water Conditions," (executive summary), June 1984, p. 8.

51. Veronica I. Pye, Ruth Patrick, and John Quarles, *Groundwater Contamination in the United States* (Philadelphia: University of Pennsylvania Press, 1983), p. 143.

4: The Treatment Plant and Beyond

1. Environmental Defense Fund, *Malignant Neglect* (New York: Vintage Books, 1980), p. 97.

2. Ibid., p. 100.

3. Patricia Roberts, "Warning: The Water You Drink May Be Dangerous to Your Health," *Town and Country*, undated.

4. Joanne Omang, "Using Chlorine in Water Raises Risk of Cancer," *Washington Post*, December 18, 1980.

5. Council on Environmental Quality, news release, December 17, 1980.

6. "Ozone: The Water Purifier That Could Edge Out Chlorine," *Business Week*, May 7, 1984, p. 118.

7. Figures provided by Predicasts, Inc.

8. *Hearing on Plastic Pipe Permeation*, California State Assembly Subcommittee No. 1 on Health and Welfare, October 19, 1983, statement of Alan Olson, p. 55.

9. Quoted in Michael Harris, "Asbestos in Drinking Water: No One's Doing Much about It," *New Hampshire Times*, January 24, 1979.

10. J. Wister Meigs et al., "Asbestos Cement Pipe and Cancer in Connecticut 1955–1974," *Journal of Environmental Health*, January/February 1980, pp. 187–91.

11. Quoted in Peter C. Karalekas, Jr., Christopher R. Ryan, and Floyd B. Taylor, "Control of Lead Pipe Corrosion in the Boston Metropolitan Area," paper presented at the annual meeting of the American Water Works Association, Miami Beach, Fla., May 16–20, 1982.

12. EPA Regional Water Supply Branches, "Lead Product Utilization Survey of Public Water Supply Distribution Systems throughout the United States," April 1984.

13. *Drinking Water and Health* (Washington, D.C.: National Academy of Sciences, 1977), Part 1, pp. v–120.

14. Peter Lassovszky, "The Health Hazards Associated with the Use of Lead to Transmit Drinking Water," paper presented at a meeting of ASME A–40 Committee on Safety Requirements for Plumbing, Denver, Colo., June 7–9, 1983.

15. J. W. Patterson, "Corrosion in Water Distribution Systems," EPA Office of Drinking Water, March 1981, cited in Karalekas, Ryan, and Taylor, "Control of Lead Pipe Corrosion in the Boston Metropolitan Area."

16. Peter C. Karalekas, Jr. et al., "Lead and Other Trace Metals in Drinking Water in the Boston Metropolitan Area," *Journal of the American Water Works Association*, June 1976, pp. 150–72.

17. Floyd Taylor et al., "Acid Precipitation and Drinking Water Quality in the Western United States," EPA Project Summary, April 1984.

18. Cited in Peter Lassovszky, "The Effect on Water Quality of Lead and Non-Lead Solders Used in Water Supply Systems: Literature Review," EPA Office of Drinking Water, June 1983.

19. *Hearing on Plastic Pipe Permeation*, testimony of Robert Harris, p. 76.

Fluoridation box

1. *Science*, July 2, 1982, p. 27.

2. Ernest Newbrun, "Systemic Fluorides: An Overview," *Journal of the Canadian Dental Association*, No. 1, 1980, pp. 31–37.

3. Quoted in Russell Wild, "Fluoride: Miracle Cure or Public Menace?" *Environmental Action*, July/August 1984, pp. 14–19.

4. Ibid.

5: The States: On the Front Line

1. Ken Stephens, "State Closes Furley Waste Dump," *Wichita Eagle-Beacon*, January 19, 1982.

2. "More Danger Signs at Furley" (editorial), *Wichita Eagle-Beacon*, March 11, 1982.

3. Robert Vinson Eye, statement before the Subcommittee on Natural Resources, Agriculture Research, and Environment, House Committee on Science and Technology, August 1, 1983.

4. The New York State Assembly Standing Committee on Environmental Conservation, *Toxic Substance Control in New York State: A Failed Effort*, March 16, 1984, p. 1.

5. U.S. General Accounting Office, "States' Compliance Lacking in Meeting Safe Drinking Water Regulations," CED–82–43, March 3, 1982, pp. 4, 7.

6. U.S. General Accounting Office, "Interim Report on Inspection, Enforcement, and Permitting Activities at Hazardous Waste Facilities," RCED–83–241, September 21, 1983, pp. 6–7.

7. U.S. General Accounting Office, "Inspection, Enforcement, and Permitting Activities at New Jersey and Tennessee Hazardous Waste Facilities," RCED–84–7, June 22, 1984, p. 5.

8. California Assembly Office of Research, *Is Our Water Safe to Drink?* April 1983, pp. 57–58.

9. U.S. General Accounting Office, "Wastewater Dischargers Are Not Complying with EPA Pollution Control Permits," RCED–84–53, December 2, 1983, p. 5.

10. Jack E. Ravan, EPA Assistant Administrator for Water, testimony before the Subcommittee on Investigations and Oversight, House Committee on Public Works and Transportation, September 19, 1984.

11. Dan Tracy, "Precautions Not Enough to Save Nurseryman," *Orlando Sentinel,* August 1, 1982.

12. Neil Skene, "Florida Bans EDB but Allows Temik," *St. Petersburg Times,* September 17, 1983.

13. Victoria Churchville, "Decision to Lift Temik Ban Runs into Opposition," *Orlando Sentinel,* October 11, 1983.

14. Barbara Hastings and Jerry Burris, "Pine Industry Urged Ariyoshi to Voice EDB Support," *Honolulu Advertiser,* September 29, 1983.

15. Christopher J. Duerksen, *Environmental Regulation of Industrial Plant Siting: How to Make It Work Better* (Washington, D.C.: The Conservation Foundation, 1983), p. xxi.

16. *Department of Housing and Urban Development—Independent Agencies Appropriations for 1985,* hearings before a subcommittee of the House Committee on Appropriations, April 10, 1984, statement of John Kerry, p. 24.

17. Ibid., statement of Donald Lazarchek, p. 32.

18. EPA, "Phase III Groundwater Monitoring Report" (draft).

19. Ibid.

20. The New York State Assembly Standing Committee on Environmental Conservation, *Toxic Substance Control in New York State: A Failed Effort*, p. 17.

21. *Department of Housing and Urban Development—Independent Agencies Appropriations for 1985*, statement of John Kerry, p. 24.

22. The New York State Assembly Standing Committee on Environmental Conservation, *Toxic Substance Control in New York State: A Failed Effort*, p. 21.

23. *Department of Housing and Urban Development—Independent Agencies Appropriations for 1985*, statement of Donald Lazarchek, p. 33.

24. The New York State Assembly Standing Committee on Environmental Conservation, *Toxic Substance Control in New York State: A Failed Effort*, p. 7.

25. Ibid., pp. 6–7.

26. *Department of Housing and Urban Development—Independent Agencies Appropriations for 1985*, statement of Donald Lazarchek, p. 33.

27. Ibid., statement of John Kerry, p. 25.

28. *Review of Ground Water Protection Strategy Recently Proposed by the Environmental Protection Agency,* hearings before a subcommittee of the House Committee on Government Operations, April 11 and 12, 1984, statement of Sidney Martin, p. 353.

29. Barry Groveman, interview with the authors.

30. Larry Stammer, "Culligan Water Firm Hit with 73 Toxic Dumping Charges," *Los Angeles Times*, December 2, 1982.

6: The EPA: A Failed Mission

1. Joanne Omang, "EPA Chief's Farewell," *Washington Post*, December 14, 1980.

2. Representative Dennis E. Eckart, "How EPA Fails to Guard Our Water Supply" (letter to the editor), *New York Times*, November 20, 1984.

3. ABC News, "Water—A Clear and Present Danger" (transcript), August 5, 1983, p. 10.

4. Philip Shabecoff, "EPA's Drift in Stalemate," *New York Times*, November 23, 1984.

5. Robert H. Harris, "The Implications of Cancer-Causing Substances in Mississippi River Water," November 6, 1974, pp. 5–7.

6. Quoted in Environmental Defense Fund, *Malignant Neglect* (New York: Vintage Books, 1980), p. 82.

7. *INFORM Reports*, March/April 1983, p. 3.

8. *Research Needs of the Clean Water Act*, hearings before the Subcommittee on Natural Resources, Agriculture Research, and Environment, House Committee on Science and Technology, June 8 and 10, 1982, statement of James Taylor Banks, p. 30.

9. Jack E. Ravan, EPA Assistant Administrator for Water, testimony before the Subcommittee on Investigations and Oversight, House Committee on Public Works and Transportation, September 19, 1984.

10. U.S. General Accounting Office, "Wastewater Dischargers Are Not Complying with EPA Pollution Control Permits," RCED–84–53 December 2, 1983, p. 7.

11. Ibid., p. 16.

12. Ibid., p. 3.

13. Environmental Safety Council publication, March 4, 1984.

14. U.S. General Accounting Office, "Wastewater Dischargers Are Not Complying with EPA Pollution Control Permits," p. 25.

15. Ibid., p. 24.

16. *Research Needs of the Clean Water Act*, statement of James Taylor Banks, p. 25.

17. Joanne Omang, "Industry Told of Easier Clean-Water Rules," *Washington Post*, January 13, 1982.

18. The New York State Assembly Standing Committee on Environmental Conservation, *Toxic Substance Control in New York State: A Failed Effort*, March 16, 1984, p. 27.

19. Ibid., pp. 28–29.

20. Jack E. Ravan, EPA Assistant Administrator for Water, statement before the Subcommittee on Investigations and Oversight, House Committee on Public Works and Transportation, March 8, 1984.

21. Hugh J. Wessinger, U.S. General Accounting Office Senior Associate Director, Resources, Community, and Economic Development Division, statement before the Subcommittee on Investigations and Oversight, House Committee on Public Works and Transportation, September 19, 1984.

22. Ibid.

23. Representative Elliott H. Levitas, statement before the Subcommittee on Investigations and Oversight, House Committee on Public Works and Transportation, September 19, 1984.

24. Environmental Safety Council, January 31, 1984.

25. NBC Reports, "Assault on Big Brother . . . Regulating the Regulators" (transcript), April 20, 1984, p. 77.

26. William D. Ruckelshaus, "Putting the Hazardous Waste Issue in Perspective," *EPA Journal*, October 1984, pp. 2–3.

27. Richard Riley, "Toxic Substances, Hazardous Wastes, and Public Policy: Problems in Implementation," in James P. Lester and Ann O'M. Bowman, eds., *The Politics of Hazardous Waste Management* (Durham, N.C.: Duke University Press, 1983), p. 35.

28. Quoted in Lewis Regenstein, *America the Poisoned* (Washington, D.C.: Acropolis Books, 1982), p. 156.

29. Jonathan Lash, Katherine Gillman, and David Sheridan, *A Season of Spoils: The Story of the Reagan Administration's Attack on the Environment* (New York: Pantheon, 1984), p. 121.

30. U.S. General Accounting Office, "Inspection, Enforcement, and Permitting Activities at New Jersey and Tennessee Hazardous Waste Facilities," RCED–84–7, June 22, 1984, p. 2.

31. "240 Waste Sites Licensed; about 5,000 to Go," *Washington Post*, October 31, 1984.

32. Lash, Gillman, and Sheridan, *A Season of Spoils*, p. 82.

33. *EPA: Investigation of Superfund and Agency Abuses* (Part 3), hearings before the Subcommittee on Oversight and Investigations, House Committee on Energy and Commerce, No. 98–94, September 27 and 28, 1983, attachment to statement of Anne M. Burford, p. 219.

34. *EPA: Investigation of Superfund and Agency Abuses* (Part 2), hearings before the Subcommittee on Oversight and Investigations, House Committee on Energy and Commerce, No. 98–94, May 2, 1983, testimony of William Hedeman, p. 160.

35. Ibid., submission for the record by Representative Mike Synar, p. 153.

36. Lash, Gillman, and Sheridan, *A Season of Spoils*, p. 19.

37. Martin Tolchin and Susan J. Tolchin, "The Rush to Deregulate," *New York Times Magazine*, August 21, 1983, pp. 34–38, 70–74.

38. William Greider, "When Big Business Needs a Favor, George Bush Gets the Call," *Rolling Stone*, April 12, 1984, pp. 8–14.

39. Howard Kurtz, "OMB's Role in Reviewing Federal Rules under Debate," *Washington Post*, October 9, 1983.

40. *EPA: Investigation of Superfund and Agency Abuses* (Part 3), testimony of John E. Daniel, p. 5.

41. Ibid., p. 8.

42. *Department of Housing and Urban Development—Independent Agencies Appropriations for 1985*, hearings before a subcommittee of the House Committee on Appropriations, April 10, 1984, statement of Representative Guy Molinari, p. 7.

43. "OMB Asks EPA to Study Repeal of SDWA in Move Suggesting 2nd Term Plans," *Inside EPA*, July 20, 1984.

44. "EPA Fights Hazardous Waste: An Interview with Lee M. Thomas," *EPA Journal*, October 1984, pp. 4–7.

45. EPA, "Phase III Groundwater Monitoring Report" (draft).

46. EPA Office of Solid Waste and Emergency Response, *Extent of the Hazardous Release Problem and Future Funding Needs*, December 1984, p. i.

47. Ibid., pp. 5–7.

48. Ibid., pp. 5–9.

49. Ibid., p. iii.

50. The Association of State and Territorial Solid Waste Management Officials, *State Cleanup Programs for Hazardous Substance Sites and Spills*, December 21, 1983, p. 2.

51. Joel S. Hirschhorn, statement before the Senate Full Committee on Environment and Public Works, September 10, 1984, p. 4.

52. Susan Kellam and Jonathan King, "Superfund Targets 15 L.I. Sites," *New York Times* (Long Island Weekly section), January 6, 1985.

53. *Waste Disposal—Establish NOPC*, hearings before the Subcommittee on Fisheries and Wildlife Conservation and the Environment and the Subcommittee on Oceanography, House Committee on Merchant Marine and Fisheries, No. 98–15, May 12 and 17, 1983, statement of William Sanjour, p. 13.

54. *EPA's Regulation for Land Disposal of Hazardous Wastes*, hearings before the Subcommittee on Natural Resources, Agriculture Research, and Environment, House Committee on Science and Technology, November 30; December 8 and 16, 1982, testimony of Kirk Brown, p. 161.

55. Ibid.

56. Ibid., p. 173.

57. *EPA's Office of Research and Development and Related Issues*, hearing before the House Committee on Science and Technology, March 14, 1984, testimony of William D. Ruckelshaus, p. 21.

58. *EPA's Regulation for Land Disposal of Hazardous Wastes*, testimony of William Sanjour, p. 192.

59. Cited in Office of Technology Assessment, *Groundwater Protection Standards for Hazardous Waste Disposal Facilities: Will They Prevent More Superfund Sites?* staff memorandum, April 6, 1984, p. 37.

60. Arlene Sheehan, environmental scientist, EPA Office of Solid Waste, interview with the authors.

61. Office of Technology Assessment, *Engineering Case Study of the Stringfellow Superfund Site*, August 1984, p. 1.

62. Cass Peterson, "Toxic Merry-Go-Round Seen," *Washington Post*, July 19, 1984.

63. Quoted in *Waste Disposal—Establish NOPC*, statement of William Sanjour, p. 14.

64. *EPA's Regulation for Land Disposal of Hazardous Wastes*, statement of William Sanjour, p. 18.

65. Eric Draper, "Victims Visit Washington," *Clean Water Action News*, Fall 1984, pp. 12–14.

66. *Waste Disposal—Establish NOPC*, statement of Lois Gibbs, p. 17.

67. Draper, "Victims Visit Washington."

R&D Cuts box

1. Environmental Safety Council, March 4, 1984.

2. Unnamed scientist, EPA Environmental Research Laboratory, Duluth, Minnesota, interview with the authors.

3. Ibid.

7: The Suffering Behind the Statistics

1. *Health Effects of Hazardous Waste Disposal Practices, 1980,* joint hearings before the Subcommittee on Health and Scientific Research, Senate Committee on Labor and Human Resources, and the Senate Committee on the Judiciary, June 6, 1980, testimony of James McCarthy, p. 6.

2. Ibid., testimony of Kathleen Benesch, pp. 14–15.

3. S. W. Lagakos, B. Wessen, and M. Zelen, *The Woburn Health Study* (Boston: Harvard School of Public Health, n.d.), p. 10.

4. Ibid., p. 2.

5. Ibid., p. 3.

6. "How Serious Are the Hazards to Reproduction?," *Conservation Foundation Newsletter*, May/June 1984.

7. Christopher Norwood, "Terata," *Mother Jones*, January 1985, pp. 15–21.

8. Robert H. Harris et al., "Adverse Health Effects at a Tennessee Hazardous Waste Disposal Site," unpublished paper.

9. Ann Gibbons, "Birth Defects High near Toxic Leak," *Peninsula Times Tribune,* January 16, 1985.

10. Jay M. Gould, "The Link Is Getting Stronger," *Council on Economic Priorities Newsletter,* October 1984.

11. Thomas Petzinger, Jr., and George Getschow, "In Louisiana, Pollution and Cancer Are Rife in the Petroleum Area," *Wall Street Journal,* October 23, 1984.

12. Edward L. Baker et al., "Phenol Poisoning Due to Contaminated Drinking Water," *Archives of Environmental Health,* October 1979, pp. 89–94.

13. Cited in Statement of Janet Hathaway before the Subcommittee on Commerce, Transportation, and Tourism, House Committee on Energy and Commerce, March 1, 1984.

14. Courtney Riordan, statement before the Subcommittee on Investigations and Oversight, House Committee on Public Works and Transportation, July 21, 1983.

15. *Amending and Extending the Comprehensive Environmental Response, Compensation, and Liability Act of 1980 (Superfund),* hearings before the Senate Full Committee on Environment and Public Works, April 11 and 25; May 16, 23, and 24; June 4 and 25; July 31, 1984, testimony of David Ozonoff, p. 49.

16. Ibid., testimony of Marvin Zelen, p. 51.

17. David Ozonoff et al., *Silresim Area Health Study: Report of Findings* (executive summary), November 22, 1983, p. 1.

18. James H. Kreiger, "More Studies Urged on Health Effects of Hazardous Waste," *Chemical and Engineering News,* June 18, 1984, pp. 21–23.

19. Gerald S. Parker and Sharon L. Rosen, *Woburn: Cancer Incidence and Environmental Hazards, 1969–1978* (executive summary), January 23, 1981.

20. Quoted in Lagakos, Wessen, and Zelen, *The Woburn Health Study,* p. 7.

21. Robert A. Neal, "Health Risks of Organic Chemicals in Water," paper presented at the Symposium on Drinking Water and Human Health, Washington, D.C., April 8, 1983.

22. Irwin D. J. Bross, *Why the Assurances That the Water Is 'Safe' Have No Scientific Validity,* testimony submitted to the New York State Assembly Committee on Environmental Conservation, November 19, 1981.

23. *Amending and Extending the Comprehensive Environmental Response, Compensation, and Liability Act of 1980 (Superfund),* testimony of David Ozonoff, p. 51.

24. Douglas M. Costle, "Pollution's 'Invisible' Victims: Why Environmental Regulations Cannot Wait for Scientific Certainty," speech to the National Coalition on Disease Prevention and Environmental Health, Washington, D.C., April 28, 1980.

25. *Federal Register,* June 12, 1984, p. 24340.

26. Ibid.

27. Halina Szejnwald Brown, Donna R. Bishop, and Carol Rowan, "The Role of Skin Absorption as a Route of Exposure for Volatile Organic Compounds (VOCs) in Drinking Water," *American Journal of Public Health,* May 1984, pp. 479–84.

28. Ibid.

29. David Weir, "Poisons in Our Food Threaten Consumers," *USA Today,* September 20, 1983.

30. Environmental Defense Fund, *Dumpsite Cleanups: A Citizen's Guide to the Superfund Program,* p. 80.

31. Frances Parsons, "Biotransformation of Chlorinated Organic Solvents in Static Microcosms."

32. Bross, *Why the Assurances That the Water Is 'Safe' Have No Scientific Validity*.

33. *Hazardous Substance Victim's Compensation Legislation*, hearing before the Subcommittee on Commerce, Transportation, and Tourism, House Committee on Energy and Commerce, No. 98–45, June 29, 1983, statement of Senator George J. Mitchell, p. 36.

34. Jeffrey Trauberman, "Statutory Reform of 'Toxic Torts': Relieving Legal, Scientific, and Economic Burdens on the Chemical Victim," *Harvard Environmental Law Review*, 1983, pp. 184–206.

35. *Hazardous Substance Victim's Compensation Legislation*, statement of Anthony Z. Roisman, p. 108.

36. *Compensation for Victims of Toxic Pollution*, report prepared for the National Science Foundation, 1983.

37. Ibid.

38. *Health Effects of Hazardous Waste Disposal Practices, 1980*, testimony of James McCarthy, pp. 36–37.

39. *Hazardous Substance Victim's Compensation Legislation*, statement of Anthony Z. Roisman, p. 105.

40. Ibid., testimony of Bruce Karrh, pp. 265, 352.

41. Geraldine V. Cox, "Causation—A Technical Aspect," paper submitted to the Keystone Conference on Public Compensation, November 3, 1983.

42. James J. Tozzi, "Evaluating the Merits of Alternative Legislative Proposals on Toxic Torts: Status Report," memorandum to the Ad Hoc Group on Toxic Torts, April 18, 1983.

43. *Amending and Extending the Comprehensive Environmental Response, Compensation, and Liability Act of 1980 (Superfund)*, statement of Ellen Silbergeld, pp. 799–800.

44. Sheila Birnbaum, statement before the Subcommittee on Investigations and Oversight, House Committee on Public Works and Transportation, July 27, 1983.

45. "Runaway Compensation" (editorial), *Washington Post*, March 28, 1984.

46. *Hazardous Substance Victim's Compensation Legislation*, testimony of Anthony Z. Roisman, pp. 258–59.

47. Trauberman, "Statutory Reform of 'Toxic Torts.'"

48. *Hazardous Substance Victim's Compensation Legislation*, statement of Senator George J. Mitchell, p. 37.

49. Ibid., testimony of Anthony Z. Roisman, p. 254.

50. Matthew Purdy, "Verdict in Water-Contamination Case Seen as a Marker in Uncharted Seas," *Philadelphia Inquirer*, November 18, 1983.

Bringing a Lawsuit box

1. Environmental Defense Fund, *Dumpsite Cleanups: A Citizen's Guide to the Superfund Program*, p. 97.

2. *Hazardous Substance Victim's Compensation Legislation*, hearing before the Subcommittee on Commerce, Transportation, and Tourism, House Committee on Energy and Commerce, No. 98–45, June 29, 1983, testimony of Anthony Z. Roisman, p. 251.

8: What Can You Do in the Home?

1. EPA, "National Statistical Assessment of Rural Water Conditions" (executive summary), June 1984, p. 7.

2. U.S. General Accounting Office, "States' Compliance Lacking in Meeting Safe Drinking Water Regulations," CED 82–43, March 3, 1982, p. 9.

3. Fresno County Health Department Division of Environmental Health, interview with the authors.

4. Sarah Adams, Ohio Department of Health Laboratory, interview with the authors.

5. Robert Garfield, "Bottled Water: A Booming Industry Built on Nothing," *USA Today*, September 30, 1983.

6. International Bottled Water Association, "20 Questions about the Bottled Water Industry."

7. Information provided by the International Bottled Water Association.

8. International Bottled Water Association, "Bottled Water."

9. Enoc P. Waters, "What about Bottled Water?" *FDA Consumer*, May 1974.

10. Carol L. Ballentine and Michael L. Herdon, "The Water That Goes into Bottles," *FDA Consumer*, May 1983.

11. William Deal, interview with the authors.

12. "The Selling of H₂O," *Consumer Reports*, September 1980.

13. Paul Pontura, Senior Public Health Engineer, Suffolk County, New York, Health Department, interview with the authors.

14. John Pekkanen, "How Safe Is Your Water?" *Washingtonian*, December 1984, pp. 73–75.

15. Paul Pontura, interview.

16. Water Quality Association, "Point of Use Water Treatment Industry Statistical and Market Information," p. 6.

17. Ibid., p. 7.

18. Carol Keough, *Water Fit to Drink* (Emmaus, Pa.: Rodale Press, 1980), pp. 60–108.

19. EPA Office of Drinking Water, Criteria and Standards Division, "Fact Sheet/Update: Home Water Treatment Units," July 1980.

20. "Water Filters," *Consumer Reports,* February 1983.

21. Ibid.

22. "Clean Water at Your Tap," *New Shelter,* October 1983.

23. Health Protection Branch, Canada, "The Hazards of Using Point-of-Use Water Treatment Devices Employing Activated Carbon," December 1980.

24. EPA, "Fact Sheet/Update: Home Water Treatment Units Contract," and R. S. Tobin, D. K. Smith, and J. A. Lindsay, "Effects of Activated Carbon and Bacteriostatic Filters on Microbiological Quality of Drinking Water," *Applied and Environmental Microbiology,* March 1981, pp. 646–51.

Quick Fixes box

1. Frank Bell, Ervin Bellack, and Joseph Cotruvo, "Water Quality Improvement in the Home," 1984, p. 21.

2. Carol Keough, *Water Fit to Drink* (Emmaus, Pa.: Rodale Press, 1980), p. 130.

9: Where Do We Go from Here?

1. Governor's Office of Technology Assessment, *Alternatives to the Land Disposal of Hazardous Wastes: An Assessment for California,* 1981, p. 183.

2. National Materials Advisory Board, *Management of Hazardous Industrial Wastes: Research and Development Needs* (Washington, D.C.: National Academy of Sciences, 1983).

3. *Waste Disposal—Establish NOPC,* hearings before the Subcommittee on Fisheries and Wildlife Conservation and the Environment and the Subcommittee on Oceanography, House Committee on Merchant Marine and Fisheries, No. 98–15, May 12 and 17, 1983, statement of William Sanjour, p. 13.

4. Rip G. Rice, "Ozone Treatment of Drinking Water—Evolution and Current Status," paper presented at the National Drinking Water Conference, Ottawa, Canada, February 7, 1984.

5. Ward Worthy, "Pesticide Chemists Are Shifting Emphasis from Kill to Control," *Chemical and Engineering News*, July 23, 1984, pp. 2226.

6. "Culprits and Savings in Waste Reduction Cited by INFORM," *INFORM Reports*, November/December 1983.

7. "Allied Converts Hazardous Waste from Environmental Liability into Asset," *Chemecology*, December 1983/January 1984.

8. "Recycling Conserves Resources, Cuts Waste Disposal Costs," *Chemecology*, February 1984.

9. 3M Company, "Pollution Prevention Pays," *Status Report*, July 1, 1984.

10. *Hazardous Waste Control and Enforcement Act, H.R. 2867 (Part 2—Innovative Technologies)*, hearing before the Subcommittee on Energy, Environment, and Safety Issues Affecting Small Business, House Committee on Small Business, October 27, 1983, statement of M. R. Speach, p. 4.

11. Dow Chemical Company, "Incineration: Its Role in Resource Recovery and Waste Management at Dow."

12. Martha M. Hamilton, "Dow Tries Burning Its Toxic Waste," *Washington Post*, October 25, 1984.

13. Ibid.

14. Joel S. Hirschhorn, "Long-Term Benefits of Waste Reduction," extended abstract of a speech to the Second Annual Massachusetts Hazardous Waste Source Reduction Conference, Boston, Mass., October 17, 1984.

15. *Hazardous Waste Control and Enforcement Act, H.R. 2867 (Part 2—Innovative Technologies)*, statement of M. R. Speach, p. 2.

Index

Y